Beasts and Gods

Dr Roslyn Fuller is currently a research associate at the Waterford Institute of Technology and has lectured in international law at Trinity College, Dublin and the National University of Ireland, Maynooth. She is also legal correspondent for *Russia Today*, contributing a regular column on issues of international law.

Beasts and Gods

How democracy changed its
meaning and lost its purpose

ROSLYN FULLER

Zed Books
LONDON

Beasts and Gods: How democracy changed its meaning and lost its purpose
was first published in 2015 by Zed Books Ltd,
The Foundry, 17 Oval Way, London SE11 5RR, UK.

www.zedbooks.co.uk

Typeset in Scala by seagulls.net
Index: John Barker
Cover design: liamchapple.com
Cover photo © Adam Gault/Getty

ISBN 978-1-78360-543-9 hb
ISBN 978-1-78360-542-2 pb
ISBN 978-1-78360-544-6 pdf
ISBN 978-1-78360-545-3 epub
ISBN 978-1-78360-546-0 mobi

Contents

PART II

Figures

Acknowledgements

It is said you should turn your passion into your work, and I have been lucky enough to do just that. This book is the final product of nearly ten years of research. What began as a doctoral thesis examining the relationship between democracy and international law has turned into something much, much bigger. I have lost count of the number of times I have written and rewritten this material, but it is all as fascinating today as it was in the very beginning. In fact, many of the issues and concepts in this book are *more* important today than they were a decade ago.

And as with any book, especially one of such breadth, this is the product of more than one person. Not only does the work presented here build on countless studies by other researchers and academics, many people also came forward to help me. Without them, this book would not exist.

Maren Stefan was especially supportive during the final days of writing, grilling me on the core ideas with a great deal of patience and insight.

My editor Kika Sroka-Miller understood what I was trying to achieve from day one, and went well beyond the call of duty in working on this manuscript. Her efforts have immeasurably improved it. Copy-editor Ian Paten later patiently accepted my many post-submission alterations while doing a fantastic job of editing the manuscript. All errors are, of course, my own.

I owe many thanks as well to the staff of Trinity College, Dublin, foremost among them my adviser Gernot Biehler. Gernot never forced me on to conventional tracks, but he insisted that whatever I did, I should do well. I will never forget the first time I spoke to him about life in ancient Athens. I happened to be wearing a Greek T-shirt, and Gernot, who didn't hesitate to throw out a phrase in Arabic or Russian if it suited him, much to my consternation, quickly began translating this T-shirt, berating me to follow along. While more conventional Greek lessons were to follow, I think that first one exhibited exactly the kind of unorthodox pragmatism that would have found full approval in Athens.

Later, Professors William Binchy and Neville Cox encouraged me to rewrite my findings as a book.

Last, but not least, my parents deserve special thanks. Of all senses, common sense is the least common, but my parents possessed it in spades, and always taught me to be open to everything but to blindly accept nothing.

Society is something that precedes the individual.
Anyone who either cannot lead the common
life or is so self-sufficient as not to need to, and
therefore does not partake of society, is either a
beast or a god.

Aristotle

Introduction

What is Democracy?

In the case of a word like democracy, not only is
there no agreed definition but the attempt to make
one is resisted from all sides. It is almost universally
felt that when we call a country democratic we are
praising it: consequently the defenders of every kind
of regime claim that it is a democracy and fear that
they might have to stop using the word if it were
tied down to any one meaning.

George Orwell

Democracy is a curiously difficult term to pin down. Ask nearly
anyone about it and they will tell you that they know exactly
what democracy is, that everyone, in fact, knows what it is.

You may be told that the current Western system of
government provides its citizens with a level of political
participation that has never been matched, either anywhere
else in the world or at any other time in history, and that this
is why it is called democracy. You may be told that democracy
is nothing more than the absence of dictatorship or absolute
monarchy, that its defining characteristic is a reprieve from

I

barefaced tyranny. You may be told that democracy is about liberty and equality, or about everyone having a say. You may hear that in a democracy ordinary people control public policy because politicians are supposed to implement the policies that those people have voted for, or that the practice of elections gives citizens the ability to ensure that their own best interests are protected and safeguarded by giving them the option of 'throwing the rascals out' at the next election.

But above all, you will probably hear that democracy is the form of government we practise, and the form of government we practise is democracy; that there can be no other meaning to the idea of popular emancipation than what is contained in this circular logic and no improvements possible because all other systems of political organization, when measured against the current one, have already been tried and proved sadly wanting.

Democracy, as we know it, is as good as it gets.

And that's just it.

But is any of this really true? Is the system of politics practised in Western nations really the best and most democratic one ever invented by humankind? Does it really allow ordinary people to meaningfully participate? Does it deliver a free and fair decision-making process that takes all viewpoints and interests into account? Does it truly make people more free and more equal than in all other societies, past, present, real or imagined?

I'm not sure that it does.

My scepticism stems from the following considerations: If we live in a country governed by the people and for the people, why is it always so difficult to find anyone who supports anything that the government does? In a land where the collective citizenry is ostensibly in total control of public policy, why is it regarded as naive to believe that a politician will implement the policies they have campaigned on once elected? Most thought-provokingly of all, if elections give citizens a way to effectively control their government, why are most people who live in what are acknowledged to be democracies becoming poorer?

I think that this last point is particularly telling. Many experts have shown that over the past thirty years governments in Western nations have consistently passed laws directly privileging only the wealthiest members of society. Although it is a well-publicized fact that these laws are causing the vast majority of citizens in Western states to become less affluent despite massive increases in economic productivity, they have not been repealed. In fact, laws that strongly discriminate in favour of a tiny minority of extremely wealthy individuals to the detriment of everyone else have often been quickly followed by *more* legislation making the same discrimination even more strongly.

How can this be happening in societies that practise majority rule? Why would not just some, but *most*, people vote for policies that produce such direct catastrophic results for so many of them? And, even more strikingly, why would they keep voting for them after the consequences of those policies become obvious? Do they *like* the idea of becoming poorer and poorer?

The way I see it, there are really only two possible explanations: either we are all so phenomenally stupid that we simply cannot help but consistently vote in our own worst interests, or something is fundamentally wrong with the system we use to convert public opinion into policy decisions.

This approach puts me at odds with most other political analysts, who push the line that our problems with democracy stem from a few 'bad apples'. These experts tend to focus on the difficulties we encounter in faithfully implementing the rules of democracy, preferring to attribute its failings to cheating or other obnoxious behaviour. They tend to accept that the political system of electoral democracy itself is good – we just aren't following it perfectly enough.

It seems to me, however, that we are following our own instruction manual of democracy with utmost precision. We hold elections regularly and within the prescribed time limits; constitutional crises are rare and often overcome with a minimum of disruption; an independent judiciary oversees all laws and their decisions are almost always respected. Flagrant violations of democratic rules are rare in Western nations. We do not normally encounter coups or ballot-box stuffing, and even campaign overspending is closely monitored and controlled. Yes, you get the odd MP attempting to claim expenses for a £2,000 ornamental duck house, as British backbencher Peter Viggers did in 2009. You get the occasional rising political star cheating their way to an improved CV, as German minister for defence Karl-Theodor zu Guttenberg was found to have done when it came out in 2011 that he had gained a doctoral degree through shameless plagiarism. You get some overstepping on travel and decorating expenses, as poignantly demonstrated by US Congressman Aaron Schock, who requested reimbursement for more official travel miles than even existed on his vehicle while simultaneously redecorating his office to resemble the set of Downton Abbey. But such misdemeanours are nearly always found out through the vigorous patrolling of journalists and opposition parties.

Viggers, Guttenberg, Schock, and many more like them, have been forced into early retirement, fined and subjected to legal investigations for indulging their reckless flights of fancy on the taxpayers' dime.

When it comes to democracy, we actually have a fairly good record of enforcing the rules of the game. We say what we do and we do what we say. To the letter. Or last ornamental duck house, as the case may be.

Yet despite the fact that the rules of democracy are nearly always enforced, few people would dispute that there is something deeply wrong, even corrupt, about our political system.

And if you implement the rules of a system reasonably well and still end up with a result that substantially differs from the one you intended to achieve, there is some logic to concluding that the problem must lie with the rules themselves. There must be a design flaw somewhere in the system that is causing this undesired result.

I began to wonder whether the problems we were having with democracy lay not in how we practised it, but in our very *idea* of democracy. Was there some glitch in the system that, somewhere between elections and implementing public policy, thwarted the will of the people from being realized? I decided to investigate.

And I did find flaws. Many of them.

I found out that the rules that govern modern democracy systematically fail to enable free and equal decision-making. In fact, the very practice of holding elections is based on assumptions about political organization that have never been proved to be true.

One of these assumptions is that in electoral democracies the government and other Members of Parliament (or

Houses of Congress in the USA) are the living embodiment of voter preferences as expressed in the last election. After all, citizens vote to determine who forms the government, so the government cannot help but represent the voters – it is always and necessarily a mirror image of the preferences they have expressed at the ballot box.

It sounds wonderful, but it's complete fiction. In something as large as a modern state, achieving accurate representation of all citizens in legislatures and governments is mathematically impossible. You just can't take the votes of millions of citizens and transform them into a chamber of only a few hundred representatives without some funny things happening.

For example, the idea behind democracy is that the candidate or party who gets the most votes should win the election. But frequently the party or candidate who wins the most votes *loses* the election. This happened in the US presidential election of 2000, when over half a million more Americans voted for Democratic candidate Al Gore than for his Republican rival George W. Bush. But because George W. Bush won more *states* than Gore did he was deemed the victor of the election, became president and implemented his own policy over the next four years. This electoral skewing opened the door for what would prove a deadly chain of events. While Bush's foreign policy was notable for its many faux pas, one decision reverberates to this day: the decision to go to war on Iraq in 2003.

It was an extremely unpopular move – the majority of Americans, after all, did not even agree with the idea of Bush being president, much less anything he did. Furthermore, Bush failed to obtain the backing of the United Nations for the war. Denied international cooperation and facing substantial opposition within his own country, Bush needed to find other world leaders willing to back him up and commit resources and credibility to the war.

Here Bush could find only one major ally – British prime minister Tony Blair. And funnily enough, Blair had come to power much the same way Bush had. In the last British election, Blair's Labour Party had taken 62.5 per cent of seats in Parliament with only 40.7 per cent of the popular vote. In other words, most British citizens voted for a party other than Labour, but still got a parliament that was mostly Labour and a government that was completely Labour! British people were even more strongly against the idea of a war in Iraq than Americans were, yet because Bush and Blair were the legitimately elected leaders, they were able to embark on this ill-considered global policy that cost so many people their lives.

Neither leader had received the endorsement of the majority of their own citizens *at any point* – yet they both came to power in accordance with all the rules of democracy.

Shocking as this case is, I discovered that such strange outcomes are not flukes, but rather a regular feature of democracy as we practise it. In electoral democracies it is not unusual for a vote cast in favour of one party to be worth up to ten times a vote for another party, and a party can even go down in the polls and up in terms of electoral success at the same time. The British national election of 1983 is a perfect illustration. In that election, the Conservative Party won one seat in Parliament for every 32,777 votes cast in its favour, while the Social Democrat–Liberal Alliance scraped together only one seat for every 338,302 votes received. End result: the Conservatives gained over fifty seats, despite losing nearly

700,000 votes from the previous election! That's right: Conservative leader Margaret Thatcher managed to lose more than 5 per cent of her voters between 1979 and 1983 and became a more successful prime minister because of it.

And these figures barely scratch the surface. We might like to believe that how people vote causes their preferred candidates or parties to win elections, but even just a quick look at the numbers proves that this is not actually the case. Only the weakest, most elastic link exists between these two events.

The representative aspect of representative democracy is little more than a myth. The truth is that citizens in 'democracies' spend up to one fifth of their lives governed by a party or candidate *other* than the party or candidate that most of them voted for at the last election, and nearly all of the rest of the time governed by a party or coalition that could not attain an absolute majority in favour of its policies. It's no wonder that it's always hard to find people who agree with the government – there just aren't ever very many of them.

Another myth surrounding our democracies is that elections are 'free and fair'. I quickly learned that elections are nearly invariably won by the side that spends the most money and that this money is almost always supplied by what are termed 'special interests' – those who stand to profit most from a certain outcome. This is not only true in countries like the United States, where campaign finance laws are notoriously loose. It happens everywhere, even in nations with tough campaign financing laws. It is almost impossible for a candidate or party that does not have connections to corporate donors or mass media to seriously contest an election, much less win one.

In Canada and the United Kingdom – two of the most developed and oldest democracies in the world – no party has ever come to power without receiving corporate backing. Ever.

That means that no one who lives in these two countries has ever spent a single day of their lives under a government that does not have corporate ties.

And the USA – the world's oldest and most developed democracy – is even worse. Study after study shows that the more money a candidate spends on his or her election, the more likely they are to win. So likely, in fact, that any candidate willing and able to double the spending of their electoral opponent increases their chances of winning an election to over 90 per cent. Ratchet that up to five times the spending, and electoral victory becomes a sure thing – 100 per cent certain.

It's a numbers game.

And it continues after election.

Representatives not only work harder to pass legislation that corresponds to the wishes of their major donors, not only do they nearly always vote in the interests of major donors, they will often switch their vote in favour of a donor that offers them more money than previous benefactors.

Exactly this happened when the US Houses of Congress debated reform on the Glass-Steagall Act during the 1990s. For years, the banking and insurance industries wrangled over reform to the Act, altering their campaign contribution strategies to ensure that no amendment to this financial legislation would be passed until it met their own commercial interests. When Democrats ruled the Houses of Congress in 1991, insurance and investment interests contributed heavily to Democrat candidates – and 74 per cent of them voted in line with insurance interests. But when reform came up again while Republicans controlled the legislature in 1998, insurance and investment interests dropped the Democrats and siphoned funding into Republican campaign coffers. Candidates in both parties responded. Democrat support for the insurance position plummeted from 74 to 38 per cent, while Republican support rose from 22 to 77 per cent. In fact, two-thirds of all representatives who voted on both pieces of legislation changed their position between votes, depending on the ebb and flow to their own campaign coffers. This responsiveness to campaign contributions on the part of representatives paved the way for repealing parts of the Glass-Steagall Act in 1999, which generated a profit bonanza for the financial sector and a deep economic recession for ordinary Americans.

Not only does campaign financing give the rich a way to control the content of legislation, the need to raise large amounts of money and to project an unrealistically clean public image acts as a gatekeeper that prevents the vast majority of people from ever running in elections. It is a vetting system that rivals the Iranian Supreme Council or the Chinese Communist Party in its effectiveness at excluding disruptive candidates. However, unlike in China and Iran, where candidates are primarily excluded from running over ideological differences, our gatekeepers ensure that elections are systematically skewed in favour of the rich.

I discovered during the course of my research that electoral systems are *always* corrupted by money, meaning that elections are by definition *never* free and fair.

How could citizens ever seek to have their will implemented in a system that was inevitably controlled by special interests and which was incapable of accurately reflecting the direction they had voted in? If things were going wrong with democracy, it looked like it wasn't the ordinary voter's fault.

However, there was one more avenue to investigate that might still let me pin the blame for all our woes on us, the people. After all, citizens in Western nations can always seek to engage in public affairs by participating outside of elections, for example by protesting or petitioning the government. If we were failing to do this, perhaps the problems with democracy could still be laid at our door on grounds of laziness. However, here too I soon discovered that while citizens can indeed protest or petition their government, it is almost impossible for them to achieve any particular goal by doing so. This is because elected officials are free to choose whether or not to respond to protesters or petitioners. The ultimate decision lies, by law, with them, and frequently they choose to either not respond at all or to double-down on their own position. For example, in 1999 over forty thousand people gathered to protest the detrimental effects of overzealous trade liberalization at the World Trade Organization's annual meeting in Seattle. In fact, protesters actually managed to shut down the meeting. Far from sending delegates out to meet with people on the street and address their concerns – the natural reaction one would expect in a society based on the principle of rule by the people – the World Trade Organization simply moved its talks to more easily controlled locations like Hong Kong and Qatar. Protesters may have won the battle but they lost the war.

Through vote-skewing, campaign financing and representatives' right to simply ignore anything that happens in between elections, the vast majority of people are systematically excluded from public decision-making. And once you know that, you don't need to be a rocket scientist to see why so many of these decisions do not seem to be in their interests.

Looking at democracy this way left me with some good news and some bad news.

The good news is that we aren't stupid. Appearances to the contrary, the majority of us are not actually in the habit of consistently making decisions in our own worst interests.

The bad news is that the flaws in our democracy are embedded in the very fabric of our political and legal system. We engage in practices like elections and protest on the assumption that they produce government by the people. But this assumption is wrong: mass representation through Parliament or Congress is hopelessly inaccurate; elections are bought and sold even where tight financing laws are in place; and non-electoral forms of participation like protest and petition are for the most part useless, not just because protest can be repressed, but because politicians know that regular voters do not really impact on their chances of winning; rather, big donors do.

Even if we're not entirely clear on what some of our big ideas about democracy mean, even if we don't always see eye to eye on what values like liberty, equality and frater-nity precisely entail or what a government of, by and for the people is really supposed to look like, I think we can all agree on one point – it's definitely not this.

Somehow the rules aren't working. And in that situation the obvious thing to do is to change them so that they do work.

But how could that be done?

This was the second question I asked myself when writing this book.

One possibility would be to try to fix democracy through trial and error. Legislators use this method to change regulations when they do not have enough information to be sure that the decision they are making is the right one. When the rules concerned are fairly limited – rules on car insurance or rent controls, for example – this can be acceptable. However, even in these cases, it is not ideal. Making rules by trial and error almost always takes some adjustment and, in the meantime, innocent people often suffer from unintended consequences. When it comes to something as important as the way we govern entire nations, I don't believe that trial and error is the best approach. We need to fix democracy to be more responsive to people, but the consequences of any major change to our government are simply so huge that it would definitely be best to try to get things right the first time.

So what about learning from someone *else's* trials and errors? What about learning from another country that had succeeded in creating a government in which this troublesome gap between citizens' preferences and public policy did not exist? Could I find such a country, figure out how they had managed to achieve democracy and then apply that knowledge to our own societies?

This seemed like a step in the right direction, but where could I look for such an example?

The majority of countries across the globe have copied, or have been forced to copy, Western laws on democracy down to the ground, and they are experiencing all of the same problems, and more, that go with them. The few countries that haven't aren't doing any better. I might not be completely convinced that people in Western states are infinitely better off than people in China or Iran, but I don't propose to copy the political systems of those nations, either.

In the end, I spent many months looking for a society that had successfully achieved a style of government in which people's preferences were not systematically thwarted by the very instruments that were supposed to implement them. I looked everywhere and at everything – from medieval Iceland to modern Bhutan to 1950s Middle East Nasserism, but came up blank. Finally, one day, in utter desperation and not expecting anything to come of it, I visited the classics section of the library.

One year later, I could not have been levered out with a crowbar. I had improved my Latin, become passable at deciphering ancient Greek, and knew more about antiquity than I had ever previously wanted to know. And in all of my studies, one particular nation fascinated me above all others: the city-state of ancient Athens.

Athens didn't just provide some handy hints about improving politics, it turned my ideas of democracy upside down. In fact, Athenian democracy first attracted my interest precisely because it revolved around a set of practices that sounded a little crazy. The Athenians chose all of their officials randomly, they paid people to vote, they purposely drafted their laws as vaguely as possible, they set up a system of democratic 'people's courts' and they actually demanded the participation of thousands upon thousands of ordinary citizens in government *every single day*. At first glance, it seemed like an absolutely bizarre way to run a country.

But here's the thing: it worked.

In ancient Athens there was no gap between what the people wanted and the policies the state implemented. In this sense, there is no doubt that Athenian democracy – unlike our version – really, truly, was government by the people, for the people.

But what struck me even more forcefully was that the Athenians had initially practised a system of electoral government similar to modern representative democracy. Only later, when they found elections unsatisfactory, had they switched over to a system that was more suited to delivering what they termed 'people power'. The Athenians, in other words, had not adopted their strange-sounding form of government because they were *less* developed than we are, but because they were *more* developed. That certainly provided some food for thought. And the more I looked into Athens, the more I realized how much we could learn from it.

I had finally discovered a society that had already gone through the trials and errors of creating a state that allowed government by the people. It just wasn't where I had expected, or rather, *when* I had expected, it to be.

And that left me with a third question: No matter how terrific government may have been in Athens, how could I possibly adapt the rules and practices of a 2,500-year-old civilization to modernity in my quest to fix our own issues with democracy?

After all, the classical world of antiquity was a very different place. Ancient peoples suffered chronic underpopulation and labour shortages, knew nothing of mass communications or modern science, and held vastly different views on topics like religion and warfare to those most of us hold today. Few things seemed more natural to the ancient mind than holding slaves or excluding women from political decision-making.

Some aspects of ancient society were inspiring, others disturbing, but I soon realized that we don't need to embrace the less savoury practices of antiquity in order to adopt the best parts of ancient democratic governance to our benefit for one very good reason: none of these issues had anything to do with democracy itself. Cultural practices like holding slaves and discriminating against women had been ongoing long before democracy was established and continued long after it ceased to exist, with few discernible alterations.

It's neither necessary nor is it my intent to re-create classical Athens down to the last marble statue. In this book I will pry open the *principles* that guided Athenian democracy and show how they could be applied to modern life to our benefit.

We know that we have made some mistakes in how we have set up democracy, but thanks to Athens, we also know that achieving rule by the people is not the product of some ineffable X-factor obscured by a complex web of hopes and dreams. Real democracy is the product of a clear-cut system of rules and laws that are suited to achieving their objective.

The Athenians weren't perfect, but they did manage to create a stable system of government that delivered far more power to its citizens than does ours; a system that did not suffer from the rampant fraud, demagoguery and creeping oligarchy that is so prevalent in modern 'democracy'. Using this template to correct some of the problems we are experiencing is certainly *more likely* to lead to success than simply casting about wildly for solutions that *don't* have any functioning precedent.

The lessons we learn from Athens may be vital to our future, because the pressure for political change is building all around us; the movement for radically different, less hierarchical decision-making well under way. From internet voting in Switzerland and Estonia to crowdsourcing constitutional change in Iceland to the participatory budget of Paris, where citizens vote directly on cultural and community projects, we can see the possibilities for a different sort of democracy emerging all around us. Change will come – the only question is whether we will be ready for it.

PART I

I

_____

Democracy in Athens:
People Power is Born

It does not matter if a cat is black or white.
As long as it catches mice, it is a good cat.

Deng Xiaoping

The ancient city-state of Athens is often credited with being
the birthplace of democracy. Although democracy was also
practised in other Greek states, the political structure of
Athens has been the subject of the most study as well as some
of the best-preserved records written by people who personally experienced it. These people woke up every morning and
went to bed every night under democracy; they witnessed
some of the most dramatic moments of history with their
own eyes, and were personally involved in the important decisions of Athenian political life. The writings of these ancient
political observers are almost like time capsules, delivering
information about their society far into the future in a way
that those alive at the time could probably never have imagined possible. And in their turn, they tell us about an ancient
system of government that is equally hard for us to imagine

today. It may have shared the name 'democracy' with our own, but it used vastly different methods of governance. So different, in fact, that they call many of our own ostensibly democratic traditions into question. To understand just how profound these differences were, it's necessary to know a bit about the culture that came up with them.

When we look at the classical marble statuary of Greek civilization in museums, we often get an impression of solemn formality but when they were created, these statues were often painted, brightly coloured masterpieces not of grave reverence, but of passion, wisdom and power. After all, the ancient Athenians lived in the dynamic atmosphere of one of the most powerful and developed cities on earth. Feats of engineering, chariot racing and risqué theatre productions – Athens had something for everyone. The philosophers who lived, studied and congregated in this city of ideas were already hypothesizing that the world was round, that the sun was a ball of fire, and that all matter was constructed from building blocks too small to see that they christened 'atoms' – all far-sighted theories that would not be conclusively proved for millennia. But what really distinguished Athens from other important cities of the time was that its citizens aspired to the good life. Socializing, satisfying meals, beautiful things, and a break from hard labour – this cultivated prosperity was what made life worth living. In this sense, the Athenians shared values with many people living in Western societies today.

But there were also important differences. At the time that the Athenian navy dominated the Aegean Sea, its architects designed the Acropolis and philosophers like Plato founded schools of thought that would influence human reasoning for thousands of years, no one really thought that democracy was a good thing unto itself or that people had an inherent right to live under this kind of government. In fact, many of the greatest thinkers of the time were convinced that other forms of rule, such as oligarchy or aristocracy, were superior to democracy. Even important and respected nations like Sparta and Rome were positively proud of their undemocratic way of life. Their citizens and rulers did not hesitate to disparage the very idea of democracy or boast that their own political practices were far more advanced precisely because they did not give 'the common people' any say in government. Democracy, in short, was not at all fashionable, and no one felt compelled to *pretend* that they lived in a democracy.

And in the absence of pretence, it was easier to get absolute clarity on what democracy was. It was measured on one thing only: who held political power? To the ancient Greeks, this was the bottom line in defining political organization, and it is reflected in the names they gave to each form of government. To us, words like 'oligarchy' or 'democracy' may sound like technical terms, but they are really just straightforward Greek descriptions of how government decisions are taken. In ancient Greek *demos* means 'people' (in the sense of the people of a nation), while *kratos* means 'power'. *Demos* + *kratos* (*demokratia* in ancient Greek) means 'people power'. By the same token *oligos* means 'few', while *arches* means 'rule'. Oligarchy therefore means 'rule by the few'.

So, when the Athenians spoke to each other in what they would have considered to be plain Greek, they literally said, 'so here we are in a people power [state]' or 'yes, of course, Sparta is a rule by the few [state]'. This is significant, because it meant that the ancient Greeks did not confuse the *means* via which decisions were made (e.g. by one person, a few people, or everyone) with the *end* they were trying to achieve (e.g. a well-run economy, sound foreign policy, etc). The Athenians would not have seen 'elections' or 'human rights' or 'economic prosperity' as signs that a nation was a democracy. Democracy simply meant 'people power'. How the people of a nation acquired that power and what they did with it were separate issues. By the same token, oligarchy did not necessarily mean 'oppression' or 'human rights abuses'. It simply meant 'rule by the few'. Whether those few were benevolent or not was another question entirely. Therefore, no matter how impressive a state's achievements might be, it could only qualify as a democracy if political power genuinely resided in the hands of the people, if they, and no one else, made *all* decisions.

While modern Western democracies are often accused of failing to deliver power to the people (a well-founded accusation, as we will see in the following chapters), Athenian democracy unarguably achieved this goal. Perhaps even more importantly, while the Athenians did not associate other goals, such as an impartial justice system, lack of corruption or real equality between citizens, with democracy in the same explicit way that we do today, their form of government did a much better job of actually delivering these goods than ours does.

So how did they do it?

How Athenian democracy worked

In modern times, it is understood that elections are the very essence of democracy, so it is reasonable to expect that the first democrats, the Athenians, also held elections to determine who their leaders would be. This assumption is correct to the extent that the Athenians were very familiar with the concept of elections and they did indeed use them to directly select government officials and a 400-member legislative debating chamber.

But they did so before they became a democracy.

Like other ancient peoples, the Athenians viewed electoral leadership as a version of oligarchy. It was rule by the few, and the fact that those few were subject to change once in a while did nothing to alter that fundamental point. In fact, Aristotle described elections as giving 'the people only the necessary minimum of power' to remain free citizens and not be classified as slaves.[1]

The Athenians, and their neighbours, agreed that in a true democracy, the people did not obey the decisions taken by those empowered to do so via election or any other means. Instead they took all decisions themselves through two important bodies: the Assembly and the courts.

Assembly: meeting of the many

While there were many important democratic practices in Athens, the Assembly was its centrepiece, and it remains the part of Athenian democracy that is most easily understood today. The Assembly was simply a gathering that every Athenian male citizen was entitled to attend by virtue of turning up at the right place and time. While regular Assembly attendance was viewed as a duty, it was also generally voluntary. There were usually between 5,000 and 6,000 people present

---

[1] Aristotle, *Politics*, at 200.

at each Assembly meeting out of a total eligible population of around 35,000 to 45,000 adult male citizens. This meant that proportionally speaking Assembly attendance ran at about 10–20 per cent of the voting population. Translated to modern terms, it would be as if 30–60 million Americans attended a meeting of Congress or 10–20 million Brits descended on Westminster. It sounds unimaginable, but such a high level of participation was everyday fare in Athens.

And the assembled Athenian citizens did nothing more glamorous than sit down together and make all of the decisions necessary to run their country. They passed laws, bestowed citizenship on others, approved state expenses, and took executive decisions, such as the decision to embark on a war. It is no exaggeration to say that absolutely every political decision was taken in the Assembly, which never delegated its powers to individual officials, even in states of emergency. As one historian put it, '[t]he week-by-week conduct of a war, for example, had to go before the Assembly week by week, as if Winston Churchill were to have been compelled to take a referendum before each move in WWII'.[2]

Despite this high level of responsibility, the Assembly was an extremely efficient body. It met only four times each month, and when it did the Athenians quickly got down to the business of making decisions in a fashion as effective as it was unpretentious.

There were no prime ministers or Speakers of the House in ancient Athens. In fact, no one was truly in charge of the Assembly. Order was kept by a panel of randomly selected officials, one of whom was (again randomly) designated

---

2 Finley, 'Athenian demagogues', 163 at 175 et seq.

the 'supervisor' for the day. It was the supervisor's not-very-illustrious job to present the various motions that had been suggested by citizens since the last meeting. The assembled citizens then voted on whether each motion should be accepted unchanged or subjected to further debate. For example, a motion might be that some form of state relief should be provided for orphans, or that the citizenship rules should be reformed, or (ever popular) that the Athenians should rip up the latest peace treaty with the Spartans and attack. However, the motion rarely said how exactly this was to be achieved, so it was usually necessary to thrash things out together in Assembly. Once debate was opened, citizens volunteered to make speeches for or against a certain view, amendment or interpretation of the issue under debate. Any citizen could choose to address the Assembly freely because each and every citizen had the right to express himself, not just publicly, but in a forum where public decisions were being made and on equal terms with all other speakers. The Athenians called this right 'isegoria'. Athenians, in other words, did not just enjoy the right to attend and vote in Assembly, each citizen had a right to share his views with it. Once this debate had been concluded, the Athenians voted for or against each motion put forward by a show of hands. Such were the workings of the Athenian Assembly, in a nutshell.

However, before anyone gets the wrong idea, it's necessary to point out that the Athenian Assembly was not by any stretch of the imagination a secluded realm of thoughtful introspection. Neither was participation at Assembly all about the grand moments of history. Most of the time, business was decidedly prosaic. On one lacklustre occasion, the assembled citizens (all men, of course), presumably wearied of handling luggage, could think of nothing better to do with their time than to pass a law stating that no woman would henceforth be allowed to travel with more than three dresses. One can only guess at how this law was received within the family home, but it didn't stay on the books for long.

The processes of the Assembly were also characterized more by pragmatism than philosophical ideals. Sharing in Assembly was not intended to be an emotional unburdening in a judgement-free zone where each thought was equally valued and respected. The assembled citizens were well aware that their time was precious. They did not like long-winded speeches (unless they were really good) and they did not have much patience for anyone who did not appear to know what they were talking about or who was failing to add anything to the conversation. And while Athenian democracy is notable for its near-complete lack of violence, heckling, being forced off stage and even the occasional death threat were all part and parcel of the action. The way the Athenians saw it, if you couldn't take the heat, you had best get out of the kitchen.

So *isegoria* was a right – an important and treasured right – but ultimately the idea behind it was for citizens to get out there and share their knowledge for the greater good of the community. It was supposed to enable people to say what they thought and to fight for what they thought. It did not, however, guarantee that others would take those thoughts seriously or hesitate to point out any shortcomings in them. This did not present any major difficulties for the Athenians, because they tended to be admirably unfazed by these social perils. We know that citizens from all walks of life did not hesitate to use their right to address their fellow citizens in

Assembly, and that often people who were normally not very conspicuous in public life chose to speak up on an issue that was important to them, and managed to carry the vote on it, even when opposed by more famous and polished speakers.

Athenian citizens did just not 'give input' or 'make their voices heard' in Assembly – the frequent demands of pro-democracy advocates today – they collectively took the final decision on their nation's policies on each and every substantive point after making an attempt to convince those present of the merits of their own views. This means that despite the robust nature of Athenian public debate, it was still a much more inclusive form of political decision-making than we practise today, because everyone, even wallflowers who never took advantage of their right to speak publicly, got an equal vote on every motion.

For these reasons, Athenian democracy is often referred to as 'direct democracy' to distinguish it from 'our' type of democracy, in which we elect individuals to make political decisions on our behalf. In reality, however, any given decision in the Assembly was usually the product of a debate conducted between 10 and 20 per cent of the population. In a sense, all other citizens were represented on that particular issue by those who happened to be in attendance on the day that it was debated. But it was a different kind of representation to what we know today because the concrete identity of the citizens in Assembly rotated constantly in unforeseeable patterns, and they were numerous enough to reproduce a more accurate cross-section of societal interests.

At first glance, that may sound innocuous, even banal, but it's not. Later on, when we look at our own modern democracies, we are going to see just how vital the ever-shifting nature of Athenian democracy really was. But before we do that, there are a few other matters to clear up, because in Athens democracy was not just a matter of *making* laws in Assembly, it was also a matter of interpreting them in the courts.

The courts: justice by the thousands

According to Aristotle, Athens' judicial system was an integral component of its political organization, and it was very different to our court system today.

To start off with, all Athenian courts were jury courts, staffed by large numbers of randomly selected jurors. The minimum jury size for a private suit was 201 jurors, which increased to 401 if the claim was worth more than 1,000 drachmae (a drachma was the Athenian unit of currency, and 1,000 drachmae would have been something like $60,000 by today's standards). In public cases, the juries were even larger. The minimum jury size for a public suit was 501, with additional jurors being added in increments of 500, depending on the importance of the case. It was not unusual to have a jury with 2,500 or even 6,000 members. This means that for matters of major importance there would be as many decision-makers sitting on the jury as there were at a typical Assembly meeting – over 10 per cent of Athens' total citizen population. In Athens, courts were not the preserve of the few, but rather a venue of mass participation that completely penetrated society so even if a citizen did not attend a specific case themselves, they would definitely rub shoulders with plenty of people who had.

The subject of debate in an Athenian courtroom could also be very different to that of a typical jury case today. While neighbourly disputes and many types of criminal behaviour were considered to be private cases, public suits tended to touch on some point of public policy, such as whether a law that had been passed in Assembly accorded with the unwritten Athenian constitution. Any citizen could prosecute a public case as these were matters of national interest. Court litigation was thus an important avenue in resolving public policy differences and the Athenians pursued it with relish. This meant that not only were there many jurors assigned to each case, there were also a great many cases to be decided. Jury duty was strictly voluntary, but to handle the caseload, it was necessary for the courts to sit approximately three hundred days a year, and that meant that each citizen had to serve on a jury once every seven days. Historians believe that elderly citizens who were no longer able to engage in extensive physical labour reported for jury duty more frequently than this and that working-age men reported less frequently, but the choice was ultimately in the hands of the individual, who was free to report for duty as often as he chose. And once he was on a jury, each citizen acquired decision-making power over the case at hand.

In modern times, we are familiar enough with juries, but we take it for granted that courts are run by lawyers, officials and judges who are all legal experts. By contrast, many readers will be delighted to hear that in Athens the profession of lawyer was, at best, an underground existence, since it was illegal to give or accept money in return for providing legal advice. And the role played by Athenian judges was scarcely more elevated. While a randomly selected judge oversaw the formalities of Athenian court sittings, e.g. keeping track of the time allotted to each litigant to make his case, he did not instruct the jury, admit evidence or make any other decisions pertaining to the substance of the case. His sole task was to maintain order in the courtroom. All of the court pleadings were made by ordinary citizens and the jurors (voting collectively) took the final decision on which party should win the case.

In making this decision, the jurors were often free to exercise considerable discretion, as Athenian law tended to leave some leeway for interpretation. To give an example, the procedure against outrage, the *graphe hybreos*, stated that anyone could be charged with *hybris* 'who commits hybris against anyone, whether against a child or a woman or a man, from among free persons or slaves, or does anything unlawful against any of these'.[3] As this makes clear, the law set out the circle of possible victims, but failed to define what *hybris* actually was, except for the literal meaning of the word, which is 'something outrageous'. Whether or not the accused had actually done something outrageous was left to the interpretation of the jurors. As one historian put it:

> [I]t would be more in accordance with Athenian habits to devise a criminal procedure without having any specific charge in mind. That is, if anyone in Athens thought that an act deserving punishment had been committed, he could report his information to an appropriate authority; he did not necessarily have to specify a substantive provision of criminal law against which the alleged act offended; he reported the act because he found it outrageous and deserving of punishment.[4]

---

3 Sealey, 'Ephialtes, Eisangelia and the Council', 310, at 314.
4 Ibid., at 316 et seq.

The Athenian citizen was expected to take an active role in deciding which behaviour to punish or reward. If a particular behaviour aggravated him, he could take its perpetrator to court, where they could conduct their argument before the people. In modern courts, we tend to be limited to debating details because the values to be applied have already been decided upon by the people whom we elect to make laws for us. By contrast, in Athens, it was the prerogative of the people to make adjustments to the law and its interpretation at any given time. Law was not so much about applying predetermined values, as about giving citizens a place to have their disputes resolved by the community.

Sometimes this emphasis on community participation over points of law can give the erroneous impression that Athens was a more primitive society than our own.

It wasn't.

The Athenian court system was *extremely* sophisticated and furnished with many special procedures that would not be out of place in a modern courtroom. And because they spent so much time in court, many jurors had an impressive grasp of Athenian legal history. The choice to keep laws flexible was an intentional one, taken precisely in order to force the disputing parties to take a case to court, where a democratic decision could be rendered.

Athenian democratic courts were thus a complement to the Assembly. Although they often reconsidered Assembly decisions from a more legalistic angle, they did not operate as a 'check' on the power of the people in the way that modern courts operating under the doctrine of a separation of powers do. Instead, as in Assembly, the people decided on matters in numbers large enough to accurately represent the entire populace. The courts thus supported the Assembly instead of detracting from it, deepening the quality of participation and democracy in Athens. This attribute was deepened further still by the remarkable way in which Athens selected its public officials.

Public officials: selected to serve

Since the vast majority of decisions were taken by citizens in Assembly, where attendance was determined on a first-come-first-serve basis, and in the law courts, where jurors were assigned to cases randomly, Athens' administrative officials (called *archai*) were not much more than a set of hands obligated to carry out the will of the people as expressed in the democratic fora. Nonetheless, while officials in Athens did not enjoy very much decision-making power, they often still had important tasks to carry out. *Someone* had to keep the bureaucracy of a powerful country like Athens ticking over on a day-to-day basis, and the Athenians had some interesting ideas on who this should be.

Everyone.

In democratic Athens, the people held all political power in the state. This meant that they had to initiate and fulfil all public matters themselves. There was no king or other authority figure that they could turn to. Since each person enjoyed the same degree of responsibility for state decisions and actions, they also had a duty to help make those decisions and actions the best ones possible. To say that a person was an Athenian citizen and that they had an obligation to participate in running the nation was redundant. Only in very rare cases, such as the appointment of military generals, ambassadors to other nations and national treasurers, were other personal qualities or attributes felt to supersede this strong principle of participatory equality between citizens. Elections were therefore reserved to these few posts, where contact with foreign powers, many of them potentially hostile, rendered expertise necessary.

Far from considering these elections the pinnacle of democracy, the Athenians dourly judged them to be, at best, a necessary evil. In their view, no election could reflect the political equality of all citizens, because elections were competitive by their very nature. This competition, far from being an expression of fairness, ensured that elections would always be more easily won by rich, powerful, popular and eloquent candidates. Not only were these attributes distributed unequally among citizens, as far as the Athenians were concerned there was no particular connection between possessing them and the ability to fulfil the vast majority of public duties. So the Athenians determined to avoid elections to the greatest extent possible. That of course meant that they had to invent another method for choosing officials. The approach they fixed upon seems like a stroke of mad genius, but it was true to their principles about democracy – they selected their officials by lottery.

Choosing officials by chance: ancient ID and a Stone Age lotto machine

To run smoothly, Athens needed thousands of officials, from the *archons* who presided over court cases to the *astynomoi* (responsible for the cleanliness of the streets), *metronomoi* (charged with ensuring that sellers used correct weights and measures) and *practores* (responsible for collecting debts and fines imposed by the courts). Simply picking all of these officials at random and assigning their duties (also at random) had the potential to be a very time-consuming task, one that came on top of the need to recruit hundreds if not thousands of jurors on a near-daily basis.

But it is in the face of seemingly insurmountable challenges like these that the extent of Athenian commitment to democracy really becomes apparent. Instead of declaring lottery selection to be too much work, the Athenians simply sat down at the drawing board and figured out a way to make it all less trouble. These efforts eventually culminated in the invention of a made-to-order allotment machine called the *cleroterion*. In one of history's comic twists, the *cleroterion* bore more than a passing resemblance to a modern Lotto 649 machine – coloured bouncing balls and all – and operating it wasn't any more difficult than drawing the lotto numbers is today.

And not only did they manage to construct a working lotto machine at a time when the crossbow was considered advanced technology, Athenian civilization had even reached the stage where all citizens were issued with identity cards. These cards were called *pinakia* and they were the ancient world's ID equivalent of a driver's licence or passport, albeit a less convenient one to carry around since they were made out of bronze instead of laminated plastic. The *pinakia* bore two or three seals and had the citizen's name, their tribe and the section of jurors that they belonged to inscribed on them.

Any citizens who wished to be chosen as an official or juror gathered at the appropriate venue and tossed their *pinakia* into a basket. The basket was then shaken to mingle the *pinakia* together and make sure no one knew where any one card was. After this step was completed, the presiding official randomly selected one of the *pinakia* from the basket. The person to whom this ID card belonged was designated '*pinakia*-inserter' for the day. This person, the *pinakia*-inserter, proceeded to randomly draw identity cards from the basket and insert each one into a groove on the face of the *cleroterion*. These grooves were neatly arranged in columns and rows, so that when the *pinakia*-inserter was finished, there would be a big square grid of properly aligned ID cards. The *pinakia*-inserter completed his work in front of the assembled citizens, who were free to wander around and have a bit of a chat with each other during the process. Once all the *pinakia* had been placed on the face of the *cleroterion*, the presiding official returned to the scene, shook up a basket of black and white balls (called *kyboi*) and poured them into a funnel that dropped them into a tube running down the side of the allotment machine. These balls all fell down in a single column next to the grid of *pinakia* that stuck out of the face of the machine. The first coloured ball to fall through the tube delivered a positive (white) or negative (black) answer regarding all those whose cards were in the first row of grooves on whether they were selected to serve as officials or jurors; the colour of the second ball determined the fate of the next row and so on.

The process was very quick and very public. Different machines were used for the various lotteries, depending on how big the pool of candidates was and how many positions needed to be filled. If drawing from a small pool, the fate of each candidate could be decided individually (single column, one *pinakion* in each row). If drawing from a large pool for many positions, the fate of five or six people would be decided at one time (five or six *pinakia* per row). Jurors,

Figure 1.1 *The cleroterion – mother of all lottos*

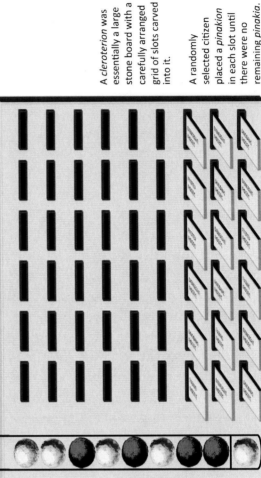

ΔΗΜΟΦΑΝΗΣ
ΚΗΦΙΣΙΕΥΣ᾽

Pinakion

The *pinakion*, or citizen ID card, was used to select officials and jurors.

On this *pinakion* the first line denotes the name and the second line the *deme* (town/village) of the citizen.

A *cleroterion* was essentially a large stone board with a carefully arranged grid of slots carved into it.

A randomly selected citizen placed a *pinakion* in each slot until there were no remaining *pinakia*.

Cut-away view of tube and *kyboi* (black and white balls).

The tube was made of metal. The Athenians released one ball at a time from the bottom of the tube to view the order in which they had fallen down.

A white ball denoted selection for the holders of all *pinakia* in that row.

A black ball meant that none of the *pinakia* holders in that row were selected.

for example, were selected using ten very large *cleroteria* that operated simultaneously.

Contrary to modern perceptions of democracy as a long-drawn-out process, the Athenians didn't like to wait around. Automation and efficiency were the rules of the day. Sometimes to assign certain duties to specific persons within a panel of officials the Athenians even used a process called *synclerosis*, or simultaneous sortition, which required two allotment machines. The cards in one machine represented the officials of the panel, the cards in the other machine represented the specific duties to be assigned. Each machine contained only one white ball and however many black ones were necessary to make up the difference. The balls were released simultaneously and the official who got a white ball for his card received the set of duties that had also received a white ball. The cards representing him and his duties were then withdrawn, the remaining cards were randomly placed in the machine again and the process was repeated. This system was so efficient that the Athenians could appoint an official and assign their duties in less time than it would take a modern hiring manager to read an applicant's CV.

But as much as the Athenians liked to keep things speedy, the lottery held an even more important advantage. Owing to the random nature of so many of the steps involved (selecting the *pinakia*-inserter, pouring the *kyboi* through the tube, etc.), it was nearly impossible to rig. Randomness was vital to Athenian democracy, because it prevented anyone from being able to exploit the rules in their favour. The fluid, ever-shifting nature of this system was aided by the fact that all posts were held only for one year and each post could be occupied by a citizen only once in his lifetime.

The lottery system worked well for the Athenians because their officials were never given any significant decision-making power. They were required to take only the most basic choices about policy implementation, and even these were subject to immediate democratic oversight. For example, those charged with keeping the streets clean could make some basic decisions about how street-cleaning was to be organized (i.e. what streets would they start on? How often should alleyways be cleaned?) or what resources were to be used (should the committee use 100 public slaves and get the job done quickly, or fifty public slaves and proceed more slowly?), provided the Assembly had not already made a decision on the point in question or directed the street-cleaning committee to make a change in its operations. However, the officials could not make more important decisions, such as whether or not to clean the streets at all or what the total public resources allotted to the task of street-cleaning should be.

This system, in which the people collectively made all decisions and attempted to avoid any distinction and competition for political power, was exactly what the Athenians – and all other ancient peoples – had in mind when they used the word *demokratia*. It was very different to what we know as democracy today, not just in the details, but in its very fabric.

Random power: the key to democratic success in Athens

Randomness is the common thread that runs through Athenian democracy. Who was admitted to Assembly was random, because it depended purely on who showed up to its sessions and how soon they did so. Likewise, selection for jury service and other official duties was made on the most random basis the Athenians could practically manage to implement, using the lottery machines.

But the preponderance of this randomness was itself no random matter; it was a deliberate choice.

It would have been much easier for the Athenians to elect or appoint officials and jurors, but instead of taking the easy route they went to some lengths to keep the identity of decision-makers uncertain until the very last moment. In doing so, they effectively obliterated focused, individualized political power. This was not an unintended by-product, but the central characteristic of democracy. No individual could have power, because the people had power. To maintain this state, democracy had to be a fluid system in which power ebbed and flowed between citizens in a manner that was pretty much impossible for any individual to manipulate on a sustained basis. Athenian democracy thus resembled in many ways what some people today would consider to be anarchy. Its basic characteristic was a near-immunity to any individual's ability to gain control of others, and it was thus an intensely egalitarian system. And more importantly, it was an egalitarian system that worked.

The Athenians were more concerned with the essence of democracy – that 'the people' should make decisions – than with any of the supposed fringe benefits, such as economic opportunity or humanitarian tolerance, that we would consider important today. However, implementing a people-power-oriented democracy proved to be an eminently suitable way to acquire these benefits. Under democracy, opportunities for political participation increased and investment in education and literacy levels rose. After all, every Athenian was entitled to give a speech in Assembly or prosecute a court case – it made sense that he would try to prepare himself to take advantage of these possibilities. Tolerance for different lifestyles, as well as more humane treatment for conquered peoples and slaves, also gained traction. In fact, die-hard conservatives often complained that it was hard for a casual observer to even tell the difference between a slave and a free Athenian citizen. And, as the icing on the cake, democratic Athens enjoyed one of the most vibrant economies on earth and everyone was allowed to participate in it and to take a hand in directing the future course of the nation. Athenian democracy, in short, was simply not subject to many of the problems we are currently experiencing: growing economic inequality, spiralling corruption and increasing political apathy. In the following chapters, I will explore some of these problems and show that – strange as it may seem to us – the Athenians were actually right in nearly everything they believed about democracy and that this is why they succeeded where we are failing.

2

The Myth of Representation

Everything should be made as simple as possible, but not simpler.

Albert Einstein

The Athenians went in for direct participation rather than representative elections because they had grasped, perhaps intuitively, something fundamental about representation that we have forgotten: that you can understand the idea of representation in two completely different ways.

One option is to accept that a representation is an artificial approximation of something real, an approximation that maintains the basic characteristics of that thing. For example, a technically accurate drawing of a tree is a representation of a tree, not, e.g., a representation of a fish. Anyone looking at the drawing will say, 'That is a tree. It has a trunk and branches and bark and leaves just like a real tree.' The more detailed the drawing is, the more specific or concrete the tree becomes. It is not just a tree, but a particular tree that cannot be mistaken for any other tree. It would be possible to look at the drawing and go out and find the real tree that it is based on, if one had the time.

Another possible definition is to say that a representation is a sign or placeholder that stands in for something else because we desire it to. For example, an artist might draw a straight line and tell others that this straight line represents a tree. The artist's viewers might accept this because they are willing to engage in an exercise of abstraction in order to understand the artist. However, the straight line certainly does not look like a run-of-the-mill tree and any person seeing it for the first time might well conclude that it represents a telephone pole or a beam of light or a skyscraper or any one of a thousand other things. The Athenians, of course, used this kind of abstract representation, too. They agreed that the sign α was a letter and that it made a certain sound, because making an arbitrary agreement like this helped them communicate. This kind of representation-pretending can be more accurately described as symbolic representation.

When it came to politics, the Athenians did not find symbolic representation helpful and so they reverted to the first understanding of representation: only something that looked like the people and preserved the basic characteristics of the people could be a representation of the people. Athenian democracy, far from being 'direct', was actually representative in this sense. About 10–20 per cent of eligible Athenian citizens attended each Assembly, while between 2 and 20 per cent sat in each court. The citizens in attendance stood in for everyone else.

By contrast, in Western nations today we elect politicians to assemble and make decisions for us. This practice is officially called 'representative democracy'. As we will see, however, this is, in many important ways, just as inaccurate as terming Athenian democracy 'direct'. In fact, while it would be more correct to call Athenian democracy 'representative democracy', it would also be more correct to call our kind of democracy 'symbolic democracy'.

This is because our elected representatives are very few in number. In Western nations they currently average between 0.0003 and 0.001 per cent of the voting population. It is mathematically impossible for such a small percentage of citizens to represent the entire nation in something as complex as political decision-making: they just cannot provide enough depth of information. Relying on such extremely small numbers of 'representatives' is the equivalent to drawing a straight line and asking people to believe that it is a tree, not a telephone pole. The representation exists only in an abstract sense and only because (some) people agree that it does. One straight line cannot convey the complexity of any particular tree. Likewise, a very small percentage of a nation's population cannot accurately reflect the characteristics and complex desires of the entire population. It is convenient to believe that they do, but this is a false belief that is not supported by the facts.

Exactly how and why this representative inaccuracy occurs varies from electoral system to electoral system, so in this chapter I will examine some of the most common electoral systems around the world, and show why the Athenians were right to reject them.

First-past-the-post: the winner takes it all

The first-past-the-post (FPTP) electoral system is virtually synonymous with the term 'democracy' in English-speaking countries. It is used in Canada, India, the United States, the United Kingdom and (before 1993) in New Zealand. When elections are held in a first-past-the-post country, the territory of the state is divided into ridings or districts. In each riding, party or independent candidates stand for election and the candidate who receives the most votes cast in the riding becomes a Member of Parliament (MP). The MPs sitting in Parliament then elect a prime minister, who is almost invariably the head of the party that won the most seats. Following his or her election, the prime minister forms a government by choosing a cabinet of ministers who each have a specific area of responsibility, such as education or health. While there is not always a formal requirement that these ministers are themselves Members of Parliament, they nearly always are, as well as being important members within the winning party. This is slightly different in the USA, where the president is elected separately from the representatives in Congress. However, the members of Congress impact on legislative activity in a similar way to parliaments in other nations, and members of Congress are chosen in the same way and with the same flaws as MPs are.

This is the version of first-past-the-post voting that we teach our children, but below its facile surface, the FPTP electoral system is fraught with difficulty.

Vote-wasting: not everything that can be counted counts

You will often hear it said, in connection with elections, that every vote counts. But this is not technically true. Many votes are wasted during the electoral process and this nearly always skews the election outcome. This is true in all electoral systems, but it is especially true under FPTP voting.

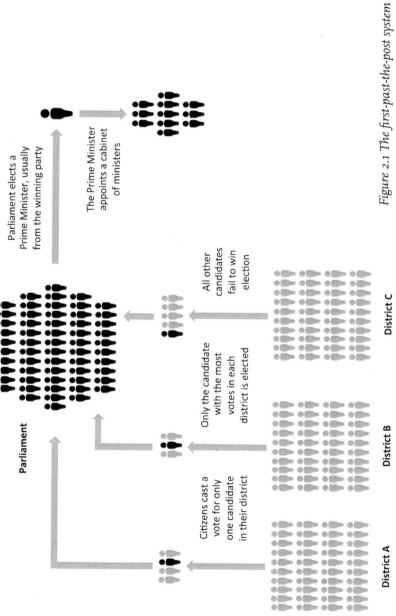

Figure 2.1 The first-past-the-post system

Parliament elects a Prime Minister, usually from the winning party

The Prime Minister appoints a cabinet of ministers

Parliament

All other candidates fail to win election

Only the candidate with the most votes in each district is elected

Citizens cast a vote for only one candidate in their district

District A

District B

District C

Under FPTP, any candidate who receives the most votes in their district wins the election and becomes a Member of Parliament or Congress. There is no minimum requirement as to how many votes this needs to be, and in multiparty systems (such as those in Canada and Britain) a candidate might win his riding with as little as 30 per cent of the vote. In the United States, because there are usually only two candidates running, the winning candidate tends to receive at least 50 per cent of the vote, and we experience the other extreme, with some candidates receiving up to 70 or 80 per cent of the vote in their district. Both types of outcome cause severe inaccuracies in the entire electoral process.

This is because the idea that the composition of Congress or Parliament truly reflects the way in which all people voted in the last election is nothing more than the purest fantasy.

We all know that an MP or Congressperson gets to where they are because a certain number of people vote for them in their riding. However, we also know that in any given election many people vote against the candidate who eventually wins. These latter votes do not transfer into a seat in Parliament for the MP of their choice for the very good reason that the person of their choice has lost the election and instead of getting a seat in Parliament has to go back to their day job. Nothing at all materializes from any vote in favour of a losing candidate – to all intents and purposes these votes disappear into thin air, and when we look at Parliament, we cannot find a single MP who owes their job to any of these voters. The ultimate outcome of the election and the composition of Parliament would have been *exactly the same* if every single person who voted for a losing candidate had stayed at home. So their votes are often called 'wasted votes'.

But oddly enough, we are asked to accept that these voters are adequately 'represented' by an MP who has publicly endorsed a platform that they voted *against*. That works only if we accept that political representation is merely symbolic. A representative might *symbolize* all voters in his or her riding in that, as the only person from the area, they act as a sort of national 'placeholder' for it, but they are hardly going to act in the interests of those who voted against them over the course of their time in office.

Suppose, for example, that a liberal voter who supports gay and lesbian rights, affirmative action, public healthcare, cutbacks on defence spending, higher corporate taxes and decriminalization of recreational drugs duly casts their vote for a liberal candidate who agrees with them on these policies. Their district, however, elects a staunch conservative who opposes all of these things and proceeds to take corresponding action in Parliament. It can hardly be said that this conservative MP is truly 'representing' the liberal voter in Parliament by doing the complete opposite of what the voter would do if they were there. The MP is merely symbolically standing in for them. In real terms, the voter who casts a ballot in favour of a losing candidate does not have any representation for the next four to five years, and therefore in the national decision-making process these people are as invisible as they are silent.

In multiparty systems, this means that quite often 50–70 per cent of the votes cast in any national election do not go on to have any impact on the composition of Parliament. They are completely wasted. In the United States, this is mitigated by the de facto two-party system, but still present. Although representatives who receive 70–80 per cent of votes cast in their district exist, representatives who receive only 50.1 or 55 per cent of the vote are not uncommon, either. In these cases, approximately 45 per cent of voters also cast wasted votes that are not reflected in the composition of Congress. These voters drop off the electoral stage and have no voice in future political decisions until the next election. Debate in Congress occurs only among the winners. The losers (a substantial proportion of the entire population) are excluded.

So Parliament is not at all a miniature version of 'the people'. It is a miniature version of *some* of the people. It does not look like 'the people' as a whole – it looks quite different. In fact, it is skewed and distorted, like a picture of a room seen through a broken mirror.

This is the first way that election skewing occurs.

The second way that elections deliver skewed results is less intuitive.

Not only are all the votes cast for losing candidates wasted, *all of the votes cast for a winning candidate which that candidate did not need in order to win are also wasted*. This is because it is irrelevant whether a winning candidate receives 30, 50 or 80 per cent of the vote; all that matters is that he gets more votes than anyone else in his riding. Any votes that surpass that mark (wherever it lies, but at a maximum of 50.1 per cent) are pointless because they do not affect the composition of Parliament or Congress. A representative who receives 70 per cent of the vote in his district gets only one vote in Congress, just like a representative who receives 50.1 per cent of the vote in his district. Therefore, those voters whose votes were not needed for the win are just as invisible as those who voted for a losing candidate. After all, they do not get an extra half-representative if their district votes overwhelmingly in favour of the winner.

Thus, the only people who are ever truly represented in a first-past-the-post system are those people who cast a vote for the winning candidate in their riding that that candidate needed to win, because these are the only people whose votes affect the composition of Parliament or Congress.

This has serious consequences for our democracies.

The high number of wasted votes makes it virtually impossible for the FPTP system to produce a parliament that accurately reflects voter preferences. These are not minor inaccuracies, but sizeable discrepancies between the real votes a party receives (known as 'the popular vote') and the number of seats it obtains in Parliament. Large parties usually receive more seats in Parliament than they deserve based on the votes acquired, and small parties generally receive fewer seats than they deserve. This ultimately means that the composition of our Parliament or Congress does not match up to the way we voted. British parliamentary elections over the last three decades show just how deeply vote-skewing affects FPTP systems:

- the British Labour and Conservative parties received just 70 per cent of the popular vote in 1983, 73 per cent in 1987 and 76 per cent in 1992, but garnered 93 per cent or more of the seats in Parliament following all three elections, an average of 20 per cent more seats than they deserved based on the direction in which British voters had actually cast their ballots;
- the Labour Party alone won 63.4 per cent of seats in 1997 with only 43.2 per cent of the vote and 62.5 per cent of seats

in 2001 with only 40.7 per cent of the vote. The Conservatives dropped to being under-represented, receiving only about 25 per cent of seats and 30 per cent of the popular vote in both elections. While Labour polled only 10 per cent higher than the Conservatives, they received 40 per cent more seats in Parliament following each election;

• conversely, Britain's 'third party', the Liberal Democrats, received 18.6 per cent of the popular vote in 1974, but only 2 per cent of parliamentary seats. Decades later, the pattern remained much the same. In 1992, the party garnered 3.1 per cent of seats in Parliament with 17.8 per cent of the popular vote and 8 per cent of seats in 2001 with 18.3 per cent of the vote.

This pattern of serious misrepresentation has continued uninterrupted to the present day: in the 2015 British elections, the Conservative Party won 331 parliamentary seats or 51 per cent of all available seats with just 36.9 per cent of the popular vote. The Labour Party received only 6 per cent fewer votes than the Conservatives with 30.4 per cent of the popular vote, but garnered nearly a hundred fewer seats in Parliament. In fact, although the Labour Party increased its share of votes by 1.4 per cent over the 2010 election, it *lost* twenty-six seats. In the same election, the Liberal Democrats received 8 per cent of the popular vote, but garnered only eight seats or 1 per cent of all available seats. The Scottish National Party (SNP) polled only half the votes that the LibDems had (4.7 per cent of the popular vote) but were rewarded with seven times as many seats in Parliament – fifty-six seats. UKIP suffered a similar fate to the LibDems – although the party attracted 12.6 per cent of the popular vote, it won only a single seat or 0.15 per cent of all available seats. The Greens also attained one seat, but with only 3.8 per cent of the popular vote. This means that in the last UK election, a vote for the Green Party was worth more than three times a vote for UKIP, a vote for the LibDems was worth twelve times as much, and a vote for the SNP about 150 times as much. A vote for the Conservative Party was worth nearly nine times a vote for the LibDems, about 1.2 times as much as a vote for Labour, and about a hundred times as much as a vote for UKIP.

Outcomes like this make a mockery of the principle 'one man, one vote', but are the inevitable consequence of restricting political participation to a number of people (MPs) so statistically small as to be unable to accurately reflect voter preferences. Had the Athenians allowed only 0.001 per cent of citizens to vote in Assembly, they would have run into this very same problem, with certain sectors of society relegated to habitual under-representation while others enjoy habitual over-representation.

This pattern is borne out across all first-past-the-post systems, because it is inherent in them:

- in the 1978 New Zealand elections, the Social Credit Party obtained 17.1 per cent of the popular vote, but only one seat (just over 1 per cent of available seats); in 1981 they won 20.7 per cent of the vote, but obtained only two seats, thereby once again being under-represented in Parliament by a factor of 10, and disappearing as a party shortly thereafter;
- in the Canadian federal election of 1980, the Liberal Party received 20 per cent of the popular vote in British

Columbia, Alberta and Saskatchewan, but no seats in those provinces, while the Progressive Conservative Party polled at 12 per cent of the popular vote in Quebec, but procured only one seat of the seventy-five seats available;

• on a national level the Canadian New Democratic Party (NDP) gained only 9 per cent of parliamentary seats with 17 per cent of the popular vote in 2006, and only 6 per cent of seats in 2004 with 16 per cent of the popular vote.

As these statistics indicate, the very elections that we so often extol as the essence of democracy are actually a crude and inaccurate method of achieving representative government, because they often fail to capture both moderate levels of support that are widely dispersed across voting districts, and high levels of support concentrated in a few districts. These votes simply do not show up on the system.

The people who sit in parliaments are not an accurate reflection of society in general, but a warped version, a reflection that has passed through the broken mirror of elections. So it is a foregone conclusion that the things they choose to do are also a warped version of what society as a whole would have chosen. When a voter casts their ballot, they have no control over which way the faulty 'mirror' of elections is going to fracture, or whether they will actually be represented in the future Parliament. They could end up over- or under-represented by orders of magnitude for reasons entirely beyond their ability to influence. That is a disturbing thought in itself, but it is just the beginning of the problems that are caused by inaccurate representation.

Manufactured majorities: warped government in every sense of the word

Where the statistical problems with skewed representation really come into their own is not in generating parliaments distorted by inaccuracies, but in leading to equally disproportionate governments. This is because vote-skewing can lead to what is known as a 'manufactured majority'. This term refers to one of two situations: the extremely frequent 'relative manufactured majority' and the somewhat rarer, but infinitely more hair-raising, 'absolute manufactured majority'.

A relative manufactured majority occurs when the governing party wins more votes than any other party in the last election, but still less than one half of all votes, i.e. the party wins a majority of what is known as 'the popular vote', but it is a relative majority. However, despite winning less than half the popular vote, this party wins more than 50 per cent of all seats in Parliament and therefore forms a single-party government.

As we have seen, this is possible because each candidate only needs to win their riding to be elected. It does not matter if they win with 30 or 50 or 80 per cent of the popular vote, because if they win they win 100 per cent of that parliamentary seat. And all a party needs to form the government is to win 50.1 per cent of parliamentary seats. It is irrelevant if they win each one of those seats with only 30 per cent of the vote. It is irrelevant if no single person in the other 49.9 per cent of ridings in the country votes for them. None of these votes matters. All that matters is that a relative majority votes for them in more than 50 per cent of all ridings.

Manufactured majorities of this type are extremely common in FPTP countries. In Canada, out of twenty-two federal elections held between 1945 and 2011, only four resulted in a party simultaneously obtaining the majority of seats in Parliament and the majority of the popular vote. All other elections resulted in either relative manufactured majorities (this occurred nine times in all or 40 per cent of the time) or minority governments, in which a party was able to form a single-party government, generally having received less than 40 per cent of the popular vote, but nonetheless governing for between one and three years. In Britain, the situation is even more exaggerated. There, no party since the Second World War has managed to procure the majority of seats and votes simultaneously. Of the nineteen British elections held since the war, fifteen resulted in relative manufactured majorities, including the latest one held in May 2015, in which the Conservative Party won 51 per cent of seats in Parliament – and therefore the right to form the government – with only 36.9 per cent of the popular vote.

The relative manufactured majority even afflicts the American presidential system. Despite the fact that this election, revolving around only one office, is supposed to represent a clear expression of majority will, Harry Truman, John F. Kennedy and Richard Nixon all became president without achieving an absolute majority of the popular vote, while in 1860 Abraham Lincoln became president with only 39.8 per cent of the popular vote.

Despite these weak showings, anyone who attains election by manufactured majority becomes prime minister or president in exactly the same manner as someone elected by popular majority. This person does not wield 39 per cent of political power or 45 per cent of political power – they wield 100 per cent of it. This can have serious effects on the future course of national politics, resulting in different policies being implemented than those the citizens of a nation would have chosen themselves. The 1988 Canadian federal election delivers a particularly clear example of just how far-reaching those consequences can be.

In that election, the Progressive Conservative Party obtained 43 per cent of the popular vote, while their closest rivals, the Liberal Party, received 31.9 per cent of the vote and the New Democratic Party attained 20.4 per cent of the vote. Although the Progressive Conservatives received more votes than any other single party, they were still well short of 50 per cent. The Progressive Conservatives, however, took 57 per cent of all available seats in the Canadian House of Commons, 14 per cent more than they were entitled to based on the percentage of the vote they received. Consequently, the Progressive Conservatives' failure, by a significant margin, to obtain a majority of the popular vote was transformed into a comfortable majority of parliamentary seats that easily allowed them to form the government without relying on the support of either the Liberals or the NDP, who between them had received 52.3 per cent of the popular vote, but only 42 per cent of seats available in the House of Commons.

This is significant, because the Canadian election of 1988 revolved around the possibility of ratifying a Free Trade Agreement (known as 'the FTA') with the USA, Canada's largest trading partner. Debate on this point was fierce; while the Progressive Conservatives campaigned in favour of the Free Trade Agreement, the Liberals and the NDP campaigned against it. The majority of Canadians voted for one of these latter two parties: in other words, *most Canadians voted for a party that opposed ratifying the FTA*. However, because the

Conservatives won the majority of parliamentary seats, they could form the national government while the other two parties could not (even if they had formed a coalition). The Progressive Conservatives proceeded to implement the election platform that most Canadians had voted against and ratified the FTA during their term in office. The treaty was soon expanded into the North American Free Trade Agreement (NAFTA), which also includes Mexico.

By ratifying first the FTA and then NAFTA the Canadian government bound itself, and therefore, indirectly, all Canadians, to abide by NAFTA's rules. This means that if Canadian laws ever conflict with these regulations any foreign company that suffers damages from that law can sue Canada. The country is effectively locked into an agreement that its citizens cannot change no matter what the incentive is to do so. To give but one example:

In 1997, seven years after the FTA and two years after NAFTA was concluded, the Canadian government (now formed by the Liberal Party) banned the use of a chemical additive called MMT in car fuel. Ethyl Corporation, an American company and the sole producer of the MMT used in Canadian gasoline, brought a case against the Canadian government alleging that the ban violated NAFTA rules. As a result, Canada repealed the ban, despite evidence that MMT may cause nerve damage when inhaled from car exhaust. Although Canadians did not vote in favour of the FTA and did not publicly debate repealing the ban on MMT, MMT went straight back into Canadian gasoline for several years before finally being phased out when car manufacturers complained that it harmed their engines. We could apply many labels to this process, but 'the will of the people' does not readily spring to mind as an appropriate term. First-past-the-post systems, however, enable exactly these kinds of inaccurate and unrepresentative outcomes to occur.

Owing to the way votes are counted in FPTP systems, it is possible for a party to come to power even when most people vote against its policies. Once that happens, it is not only possible for that party to impose its policies on the nation during its time in office, it can use an international treaty to lock the country into that policy *forever*. This electoral outcome is not foreseeable by the voters, nor do they have any control over it. If they did, the Conservatives would never have attained 57 per cent of seats in Parliament in the 1988 Canadian federal election. They would have received the 43 per cent of seats that Canadians chose to allot them. However, since our representation is too thin to be accurate, it is possible for this kind of rupture to occur between the way people vote and the government that they ultimately live under.

The case of the Progressive Conservative 'victory' and the FTA is certainly mind-boggling enough for anyone's taste, but pause for a moment to consider that this is only the beginning of the mayhem caused by attempting to run a representative government with only minuscule levels of representation. Over time, the inaccuracies engendered by this approach make it nearly impossible to even determine what the majority will is on any given point. To continue with the example of NAFTA:

The Liberal Party that succeeded the Conservatives and banned MMT came to power on the back of a majority that was *even more skewed* than the Progressive Conservatives' had been (the Liberal Party won 60 per cent of seats in 1993 with 41.24 per cent of the popular vote and 51.5 per cent of seats in 1997 with 38.46 per cent of the popular vote). Not only that, it was this Liberal (manufactured majority) government that expanded the FTA to include Mexico and become NAFTA. So, by (sort of) voting in a Liberal government in another manufactured majority that not only condoned the FTA but expanded it to include Mexico, did Canadians somehow retroactively agree to (NA)FTA and having MMT in their gasoline, even though the Liberals banned it?

It is anyone's guess.

The only certainties are that the MMT ban was repealed because Conservatives and Liberals successively locked Canadians into a lopsided international free trade policy after a majority of them had voted for opposing parties in 1988, 1993 and 1997, and that they were able to do so because the composition of Parliament did not accurately reflect the way Canadians had voted. Had the composition of Parliament been an accurate reflection of Canadian voting preferences, all of these governments would either have formed the opposition or been forced to go into coalition.

The inaccuracies of this style of 'representation' mean that people who live in FPTP systems almost invariably live under a government that the majority of voters voted *against*. Even if parties faithfully stick to their election promises, chances are that whatever they do – from education to healthcare to taxation to foreign policy – it will be something that *most* people have not endorsed. And this, unfortunately, is only the beginning of our problems, because FPTP systems not only produce relative manufactured majorities, they also produce absolute manufactured majorities.

In the absolute manufactured majority, the governing party (Party A) fails to win as many votes as one of its competitors (Party B). Nonetheless, Party A wins the most seats in Parliament and therefore forms the government, while Party B becomes the opposition. This means that the party that won the most votes does *not* become the government.

To take some real-life examples: In the 1896 Canadian federal election, the Liberal Party received 45.1 per cent of the popular vote and won 118 seats in Parliament (55 per cent of all available seats). Although the Conservative Party won 46.1 per cent of the vote – 1 per cent more than the Liberals – they obtained only eighty-eight seats in Parliament (41 per cent of all available seats) and therefore had to be content with forming the opposition. The situation was reversed in the federal election of 1957. This time the Progressive Conservatives won only 38.9 per cent of the popular vote, but received 112 seats in Parliament, whereas the Liberal Party won 40.9 per cent of the popular vote, but only 105 seats in Parliament.

Following each of these elections, Canadians did *not* get the government they had voted for. Instead, mind-boggling as it is to contemplate, they ended up being governed by the losing party. It is impossible to reconcile such an outcome with the idea that modern democracies are based on the will of the people or that there is any kind of rational connection between the way citizens cast their votes and the policies their nation ultimately pursues. How can the government possibly be said to represent the people when it is beyond dispute that those people preferred to have a different government?

And although it sounds very strange, absolute manufactured majorities are far from rare occurrences. In fact, a high percentage of governments in FPTP systems that are not relative manufactured majorities are absolute manufactured majorities. Consider the following:

- of the fifteen British elections held between 1918 and 2010, three of them resulted in the party that had won the popular vote failing to secure enough seats in Parliament to form the government. Instead, this privilege went to the party that had *lost* the popular vote. This occurred in 1929 and 1974 to the advantage of Labour (in 1974 Labour was able to form a minority government, as it secured four seats more than the Conservatives despite having received 0.7 per cent less of the popular vote) and in 1951 to the advantage of Conservatives. This means that during the past century, British citizens spent nearly a decade governed by a party that – but for statistical inaccuracies – should have formed the opposition instead of the government;
- in the 1978 national election in New Zealand, the National Party won 55 per cent of all seats and therefore formed the government, despite the fact that it had won only 39.8 per cent of the popular vote, while the Labour Party had won 40.4 per cent of the vote. This was repeated in 1981: Labour received 39 per cent of the popular vote, just ahead of the National Party with 38.8 per cent, but the National Party retained 51 per cent of seats and therefore formed the government;
- with perhaps the gravest consequences of all, in the 2000 US presidential election Democratic Candidate Al Gore won the popular vote with 48.38 per cent, while his rival George W. Bush received just 47.87 per cent of the popular vote – half a million votes fewer than Gore – but nonetheless became president.

It is absolutely staggering that we are willing to label these bizarre outcomes a 'representative system' of 'majority rule'. Much of the time it is patently not. For the ordinary citizen, it all seems random. There is no causal connection between the way they cast their vote and the policies the nation pursues, because reducing representation rights to less than a hundredth of a per cent of the population breaks the accuracy of this connection. There are simply too many ways in which votes can be wasted for things to be otherwise.

Since the connection between how people vote and the election outcome is skewed through these extremely low representative ratios, acquiring political power is not a matter of winning votes, it is a matter of winning seats. And this is where things really begin to go awry, because winning seats has little to do with being popular and everything to do with gaming the system.

Parties: cracking, packing and blasting to a manufactured victory

There is one set of people to whom a manufactured majority never comes as a surprise. In fact these people often work very hard to bring about manufactured majorities. These are, of course, professional politicians.

The possibility of forming the government on the back of a manufactured majority is so widely known within political circles that most parties actively attempt to take advantage of it by engaging in tactics that let them focus on winning districts instead of winning votes. Since everyone knows that FPTP is mainly inaccurate because it wastes so many votes, a shrewd politician will try to ensure that only the 'right' votes are wasted, i.e. votes cast in favour of his or her opponent.

Because merely gaining votes does not necessarily help a candidate or party come to power, gaming the system this way is often a far more effective method of getting elected than any amount of campaigning. It's not charisma or expertise which make a truly successful politician, but their willingness and ability to engage in a bit of creative accounting by cracking, packing and gerrymandering electoral districts to their own advantage.

Cracking is the art of splitting up an electoral district so that the voting majority of that district becomes a minority in two or more districts. Cracking effectively devalues certain citizens' votes by ensuring that those votes become 'wasted votes' in the new districts, unable to have any impact on the formation of government. If this does not deliver the desired results, the interested parties can always choose to 'pack' instead. Here, the electoral boundaries are drawn to swoop around pockets of certain voters and 'pack' them all into one district where they will form the majority and drown out minorities who may already be there. A particularly crass example of packing is the situation in Northern Ireland, where in 1920 the British government drew a boundary line that incorporated the maximum number of Unionists and the minimum number of Irish Republicans, thereby ensuring that Northern Ireland would vote to remain part of Great Britain for decades to come.

When they use packing and cracking, governments and parties effectively deprive certain people of their right to a meaningful vote so that they can obtain a manufactured majority for themselves. In other words, our electoral system rewards politicians for their willingness to cheat citizens out of a say in their nation's politics. Unlike in Athens, where a citizen could have a favoured policy implemented only if he persuaded a majority of his peers to approve it, our system gives the most power to those who are best able to cut others out of the decision-making process.

One need only look at the unnatural contours of voting districts in the USA to see evidence of the time and effort that parties put into ensuring that their opponents' supporters cast their votes in vain.

It is obvious from the effort that went into designing these districts along artificial lines that manufactured majorities are not occasional, regrettable blips on the path of representative democracy, but a well-known and cherished method of winning elections, a method which parties are willing to pursue with a level of whimsy and imagination that would have stopped Salvador Dalí dead in his tracks.

In some countries, where packing and cracking are not as easy to use, parties turn to other tactics, such as malapportionment (i.e. varying the number of voters in voting districts to dilute the voting power of those in larger districts and magnify the power of those in smaller districts) or simply targeting their advertisement and election efforts in certain districts. After all, as long as the party wins the requisite number of seats, it does not matter if the voters in neglected ridings agree with their policy or not. The party simply cuts these people out of its calculations and does not bother to engage with them.

And the fact that all political parties engage in this behaviour does not by any means cancel out its effects or transmutate it into 'rule by the people'. The one thing common to manufactured majorities is that they result from the majority of people voting *against* the electoral victor.

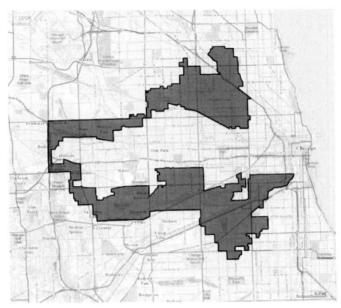

Illinois – 4th District

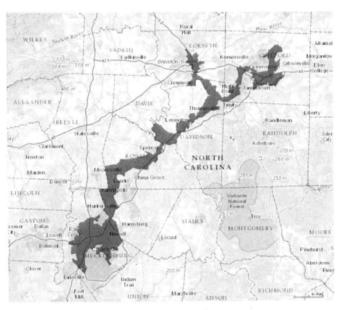

North Carolina – 12th District

Figure 2.2 American voting districts – an art form bounded only by imagination

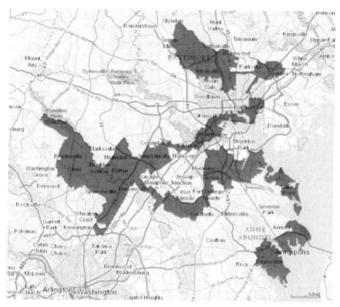

Maryland – 3rd District – 'The Praying Mantis'

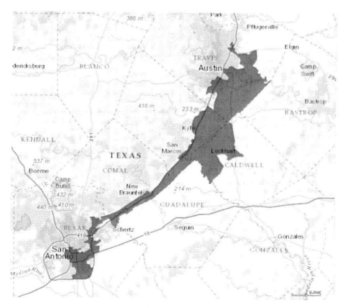

Texas – 35th District

Regardless of the number of parties engaged in attempting to achieve a manufactured majority, success is always – by definition – contrary to the will of the majority.

To voters, electoral outcomes are like lotteries; the people may or may not get the government that they voted for. Whether or not they do is beyond their control. But for politicians, election outcomes are foreseeable and manipulable. Elections, therefore, are not just a lottery, they are a rigged lottery. This is the absolutely inescapable consequence of handing power to a number of people so small that they are unable to accurately reflect the society as a whole. When this happens the chain of causality between the representative and the represented is broken. Representation is not real, but merely symbolic; a matter of belief instead of reality. The identity of the representatives does not depend on majority will, but rather on their ability to game the system, and therefore this is precisely what they focus their energies on.

And this is *exactly* why the Athenians avoided elections whenever they could – elections tempted candidates to adopt corrupt practices in order to garner votes. The Athenians were right to have such a negative view of elections, and not only with regard to first-past-the-post voting.

Other electoral systems

In recent years, the issues surrounding first-past-the-post systems and their potential for abuse have become more well known and support for swapping FPTP for other voting systems has increased. New Zealand, which had particularly suffered from manufactured majorities, replaced FPTP with the personalized proportional vote in 1993, while voters in the Canadian province of British Columbia voted to replace first-past-the-post with the single transferable vote in 2009.[1] However, although some electoral systems are *more* accurate than FPTP, they are still not *actually* accurate. All electoral systems can produce manufactured majorities, not to mention other statistical irregularities, because the basic problem – the impossibility of electing a large enough percentage of the population to be statistically accurate – is still present.

The single transferable vote: musical chairs

The single transferable voting system (STV) is used in Ireland, Tasmania and Malta. STV, it must be confessed, vaguely sounds like the kind of disease that comes as a consequence of a particularly wild night out – an association that, as we will see, is not entirely inapt. Under STV, the voter does not cast a ballot in favour of one candidate, thus implicitly rejecting all others. Instead, he numbers each candidate (or as many as he likes) in order of preference, i.e. he gives the candidate he likes best a '1', the candidate he likes second best a '2' and so forth. In each riding not one but several candidates are elected. To be deemed elected a candidate must procure one vote more than the total number of votes cast, divided by the number of seats contested in the riding plus one. For example, if there are three seats in a riding and 30,000 votes are cast, a candidate has to receive at least 7,501 votes to get elected. Whether or not a candidate has

---

1 As a 60 per cent vote in favour would have been required to effect this change, the motion was narrowly defeated (Statement of Votes, Referendum on Electoral Reform, 12 May 2009 (Elections BC, 15 January 2010), www.elections.bc.ca/docs/rpt/2009Ref/2009-Ref-SOV.pdf).

Figure 2.3 The single transferable system

First Count

In each district, there are several seats to be won. A quota is determined by dividing the number of votes by the number of seats + 1

A	....5,901 votes	→ Eliminated
B	....325 votes	
C	....**9,602 votes**	→ Elected
D	....863 votes	
E	....3,512 votes	
F	....6,912 votes	
G	....2,885 votes	

30,000 total votes
3 seats
Quota: 7,501

Candidates, who have obtained the quota of first preference votes are deemed elected. Candidates with the lowest votes are eliminated.

Redistribution of
- 325 votes of eliminated candidate
- 2,101 excess votes of elected candidate

A	....5,901 + 969 = 6,870 votes	
B	....325 votes (-325 transfers)	→ Eliminated (1st count)
C	....9,602 votes (-2,101 transfers)	→ Elected (1st count)
D	....863 + 82 = 945 votes	
E	....3,512 + 206 = 3,718 votes	→ Eliminated (2nd count)
F	....6,912 + 802 = **7,714 votes**	→ Elected (2nd count)
G	....2,885 + 367 = 3,252 votes	

30,000 total votes
3 seats
Quorum: 7,501

Candidates, who have obtained the quota after the second count are deemed elected. Candidates with the lowest votes are eliminated.

Citizens vote

by ranking

candidates in

order of preference

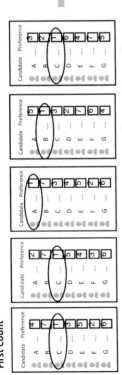

Second Count

In the second count, all second preference votes from eliminated candidates and the excess votes from elected candidates are counted

As C was elected, the second preference for F is counted in the second count

As B has been eliminated, the second preference for D is counted in the second count

A is still in the running, so second preference votes on these ballots will not be considered yet

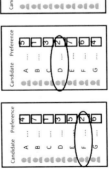

Subsequent Counts: Counting, electing, eliminating and re-distribution of votes continues until all seats for the district have been filled.

reached that quota is often determined over several rounds of calculation.

When a voter gives a candidate a '1' this is known as a first-preference vote. If a candidate receives more first preferences than he needs, he is deemed elected and his excess votes are redistributed among the remaining candidates according to the second preferences marked on the ballots. In the absence of excess votes for redistribution, the lowest polling candidate is eliminated and his votes are redistributed among the remaining candidates according to the second preferences marked on them. The redistribution is performed as many times as necessary until the seats for the riding are filled.

As this indicates, vote-counting under STV is a complicated and time-consuming process. In fact, tabulating the results of a national election can sometimes take *days*. However, the problems with STV have nothing to do with its ability to subject hopeful candidates to so many hours of agonizing tedium – on the contrary, one could see this as one of its more satisfying elements. Once again, the issue lies in the numbers.

Because STV requires so much effort, there is a certain inclination to believe that it must surely deliver some stellar results. And on the face of it, STV does look very satisfying. In fact, it seems as if the voter is getting a terrific bargain, because he gets a say on every candidate. If his first choice does not make it into the Parliament or Congress, his second choice might, because his vote continues to be transferred down the line. Therefore, it appears that STV does not waste votes, and since wasted votes are the root cause of our 'unrepresentative' democracies, that the problem has been solved.

But this is deceptive. Votes can be wasted under the STV system, and indeed are wasted whenever a ballot becomes non-transferable. This happens when election officials attempt to transfer a ballot, but all of the candidates (if any) for which the voter has given his lower preferences have already been either elected or eliminated. The ballot has nowhere to go, so it is wasted. It is also possible for the vote to be wasted if it is given or transferred to a candidate left in the count after the quota of candidates has been elected. The candidate gets the vote, but it does not lead to any results in the real world.

Just as problematic is the fact that STV also fails to ensure monotonicity (i.e. the principle that a vote in favour should always help and never harm a candidate), because the candidates eliminated are always the lowest-ranking candidates *at the time*. If the counting continued it would be theoretically possible for a candidate lagging behind in the first few rounds to overtake a candidate who was temporarily farther ahead of them at the time they were eliminated. Because in STV systems which candidate is eliminated with each round is strategically important, it is possible for a candidate to garner too many first-preference votes in the first round, thus causing the elimination of another candidate whose transfers go to a third candidate who then overtakes and beats the original candidate to the quota. That means that a vote in favour could help a candidate win election or knock him out of the race. Needless to say, from the point of view of the voter, this is about as random as it gets. When he casts his vote for someone, he wants to help that person get elected, not contribute to eliminating them from the competition. But under STV it is possible to end up ruled by a 'representative' whom you voted against because they directly benefited from that vote against them.

In consideration of these facts, it should come as no surprise that manufactured majorities are as endemic to STV as they are to first-past-the-post systems. Manufactured majorities occur about one third of the time in the Australian Senate and about 20 per cent of the time in Ireland, while four of six Tasmanian elections held under STV between 1916 and 1969 brought a party to government with fewer votes than those procured by the other main party. Thus, despite STV's tempting complexity, it is not any more accurate than FPTP voting. There is often no direct link between how voters cast their ballots and the government whose policies they end up living under.

The alternative to these candidate-centred systems is the proportional voting system, widely used in Europe. It can be divided into two main branches: the personalized proportional vote and the pure proportional vote. The fact that these systems have the word 'proportional' in their names is pretty hopeful, because it indicates that someone was at least thinking about that point and they are *better* in this regard – just not good enough to really be called democratically accurate.

Personalized proportional voting: one man, two votes

In the personalized proportional system used in Germany and (since 1993) New Zealand each voter has not one but two votes. The first vote is cast directly for a local candidate, while the second vote is cast for a party. The Parliament is divided (for the purposes of tabulating the election results) into two halves. The seats in the first half are filled by all the candidates who were elected directly by winning at least the relative majority of the first votes in their ridings. The seats in the second half are filled by party members, whose names have been compiled in set lists prior to election, in accordance with the percentage of second votes received by that party. This calculation is processed in several steps. First, the percentage of votes one party receives nationwide[2] is calculated, which determines the percentage of seats it has a right to fill in Parliament. For example, if a party receives 35 per cent of all votes, its members are entitled to fill 35 per cent of parliamentary seats. The number of seats that the party has already filled with their directly elected candidates is subtracted from this number. The remaining seats (if any) are then filled from the parties' lists. The process continues until all seats in the Parliament are filled.

The fly in the ointment is that parties sometimes win more direct seats in Parliament than they have a right to given the percentage of the vote they received as a party, e.g. a party could fill 40 per cent of all seats in Parliament with directly elected candidates, but win only 35 per cent of the proportional second vote. In this case, extra seats are tacked on to the Parliament (known as 'overhang seats') to accommodate all of the directly elected candidates. And this practice unfortunately breaks the link between representation and the way people voted, opening up possibilities for exploitation.

Through the possibility of acquiring overhang seats it becomes possible to game the system on a wide scale, and parties in PPV nations try to do so by indulging in a practice known as vote-splitting. Vote-splitting occurs when two

---

2 Or sometimes province-wide, depending on the case.

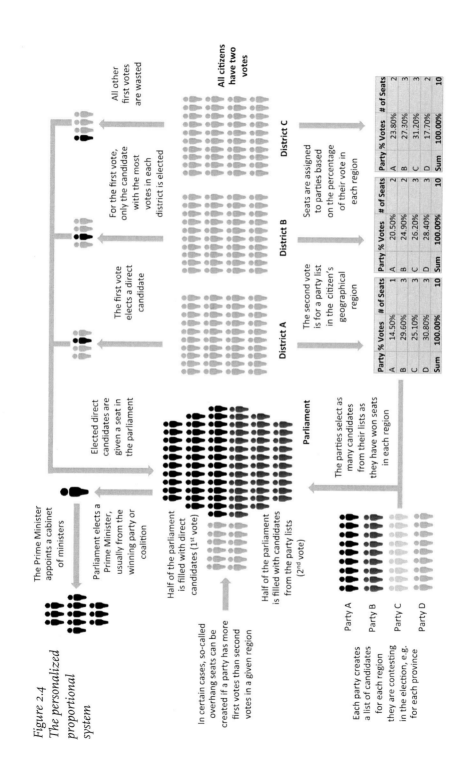

Figure 2.4
The personalized
proportional
system

All other
first votes
are wasted

**All citizens
have two
votes**

For the first vote, only the candidate with the most votes in each district is elected

The first vote
elects a direct
candidate

District A

District B

District C

The second vote
is for a party list
in the citizen's
geographical
region

Seats are assigned
to parties based
on the percentage
of their vote in
each region

Party	% Votes	# of Seats
A	14.50%	1
B	29.60%	3
C	25.10%	3
D	30.80%	3
Sum	100.00%	10

Party	% Votes	# of Seats
A	20.50%	2
B	24.90%	2
C	26.20%	3
D	28.40%	3
Sum	100.00%	10

Party	% Votes	# of Seats
A	23.80%	2
B	27.30%	2
C	31.20%	3
D	17.70%	2
Sum	100.00%	10

The Prime Minister
appoints a cabinet
of ministers

Parliament elects a
Prime Minister,
usually from the
winning party or
coalition

Elected direct
candidates are
given a seat in
the parliament

Parliament

The parties select as
many candidates
from their lists as
they have won seats
in each region

Half of the parliament
is filled with direct
candidates (1st vote)

In certain cases, so-called
overhang seats can be
created if a party has more
first votes than second
votes in a given region

Half of the parliament
is filled with candidates
from the party lists
(2nd vote)

Party A

Party B

Party C

Party D

Each party creates
a list of candidates
for each region
they are contesting
in the election, e.g.
for each province

parties with a coalition agreement encourage their combined voters to give their first vote to the larger party (which will then be over-represented via its direct candidates) and their second vote to the smaller party (which then collects an inflated number of second votes and is therefore over-represented via the lists). Because this trick involves two separate parties the direct votes and list votes cannot be tabulated against each other. If done successfully, vote-splitting always results in over-hang seats. Therefore, although the personalized proportional vote results in better representation of smaller and special-interest parties than can generally be found in first-past-the-post states, it is still open to representational deviations. If the discrepancy is in favour of the ruling party, it gives them an increased ability to pass legislation that does not enjoy much support within the party by giving the party an inflated position of strength within the legislature. Conversely, if the ruling party is weakened by an inaccuracy against it, it may be forced to go into a broader coalition and/or may be reluctant to introduce legislation for fear of further undermining its position within the Parliament.

Even more relevant, however, is the fact that, like STV, the personalized proportional vote lacks monotonicity, which can lead to what is known as 'negative vote weight' or 'inverse success value' of ballots cast. The German federal election of 2005 gives a perfect example. The election was hotly contested with results so indeterminate as to temporarily produce a hung parliament. To complicate this situation, one of the candidates for a riding in Dresden had died shortly before polling day. As a result, ballot papers in her district (Dresden-I) had to be reprinted, delaying polling there until several weeks after the national vote had been conducted.

Because the general election produced such an inconclusive result and coalition negotiations were still ongoing when residents of Dresden-I finally voted, the constituency became a topic of national focus. Sensationally, this focus was not directed at who would *win* the vote in Dresden, but rather at who would lose it, for the need to recalibrate parliamentary composition based on the outcome of this vote meant that winning the second ballot in this district would cause the CDU – which was then wrangling to form a coalition government and obtain the office of Chancellor for its candidate Angela Merkel – to lose seats in Parliament, something the party could ill afford given how tight the election race was. In fact, by polling day it was common knowledge that the CDU could not afford to receive more than 41,226 second votes in Dresden-I.

However, losing the second vote in Dresden was only half the battle. Not content to merely avoid losses, the CDU committed to maximizing their seat gains by winning the first ballot (the direct seat) while simultaneously losing the second ballot (the proportional vote). In order to make that happen CDU supporters had to go to the polls, giving their first vote to the CDU direct candidate, Andreas Lämmel, and their second vote to any party except the CDU. If this was done successfully, the CDU would then gain a further overhang seat in Mr Lämmel while not losing any of the other overhang seats that they had already gained.

Effectively shooting themselves in the foot this way was not easy since the CDU had traditionally polled very well in the district, normally receiving over 30 per cent of all second votes. However, the party was able to successfully communicate its strategy to its followers. Lämmel was elected with 37 per cent of all direct votes, while the CDU plummeted on the proportional vote to only 24 per cent. This represented an extreme level of vote-splitting and ensured that the second vote came in at numbers well below what the party needed to avoid a recalculation of proportional parliamentary seats. The CDU gained another badly needed seat at a time when the very formation of the government stood in doubt, to say nothing of Angela Merkel's extremely precarious position both as elected Chancellor and as the CDU's top candidate, and they did so purely by convincing their supporters to vote for other parties!

Seen against this background, it's small wonder that Germany has been the birthplace of so much high philosophy: in a country where politicians are able to successfully explain to tens of thousands of voters that is imperative for them to go out and simultaneously vote for and against them, the occasional musing on dialectical materialism or categorical imperatives surely holds no terrors.

As the 2005 election in Dresden-I so admirably shows, although the personalized proportional vote is generally *more* accurate than either FPTP or STV, it is not actually accurate enough to be statistically accurate or to prevent politicians from gaming the system to produce ever greater inaccuracies in their own interests. The German Constitutional Court finally declared an end to the problems exemplified by Dresden-I in 2012 and Germany now compensates parties for any overhang seats that one party may accrue to the detriment of the others. However, it is worth noting that this decision was only rendered after the electorate had put up with the flawed system for nearly sixty years. While other personalized proportional systems could of course follow suit, such changes only succeed in transforming the personalized proportional vote into something very like a pure proportional system.

Pure proportional voting: less skewed, but skewed still

At first glance, the pure proportional vote finally seems to be the answer to our problems with electoral democracy because it involves a system of proportional voting, but dispenses with the problematic overhang seats. In the pure proportional system, political parties select lists of candidates to run in multi-member districts, voters cast one vote for the party of their choice and parliamentarians are selected from the party lists according to the proportion of the vote the party has received.[3]

Here too, however, votes are wasted, because the results for each district must be rounded and the resulting inaccuracy aggregates nationally. This means that the degree of actual representation delivered by the pure proportional vote can still vary widely, and this, indeed, often occurs in the many Continental European nations where it is most commonly used.

For example, in Finland, where broad coalitions are not uncommon, the popular vote and the seats obtained by each party usually deviate by between 0.2 and 3 per cent. It sounds small, but this difference nearly always accrues to the larger parties to the detriment of the smaller parties, and since these are the parties which are more likely to form a viable coalition, this means that a bigger bump accrues in favour of

---

3 In some systems, the voters are allowed to express a preference for one or more candidates in the party list and these must be taken into consideration when deciding which party members will enter Parliament.

Figure 2.5 The pure proportional system

Parliament elects a Prime Minister, usually from the winning party or coalition

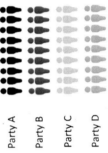

The Prime Minister appoints a cabinet of ministers

Parliament

The parties select as many candidates from their lists as they have won seats in each district.

Party A		
Party B		
Party C		
Party D		

Each party creates a list of candidates for each district they are contesting in the election

Party	Average % Votes	# of Seats – added up from districts	# of Seats deserved based on average vote percentage
A	19.60%	5	6
B	27.27%	8	8
C	27.50%	9	8
D	25.63%	8	8
Sum	**100.00%**	**30**	**30**

Based on just three districts, party C already gained one more seat than it should have received while Party A lost a seat for the same reason

Due to the small number of seats per district, statistical skewing occurs regionally and compounds nationally

Party	% Votes	# of Seats
A	23.80%	2
B	27.30%	3
C	31.20%	3
D	17.70%	2
Sum	**100.00%**	**10**

District C

Party	% Votes	# of Seats
A	20.50%	2
B	24.90%	2
C	26.20%	3
D	28.40%	3
Sum	**100.00%**	**10**

District B

Seats are assigned to parties per district based on the percentage of their vote

Party	% Votes	# of Seats
A	14.50%	1
B	29.60%	3
C	25.10%	3
D	30.80%	3
Sum	**100.00%**	**10**

In each district citizens vote for one party

District A

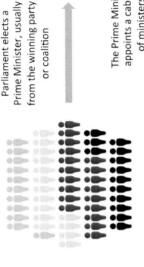

the government. In the 2007 Finnish national election, the winning coalition formed by the Centre, National Coalition, Greens and Swedish People's Party received 4.5 per cent more seats in Parliament than it deserved based on the number of votes received. The Centre and National Coalition would have been capable of forming a governing coalition on their own by a bare majority of 101 out of 200 seats solely by virtue of having accrued between them 5.5 per cent or twelve more seats than they were entitled to based on the popular vote. Had the seats been awarded accurately based on the popular vote, the Greens (who received two fewer seats than they were entitled to) would have been essential to the eventual coalition (putting them in a different negotiating position throughout the government) and that coalition would have totalled 115 seats instead of 125. Similarly, in 2015, the Centre Party received 3.5 per cent more seats than it was entitled to based on the popular vote, while the Finns received 1.4 per cent more seats. The National Coalition, the third party in the government coalition, received 0.4 per cent more votes than the Finns, but one seat less in parliament. Overall, the coalition government therefore has 4.6 per cent more seats in parliament than it is entitled to based on the vote.

The situation is similar in Belgium, where in 2014 the Reform, Open VLD and CD&V parties all received approximately 10 per cent of the vote, but Reform gained twenty seats in parliament (13 per cent of all available seats), whereas the CD&V and Open VLD were left with only eighteen and fourteen seats respectively (12 and 9 per cent of all available seats). At the same time, the Socialist Party gained twenty-three seats (or 15 per cent of all available seats) with only 11.7 per cent of the vote. That means that with only 2 per cent more of the vote, the Socialist Party gained 6 per cent more seats in Parliament than the Open VLD, while Reform received 4 per cent more seats in Parliament despite having polled slightly *lower* than Open VLD on the popular vote (the two parties received 9.64 and 9.78 per cent of the popular vote respectively).

As in other systems, under pure proportional voting it is not so important that a party *wins* a vote as *where* it wins that vote. Under the pure proportional system, it remains advantageous to a party to win the bare minimum of votes required to pick up the seats in a district. If it can multiply this effect, it can maximize its seat-to-vote ratio and ensure that each vote cast for it counts for more than a vote in favour of one of its rivals.

Both Belgium and Finland, however, are mild cases of pure proportional vote skewing. Things can and do get much worse.

Spanish politics, where the pure proportional vote is also used, has been dominated by two large parties, the centre-right Popular Party (PP) and the centre-left Spanish Socialist Workers' Party (PSOE), since shortly after the end of Franco's rule in the mid-1970s. Although three or four much smaller parties also seriously contest elections, in Spain the advantage accruing to the larger parties is more obvious than in Finland or Belgium and comes close to that experienced in first-past-the-post systems. In the three most recent elections (2004, 2008 and 2011) the PP and PSOE always gained more seats in Spain's Congress of Deputies than they were entitled to based on the popular vote.

Of course, we now know that Spain's next elections in late 2015 may have a very different outcome. The rise of the new party Podemos (which at the time of writing consistently polls at around 20 per cent of the vote) means that the PP and PSOE are no longer necessarily on firm ground. But, as inspiring as the development of Podemos is, on a structural level it is a predictable *result* of the electoral system's long-term ineffective representation, not – in a systemic sense – an alternative to it.

The stranglehold of PP and PSOE over Spanish political life for more than thirty years has contributed to a culture of rampant and deep-rooted corruption that penetrates nearly all levels of society and which systematically favours the wealthy. As a result, the economic hardship engendered by the 2008 financial crash has been particularly severe in Spain, with unemployment riding at 25 per cent for all adults and at over 50 per cent for young people. While there are great hopes that the rise of Podemos may change politics for the better, it is important to remember that Podemos has become a viable force only following seven years of economic tailspin.

That is, quite literally, a biblical level of suffering.

And while some voters may view PP and PSOE politicians as little better than a plague of locusts, one cannot help wonder that in modern times we persist in using such an inefficient political system, in which the need to organize to contest elections perforce dictates that reaction to crises remains uncertain, and, most of all, slow. Podemos may well succeed, but to say that the structural bias of political representation can be broken with great effort in times of serious crisis is not a long-term solution to the basic issue of skewed representation, because even if Podemos were to win election in Spain in 2015 and destroy the traditional parties' respective positions, political representation in Spain *would still be skewed and inaccurate*. Retaining that system means that skewed representation will inevitably repeat itself with a slow build-up to destruction and suffering, followed, after a great deal of time and effort, some years later, by a brief period of restructuring. Wash, rinse, repeat.

This is why even a movement as important and successful as Podemos can only ever provide a partial and temporary respite from the flaws of electoral democracy.

Like all other forms of electoral representation, the pure proportional vote systematically discriminates against smaller parties and allows those parties with the most resources to manipulate election outcomes in their favour. This means that, just as in other systems, electoral success does not depend on how the people of a nation genuinely voted, but on which party statistical inaccuracies favour most.

While manufactured majorities are not as endemic to proportional systems as they are to STV and FPTP, they are still possible. Indeed, following each of the last three Spanish elections, one party went on to form a single-cabinet government on the back of a relative manufactured majority. Here too there is a skewed relationship between how people voted and the government they end up living under.

Modern democracy as symbolic democracy

When citizens cast their vote, they are aware that their preferences may be shared only by a minority and that the party whose policies they endorse may be beaten at the polls by a majority preference. This is widely viewed as an acceptable outcome, one that is part and parcel of democratic governance. After all, if the majority of a citizen's peers honestly disagree with them, they still have the option of trying to change their minds and at least the satisfaction of knowing that they were fairly beaten.

In ancient Athens, this was the case: all decisions were the result of debate and voting in the Assembly and courts, a process that any citizen could participate in. Those who chose to participate on any given day were always numerous enough to include citizens from all walks of life who came with a varied array of interests, views and experiences. The decisions that these citizens made could not be skewed by intervening processes for the simple reason that there weren't any. The Athenian political system thus could not help but accurately reflect the expressed preferences of its citizens. While the individual citizen might not be happy with any particular decision of the Assembly, he at least knew that it was a genuine decision that the majority of his peers backed. Even if he had been unable to personally attend Assembly that day, he could rest assured that his interests would almost inevitably have been embodied by many other similarly situated citizens. By demanding a great deal of direct participation, Athenian democracy succeeded in being fairly representative.

Our system, on the other hand, cannot be a 'representative' democracy in the conventional meaning of the term, because the parliaments that make decisions do not take in a large enough cross-section of people to allow them to be representative. It is impossible to take something as big as a nation, shrink it so small and preserve accuracy. In attempting to do so, we have pared our 'representation' down to an absurdity. Rather than serving as a faithful reflection of society, modern parliaments are representative of 'the people' in only the most symbolic sense – it is agreed that they stand in for the people of a nation because it is convenient to believe that they do.

But in truth, because they lack a strong connection between the preferences of citizens and the composition of parliament, elections are a free-for-all grey zone that bears little relation to outside realities. This gives parties a free pass to ignore real voter preferences and instead to manufacture majorities for themselves using all sorts of sophisticated strategies, none of which would work if the basic electoral system did indeed reliably produce representative government.

As demonstrated most pointedly by the 1988 Canadian federal election and the 2000 US presidential election, these manufactured majorities can have consequences long after the electoral term concerned is over. Over twenty years after the Canadian Progressive Conservative government that signed the FTA was swept from power (losing all but two seats in Parliament), its successor NAFTA now forms part of a global web of similar trade liberalization treaties. Similarly, six years after George W. Bush – a president that most Americans did not initially elect – left office, the detention facility at Guantanamo Bay continues to operate; American troops are still in Afghanistan; American taxpayers have been subjected to a crippling debt, caused in part by the Bush administration's costly foreign policy decisions; and hundreds of thousands of people have lost their lives in the controversial Second Iraq War. Added to this is the fact that Bush was aided in pursuing the Second Iraq War by a British Labour government that had received 22 per cent more seats in Parliament than it was entitled to, having secured a mere 40 per cent of the popular vote at the last election. Because the discrepancy between the popular vote and seats received was so great, Labour was able to survive defections from senior party members and implement its deeply unpopular policy with regard to the Second Iraq War. In this case, two governments, each elected by manufactured majority, combined forces to give the impression that their views enjoyed widespread support both at home and abroad, and to silence opposition to a set of policies which were not only disastrous but which most people had never, even indirectly, endorsed. Such are the consequences of a 'representative' system that is not firmly grounded in reality.

It is disturbing to think that despite the obviously symbolic value of our representation, we accept elections as a means of legitimizing the power of politicians for a four- to five-year period, inevitably sometimes granting this legitimization to parties that pursue policies we do not even want. The citizen does not know when such outcomes will occur and has no control over them; he must simply cast his vote and hope. Thus, from the point of view of the citizen, election outcomes are random and unpredictable. In addition to not knowing whether he will be joined in his views by the majority, the individual also does not know whether it will even matter if he is. From the other end of the spectrum, however – that is, from the politicians' point of view – election results are considerably more foreseeable, as they are able to engage in gerrymandering and vote-stacking to produce manufactured majorities.

Thus, in the absence of mass participation, as voters we suffer from all of the drawbacks of randomness in the way we choose our officials (lack of control, danger of incompetency, reduced planning ability) without any of the benefits that a truly random system like the Athenian lottery method brought (equality, dispersal of political power, lack of corruption). And, if we are unflinchingly honest, that leads to one inescapable conclusion: direct voting in Assembly combined with lottery selection for most officials was – from a democratic point of view – *more* responsible and sophisticated than modern elections are. It delivered absolute clarity on what the majority desired along with the ability to faithfully implement those wishes – the ostensible goals of democracy. The Athenians *knew* that this system was more accurate than elections, which is why they abandoned elections wherever possible.

We might like to believe that things are different now and that elections work well in a modern democracy, but, as this chapter has shown, a look at the hard numbers proves otherwise. And if we are not getting what we want out of elections, i.e. a government that reflects the preferences of the people, we should ask ourselves whether it might not make sense for us to follow the Athenians' example and consider moving beyond them.

This is all the more so as the Athenians' knowledge about elections did not stop with their fundamental inaccuracy. Throughout democracy, the Athenians were concerned, and even obsessed, with the role that money could play in politics. That elections were more easily won by the rich and therefore functionally equivalent to oligarchy was an article of faith to most Athenians, a piece of knowledge that we are only beginning to discover ourselves, as the next chapter explores.

3

Buying and Selling Elections

It is clear that the principle of representation
was neither unknown to the ancients nor wholly
overlooked in their political constitutions. The
true distinction between these and the American
governments, lies IN THE TOTAL EXCLUSION OF THE
PEOPLE, IN THEIR COLLECTIVE CAPACITY, from any share
in the LATTER.

> James Madison, fourth president
> of the United States of America

The issue of representation is not the only thing the ancient
Athenians were right about. They were also right about the
effects of money on politics. They recognized that *any* electoral system would inevitably be dominated by the wealthiest
members of society, because the wealthy were more likely
to win elections. This was the case with their own residual
elections and it still holds true today. In this chapter, I will
look at *why* this is true, what the consequences are and what
we might be able to do about it.

The high cost of campaigning

Talk is cheap, but gathering a mass audience to hear that talk is not. Political parties and candidates spend vast amounts of money on propagating their views to as wide an audience as possible. That this expenditure on campaigning is critical to their success can be seen from the sums that parties and candidates are willing to part with in pursuing it:

- the 1997 Irish national elections cost parties and candidates approximately 3 million euros, a figure which tripled to 9.24 million euros in the 2002 elections, before rising still further to 11.08 million euros in 2007;
- in the UK, the Conservative and Labour parties each spent nearly £18 million in the 2005 election. Conservative spending remained at nearly the same level in the 2010 election at over £16 million, while Labour spending nosedived to £8 million with disastrous results for the party at the ballot box. In 2015, spending skyrocketed to even greater levels with the Conservatives raising nearly £29 million in 2014 alone, with Labour trailing at around £19 million;
- in the 2008 Canadian federal election, the Liberal Party spent $14 million, the NDP nearly $17 million and the Conservatives $19 million. By 2011, this had risen substantially, with the Liberal and Conservative parties each spending approximately $19.5 million, while the NDP spent $20.3 million. Total spending for the autumn 2015 elections is expected to be higher still, with even the Green Party lavishing millions of dollars on its campaign;

- in the USA, candidates spent over $1 billion on the 2008 presidential election alone; by 2012 it was $5 billion – more than the national gross domestic product of Liberia.

It is not easy for political parties to raise so much money. Much of it comes from private donations, and there are only two kinds of contributor who are able to donate sums large enough to make a measurable difference to a campaign: large corporations and individual millionaires and billionaires, who generally derive their income from ownership of large corporations.

These donations may be difficult to obtain, but they are pivotal to a party's success at the polls. No party in either Canada or the UK, two of the world's largest and most stable democracies, has *ever* won a national election without receiving corporate financing. With such incentives in place, it's hardly surprising that politicians actively solicit corporate donations in return for political favours.

For example, in the late 1980s a fraudulent attempt by drinks manufacturer Guinness to take over its rival Distillers was uncovered in Britain. Ernest Saunders, one of the men convicted in this plot, later gave an interview in which he described his attempts to convince the government to approve the takeover. According to Saunders:

> One of them, a very senior figure, came straight out while I was doing my sales pitch ... and he said he noticed we did not contribute to the Conservative Party and when were we going to do. I think there were three occasions during the period when the question of our non-contribution came up, not in any way as a threat, but it came up sufficiently

for me to realise that if we were going to go on rolling,
I would have to put this matter to the board.[1]

In other words, Saunders' negotiation partners were letting
him know that money in their campaign coffers would make
them feel a lot happier about signing off on his company's
takeover bid.

In the USA, of course, the cost of a successful political
campaign is even higher. Many of the private donations
received by American candidates come from political action
committees (PACs). PACs are organizations that gather
funds from members and then either donate them to candidates or spend them on other forms of political campaigning.
Between 1980 and 2004, the level of direct PAC donations to candidates more than doubled, with contributions
to federal candidates reaching $205.1 million in the eigh-
teen-month period leading up to June 2004.[2] From January
2005 to June 2006, PAC donations increased even further
to $248.2 million.

These generous political action committees are, by and
large, not groups of ordinary people banding together to
support a candidate who enjoys their admiration. The PACs
that contribute the most to candidates predominantly represent corporate interests. In 2013–14 these included:

- Honeywell International (number 1 with donations of
$5,134,461);
- Lockheed Martin (defence contractor, number 2 at
$3,723,500);

---

1 Linton, *Money and Votes*, at 72.
2 When figures are adjusted for inflation.

- AT&T (communications, number 4 at $3,598,000);
- Raytheon (defence contractor, number 6 at $3,292,500);
- General Electric (number 7 at $3,177,000);
- Boeing (aircraft manufacturer and defence contractor, number 9 at $2,835,000);
- Koch Industries (number 12 at $2,665,500);
- Walmart (number 18 at $2,116,000);
- Pfizer (pharmaceuticals, number 26 at $1,730,480); and
- Exxon Mobil (oil and gas, number 28 at $1,641,000).

Other heavy donors included Google, Goldman Sachs, J. P. Morgan, Citigroup, Verizon, Merck and General Motors.

The value of each dollar contributed is further enhanced by the fact that PACs spend their money strategically on 'those who are more likely to win and have useful influence in Congress'.[3] In other words, PACs prefer to sponsor candidates who are likely to gain a leadership position on the congressional committees that are responsible for drafting legislation that could affect their interests, giving double the money to potential committee chairs as they give to ordinary candidates.

You get what you pay for: the vicious circle of political donations and government action

While in many countries the data on corporate donations to politicians is well-publicized, there is an esoteric yet persistent stream of thought that holds that campaign spending does not affect election outcomes or government action. Instead,

---

3 Wright, 'Money and the pollution of politics', at 615.

we are asked to believe that by some mysterious process of black magic the campaign spending all cancels itself out and that therefore money in politics is nothing for the ordinary citizen to fret about.

But that raises some serious questions.

People who can command millions or even billions of dollars are by and large not stupid, nor are they notable for their lack of pragmatism. In particular, they are not stupid about money matters. This is, after all, their core of expertise and the foundation of all their success. So one has to wonder why these highly successful individuals who have made a career out of focusing on profitability would voluntarily give away millions of dollars to no purpose. Why would Boeing or Raytheon's shareholders, for example, ever allow the company to give away *their* profits if there were nothing to be gained by doing so? Even more to the point, why would professional parties and politicians waste their time raising and spending money that doesn't help them reach their goals? By this logic, the most successful politician would be the one who never squandered a moment of their lives either raising or spending money.

But we know that that is not the case.

The idea that professional politicians and business leaders would all voluntarily engage in wasting so much of their own time and money on campaigns is ludicrous. They do it for the reason that they do everything else: because it pays off. Other factors may influence who wins elections or how representatives vote once they are in power, but one factor trumps all others again and again: money.

More money, more victory

Corporate donations to politicians matter because the candidate or party that spends the most has a far greater chance of winning election. This is true even when the difference in spending between candidates is slight, and the likelihood that the side that spends the most will win only increases the greater the spending discrepancy between the parties, candidates or sides is. It is a pattern that can be observed over the last forty years in election after election.

In 1978 there were 307 contested races for seats in the US Congress:

- the candidate who spent more on their campaign won the seat 78.8 per cent of the time;
- in 159 out of the 307 races one candidate outspent the other by a ratio of more than 2 to 1; that candidate won 93 per cent of the time;
- in fifty-eight of the contested elections, one side outspent the other by a ratio of more than 5 to 1; in 100 per cent of those cases the winner was the bigger spender.

Nearly forty years later, these statistics are nearly identical. Following the 2011/12 election cycle, eighty-four seats in the US Houses of Congress changed hands:

- of these eighty-four races, the candidate who spent more on their campaign won 78.3 per cent of the time;
- in fifty-one races, one candidate outspent the other by a ratio of 2 to 1 or more, resulting in electoral victory 92 per cent of the time for the bigger spender;

- in thirty-four races, one candidate outspent the other by a ratio of 5 to 1 or more, resulting in electoral victory 100 per cent of the time.

The Athenians were right – elections are disproportionately won by those who can afford to lavish resources on an expensive campaign.

More victory, more money

The prize for winning an election is that the victor acquires the right to make the rules and laws that are most pleasing to them without being constrained by the need to consult others. It is a quite substantial prize and it does not require any great leap in logic to think that when different people have worked together to win a prize, it is only natural that they should share it. In the case of elections, political candidates and corporations work together to win. But how do they share the prize? Who has the upper hand? The political candidate who lends his name and face to the campaign or the corporate and financial sponsors who pay his expenses?

The answer is obvious, because one factor in this equation – the candidate – is easily replaceable. After all, the statistics do not indicate that elections are predominantly won by smart, or interesting, or honest people. They show that elections are won by the person with the most expensive campaign. Thus, the only quality that a candidate really needs to have is a willingness to accept large donations. And in societies where only 0.001 per cent of the population can become a political representative, even if only one in a hundred people are willing to run for office and accept corporate donations for their election campaigns competition for these positions will be fierce. And because the personal accomplishments or characteristics of these candidates do not significantly affect their chances of success, they are all ultimately interchangeable and therefore disposable. One is as good as another.

But, while there is no shortage of potential political candidates, there are not many entities or wealthy financiers who are willing to give an aspiring politician millions of dollars. They, and not the candidates they donate to, are therefore in a position to set the conditions for their support.

And there is only one part of winning an election that matters to corporations and those who own them: the ability to ensure that their interests are reflected in political decisions, i.e. the ability to ensure that legislation does not interfere with the primary activity they engage in: making money.

Because big donors can live without any given candidate, but no candidate can survive for long without their financial support, it is not difficult to ensure that the donor's wishes are taken very seriously.

To give just a few examples:

- The National Association of Realtors (NAR), one of the top-contributing PACs over the last forty years, supported a motion to eliminate enforcement powers against fraudulent realtors in 1978. To this end, NAR made contributions to the election campaigns of fifty-one out of the seventy-one Congressmen elected for the first time in 1978. When the bill was debated in 1979, forty-three of these fifty-one Congressmen supported the motion (a success rate of 84 per cent for NAR). Of the twenty first-time Congressmen who opposed the bill, thirteen had received no funding from NAR. During the same election period, a study showed that 95 per cent of Congressmen who received more than $2,500 in campaign contributions from oil-industry PACs voted to reduce windfall profits tax to the benefit of oil companies.

- A further study saw financial contributions not so much in terms of buying votes as in terms of buying the time of committee members. This study focused on three pieces of legislation:
  - the Natural Gas Market Policy Act (1983–84), which deregulated natural gas prices to the advantage of natural gas conglomerates and the disadvantage of consumers and smaller natural gas enterprises;
  - the Job Training Partnership Act (1982); and
  - the Dairy Stabilization Act (1982), which would decrease the price of milk and lead to an estimated 30 per cent decrease in dairy farmers' profitability.

The study found that in all three cases politicians who received contributions from these industries were more likely to speak on their behalf, negotiate with other representatives for them, attach amendments to the draft laws and to show up and vote at sessions to debate and amend draft legislation.

- Yet another study, published in 2006, revealed a direct relationship between campaign contributions received from internationally lending banks and a politician's support for quota increases at the International Monetary Fund. The banks desired these increases because they reduced their own lending risk by ensuring that the IMF had sufficient funds to bail out nations that the banks had loaned money to.

As these studies show, the chances of a politician supporting legislation are directly linked to the campaign contributions they have received from the bill's beneficiaries, which means that wealthy entities can literally purchase the laws that they desire. In all of the cases listed above, campaign donors received a solid return on investment. They may have had to give candidates and parties some money, but the rewards they received in the form of tax breaks and deregulation of their industries meant that they ultimately saved more than they spent.

This isn't a coincidence.

Electoral democracy creates the perfect conditions for the relationship between campaign contributions and representatives' actions to flourish. Wealthy individuals and entities buy election outcomes because it is possible to do so and because success is well rewarded. If it were not possible to buy election outcomes, no one would attempt to, no matter what the rewards for completing this impossible task could theoretically be. Conversely, even if it were possible to buy election outcomes, no one would be motivated to do so without the presence of some considerable incentive that outweighed the risks and costs.

The Athenians recognized this. They knew that attempting to eliminate each individual's drive to act in their own narrow short-term interests was a project that was simply too big, assuming that such an achievement was even possible. So instead of waiting for this utopia, where the rich would not succumb to the temptation to use their wealth for political ends, the Athenians simply removed the temptation.

In Athens, it wasn't worth the effort to manipulate elections, because there weren't very many and none of them conferred very much power. Equally, it was pointless to give an official a donation, because he had no power to make policy decisions, and the people in Assembly were simply too numerous to bribe. The Athenians, in short, created the right conditions for the type of government that they wanted to live under.

Not only do we maintain elections, however, we ensure that the incentive to win them is extremely high, because the winner – and only the winner – acquires the right to set the national agenda and to use the nation's policies and resources to reward his beneficiaries to the exclusion of all others. When an advantage of this magnitude exists, along with the real possibility of acquiring it for oneself, it is unrealistic to expect that some people will not try to win by any means they can. And while winning might be temporarily good for them, it is not good for society as a whole. Like the manufactured majority, the effects of corporate donations on political decision-making have consequences as long-term as they are severe.

Financial disservices: the demise of the Glass-Steagall Act

Perhaps the most dramatic example of vote-buying at work is the fate of the now-famous Glass-Steagall Act. The Glass-Steagall Act originated in the early 1930s and prevented commercial banks from engaging in investment banking activities. Commercial banks were particularly forbidden from affiliating themselves with stock market activity or underwriting speculative financial transactions. At the same time, investment banks were prevented from taking deposits. In other words, the Act drew a clear line between high finance and speculative investments on one side, and individual deposits and loans on the other. This minimized financial risk for small deposit-holders and borrowers. Such limitations represent nothing more exotic than the basic lessons learned during the stock market crash of 1929 and ensuing Great Depression.

Over the years, however, the Act became the subject of numerous controversies, reforms and attempts at reform. Two of these occurred in 1991 and 1998. In the 1991 Glass-Steagall reform effort, one of the proposed amendments would have allowed commercial banks to participate in investment banking activities. However, the amendment failed to pass the House of Congress by a vote of 200 for to 216 against. Seven years later, in 1998, a similar reform allowing affiliations between banks, insurance and securities companies passed by a vote of 214 to 213. On the surface, this would appear to represent a tiny shift in representatives' opinion, with support rising from 200 votes in favour to 214. However, these numbers belie a far more considerable alteration in voting behaviour that is itself the product of a shifting campaign finance strategy.

While the amendments were similar, their content was not identical. In fact, the fate of both amendments represents a struggle between banking and investment interests as to which industry would get the upper hand following any reform. The 1991 amendment favoured banking interests while the 1998 amendment favoured insurance and investment interests. Consequently, the insurance and investment industries opposed the first amendment and supported the second one. To this end, in the run-up to the vote on each amendment the investment and insurance industries chose to throw their financial backing behind the party with the most seats in the Houses of Congress in the hope of influencing the vote on the amendments. This was crowned by success on both occasions. In 1991, the Democrats had the most seats in Congress and received substantial donations from investment and insurance companies. At that time 74 per cent of Democrats voted in line with insurance/investment interests, joined by only 22 per cent of Republicans.

In 1998, however, the Republicans held the majority in both Houses. As a result, insurance and investment interests significantly increased their contributions to Republicans and significantly decreased their contributions to Democrats. The banking industry, which opposed the second amendment, kept its contributions to candidates in both parties stable.

This time, 77 per cent of Republicans voted in line with insurance/investment interests with only 38 per cent of Democrats doing the same. Although it appears on the surface that opinion had not changed much on the issue of appropriate financial reform, it actually underwent a sea change that closely corresponded to the benefits that investment and insurance interests expected to receive from each reform and the responsiveness of politicians to their desires.

One hundred and eighty-two representatives voted on the legislation under review in both 1991 and 1998, with two-thirds of them switching their allegiance from being in favour of the banking position on reform to backing the insurance position or vice versa. When Democrats received money from insurance companies, they voted in their interests. When that money dropped off, they returned to the banking industry, which continued to line their pockets in stable fashion. And the same could be said of the Republicans in reverse order. They supported the banking position until the insurance industry offered them more money. In doing so, the Republicans proved themselves willing to hold out for a good deal – the more banking interests gave to a candidate, the less likely they were to switch their vote in response to the increased contributions from investors and insurers.

One might like to believe that representatives vote on a law according to their own perception of its merits, but the case of the Glass-Steagall Act shows otherwise. The majority of representatives from both parties switched their opinion on the validity of a law affecting the entire nation according to who was willing to give them the most money, selling off the entire political process to the highest bidder.

These manoeuvres, however, were quickly eclipsed by a more momentous event, when only one year later banks and insurance companies finally agreed that it would be advantageous to allow cross-ownership of banks, brokerages and insurers. In a new spirit of harmony, both the banking and investment industries were finally singing from the same hymn sheet and giving their beneficiaries in Congress identical instructions. This resulted in an almost instantaneous repeal of the relevant provisions of the Glass-Steagall Act on 1 July 1999, with a landslide vote in favour: 343 to 86. This move, which served to loosen up the banking industry, is widely held to have contributed to the financial crisis of 2008, plunging the world into what is currently the seventh year of economic stagnation in which millions of people have lost their livelihoods. It is alarming that two relatively evenly matched interest groups can out-buy each other at will, and even more disturbing that the moment these interest groups manage to agree on the desired outcome of a vote that outcome becomes a foregone conclusion, as if there are no further interests to be taken into account. Together they own the entire legislative branch of government.

All of this bribery and counter-bribery makes for an exciting political game, but it is played out by only a few corporations and representatives and not by any of the people who are allegedly the real power in a democracy. The greater one's wealth, the more decisive one's influence, and most citizens, of course, have no wealth to speak of, making politics a game they will simply never get in on.

A fistful of euros: buying Irish local elections

Readers from Canada, Britain and Australia might absorb all of these statistics and examples with a feeling of confidence that elections turn out differently in their own more 'restrained' cultures, that the problem is not democracy, but with loose American campaign finance regulation.

Sadly, this is just not the case.

Wherever elections exist, money is spent to win them. While this money may be spent in lesser sums, it is still a decisive factor in *all* election outcomes and puts competing for election beyond the means of the average person. This is true everywhere, even in what could be regarded as the other extreme of the election finance spectrum: local elections in Ireland.

Ireland is a small country in terms of both population and geography. It is only about the size of Massachusetts and has just 4 million residents. In addition to its central national government, the Republic of Ireland is divided into twenty-six counties that are each administered by a council of locally elected politicians. Although there are no intermediate levels of government between the county and the nation, local councillors are limited to making decisions on what many would regard as necessary but mundane affairs, such as the placement of bicycle paths or the upkeep of local heritage sites. While acting as a country councillor can be a stepping stone to a candidacy in national elections, the position itself is of little interest to corporate entities or other special-interest groups, who therefore have no incentive to support any particular candidate. Moreover, because counties are very small and a candidate's family has typically lived in his or her county for several generations, very little effort is required to publicize their name and reputation. Therefore, it should come as no surprise to learn that in the 1999 Irish local elections median candidate spending was just 1,500 euros.

Nonetheless, while the *absolute amount* of money a candidate spent was very low, the amount spent *relative to the other candidates* in the district was clearly linked to electoral success:

- A 1 per cent increase in a candidate's spending as a share of their party's total spending resulted on average in that candidate receiving a 0.45 per cent greater share of that party's first preference votes.
- The candidates studied received anything from 22 to 72 per cent of their party's spending in their respective district. A shift from a 22 per cent share to a 72 per cent share resulted in a 22.3 per cent increase in first-preference votes, meaning that those candidates on whose behalf the most money was spent had a much higher chance of being elected than those candidates on whose behalf the least was spent.

- Similarly, without taking parties into consideration, a candidate who spent 25 per cent of all election money in a district received on average between 5.98 and 6.68 per cent more first-preference votes than those who spent only 2 per cent of the campaign money in that district. This is significant, because on average candidates receive only about 8.6 per cent of all first-preference votes. According to the study's authors, even moving from 2 to 5 per cent of total spend for a district 'basically doubles a challenger's chances of winning a seat'.[4]

- The level of funding necessary to win an Irish local election can be estimated with astonishing accuracy. A candidate who increases his spend from 500 euros to 1,000 euros will receive an additional 1.27 per cent of first-preference votes, while a candidate who jumps from 500 euros to 5,000 euros can expect this to bring him a further 4.2 per cent of the vote, a decisive margin.

As the scholars who compiled this research noted, the link between spending and electoral success in a system as small as the Irish local elections is strong evidence that finance generally plays a decisive role in any election.

In a typical Irish local election, spending 500 euros is a waste of money, but if a candidate (or their party) is willing to spend 5,000 euros, an amount of money that most people cannot afford to spend on non-necessities, they are virtually assured a victory. Better-funded parties and candidates in upper-income brackets can thus use the funding 'weapon' to assure success at the polls.

---

4 Benoit and Marsh, 'For a few euros more: campaign spending effects in the Irish local elections of 1999', at 573–6.

In larger and more important elections the level of funding required to win is so high that it ceases to be provided by the more affluent candidate himself and is instead provided by corporate interests and individual billionaires. Perhaps Lord McAlpine, a long-time treasurer of the British Conservative Party, put it best when he boasted that he could 'persuade the public to believe virtually anything, given enough money. "A poster campaign costing £1 or £2 million is a waste of money," he once told a reporter, "but give me £8 million and I will deliver whatever you want."[5]

Representative democracy: second place is the first loser

By providing a bottleneck that separates the few people who will make political decisions from the multitude who will not, elections deliver wealthy individuals and entities the chance to buy participation rights in a competitive process. If you win, you're in, and if you lose, you're nobody. So the key is to win – at any price – and then to do as one likes from a position of unassailability. Purchasing compliance this way is a tactic that would never work in a democracy with mass participation like Athens, because it would not be possible for even the richest corporations to constantly bribe 10 or 20 per cent of the population.

But when only a tiny proportion of all citizens are granted political power by virtue of winning an election they form an easily quantifiable set of variables whose desires and interests it is entirely affordable to influence. Once these few

5 Linton, op. cit., at 29.

citizens are in power, donors expect their candidates to lend them a sympathetic ear. It may not always work, there may be a power struggle between candidate and donor, but the relationship exists and it yields dividends often enough to be worthwhile. Thus, wealth equals power and power equals wealth. Wealthy individuals and corporations bankroll their preferred candidate so that he or she will write laws that favour those same individuals and corporations and allow them to make even more money. That this relationship exists is clear. The question is, what can we do about it?

Why referenda fail

One of the most common answers to the question of how one could 'clean up' politics is to hold referenda; that is, to leave the electoral system intact, but to let 'the people' decide directly on certain matters. However, unfortunately, using referenda as an occasional complement to the electoral system has little effect on the relationship between corporate finance and political outcomes.

The Athenians knew that democracy did not simply require a lot of people to participate, it required a lot of people to participate *a lot*, i.e. on at least a weekly basis. By contrast, the way in which we use referenda in modern democracies allows mass participation, but only in very infrequent bursts, often separated by months or years of inactivity. When referenda are held infrequently, they provide a focal point for the wealthy to exercise their influence that is not much different to an election campaign. It does not matter what people think a week before a referendum or a week after a referendum, as long as they vote a certain way on just one day the political issue at stake can effectively be closed off for years. Thus, while vested interests have to be able to influence many people to vote a certain way in a referendum, they only need to maintain this influence for a very short period of time. For those with enough resources at their disposal this is an expensive but still entirely achievable objective. If we look at referenda around the world, we will see that they often attract enormous levels of investment from individuals and companies whose interests are at stake and that this financial sponsorship clearly affects referendum outcomes.

$46 million and a false professor: GMO labelling in California

On 6 December 2012, Californians voted on a state-wide referendum known as Proposition 37 (or 'Prop 37'), which, if passed, would have required genetically modified food to be labelled as such. Initially, support for mandatory GMO labelling ran high. Polling on 15 September 2012 (twelve weeks before the referendum) indicated that 65 per cent of voters were in favour of Prop 37 with only 20 per cent against. Alarmed at this development, manufacturers of genetically modified seed, groceries and pesticide poured their resources into the 'no' campaign.[6] While Prop 37 supporters raised $9.4 million, mainly from health food suppliers and Hollywood celebrities, the 'no' campaign reportedly spent up to a $1 million publicizing their views *every single day*, with $46 million spent on television advertising alone over the course of the campaign. Much of this money was used to broadcast misleading claims, such as that the price of groceries would

---

6 Donors included Monsanto ($7 million), Kraft, Heinz, Sara Lee and Pepsico.

go up if Prop 37 passed and that the 'no' campaign's lead scientist was a Stanford professor (he was actually a research fellow at a think tank based on Stanford's campus and had previously worked for the tobacco industry in an attempt to discredit the links between cigarettes and cancer). This spending spree may have been crass, but it produced results. By 23 October (six weeks before voting) the 'yes' campaign's lead had been whittled down to only 8 percentage points. The corporate giants continued their highly successful media onslaught and by the time voting took place on 6 December, Prop 37 was defeated by 53 per cent against to 47 per cent for.

Any vote you want as long as it's yes: the Nice and Lisbon treaties in Ireland

Corporate interests drown out their opponents in European referenda, too. Most European countries do not require a referendum to transfer powers to the European Union (EU). However, owing to Ireland's unique history as a colonized nation within Europe, such a power transfer can occur only following a national referendum. Thus, in 2009 Irish citizens were asked to vote on whether they consented for their government to ratify the Lisbon Treaty, which deepened cooperation within Europe and altered voting quotas at the EU. The 'no' campaign leader Libertas (an Irish lobby group run by business mogul Declan Ganley) admitted to spending 1.3 million euros during the first Lisbon referendum, which the 'no' side won. While the Irish government negotiated some very minor alterations to the agreement following the referendum's defeat, a second referendum (Lisbon II) was held the following year on what was essentially the same package. In the meantime, however, the political parties and corporations that favoured deepening EU integration had learned their lesson. During Lisbon II, Ireland's three largest parties spent a combined 1 million euros on the 'yes' campaign, while private businesses such as Ryanair (500,000 euros), Intel (300,000 euros) and the Irish Business and Employers' Confederation ('IBEC', 150,000 euros) also spent significant amounts. On the 'no' side Libertas spent only between 100,000 and 120,000 euros, the UK Independence Party spent 190,000 euros and Cóir (an organization which promotes what it considers to be traditional Irish values), the biggest 'no' spender during Lisbon II, spent 250,000 euros. The better-financed 'yes' side easily won Lisbon II. As the issue at stake was essentially the same as in Lisbon I, a deciding factor in the referenda outcomes was financing, which permitted first one side and then the other to outspend the opposition and sway the electorate to their views.

The earlier Nice referenda concerning the expansion of the European Union had followed a similar pattern. After an Irish 'no' vote on Nice I, a second referendum was held seventeen months later. During Nice II, 'yes' vote supporters contributed substantially to the campaign with IBEC spending at least 400,000 euros and the Business Alliance for the Yes Campaign spending 500,000 euros, while non-party-affiliated 'no' groups spent only 50,000 euros between them. Once again, their ability to heavily outspend their opponents resulted in success for 'yes' campaigners.

Swiss referenda: a lot to gripe(n) about

Of course, Switzerland presents the pre-eminent example of referenda in Europe. The mountainous central European nation has exercised an electoral democracy that allows for national referenda for over 150 years. These referenda are held at the initiative of citizens, provided that they are able to gather 100,000 signatures in favour of holding the referendum within eighteen months. In some years only one or two referenda may be held, but in other years there can be as many as eleven or twelve. However, since this means that referenda are still held relatively infrequently (the average Athenian would have voted in hundreds of 'referenda' over the course of a year, instead of a mere dozen), they remain subject to financial influence because it is easy to focus that influence on a single issue over a short period of time.

When in 2014 Swiss voters were asked to overturn the free movement of workers between Switzerland and the European Union, Christoph Blocher, a wealthy Swiss industrialist, politician and long-time opponent of free immigration, supported the 'yes' side with 3 million francs (US$3,300,000). The referendum passed with a narrow margin (50.3 per cent) in favour.

Another 2014 referendum on military spending had a similar outcome. Several years previously, the Swiss government had decided to replace its military aircraft with twenty-two new Gripen-model jets produced by Swedish manufacturer Saab at a total cost of $3.5 billion. Switzerland, however, is a neutral country, which means it is prohibited from participating in foreign wars. This circumstance combined with its location, surrounded by friendly countries in the heart of Europe, means that the nation's air defence needs are pretty minimal. Swiss chocolate may be delectable, but no one is likely to send out the air force to get hold of some any time soon. So, all things considered, it isn't surprising that some Swiss citizens objected to the high cost of the new Gripen jets and brought a motion that would force the government to cancel the deal.

Instead of letting the matter run its course, Saab colluded with the Swiss and Swedish governments to crush the citizens' initiative. Saab, a foreign company, attempted to interfere in the Swiss referendum process by donating 200,000 francs (about US$220,000) to 'yes' supporter 'Association for a Safe Switzerland', while at the behest of Swiss defence minister Ueli Maurer, the Swedish embassy in Bern and the Swedish Foreign Ministry prepared to support the 'yes' side by running a 'soft, focused and positive' public relations campaign in the run-up to the referendum 'that would pitch Sweden in a good light with voters'.[7]

These activities may well have succeeded in changing the referendum outcome if they had not been leaked to the public before the vote took place. In the storm of public outrage that ensued, Sweden had to cancel its PR campaign and the Association for a Safe Switzerland was forced to return Saab's donation. Despite the ultimately positive outcome, the normality of these actions – and how often they go undetected – is apparent from Saab's unapologetic reaction. The company's spokesperson stated that it would have been unusual if the company had *not* contributed to the 'yes' campaign. In other words, in his view, it would have been unusual had his company *not* spent money to try to influence voters in a foreign country to vote in favour of purchasing its products. And the reason that Saab did not view its behaviour as unusual is because it works. Throwing money at referenda influences results. It's tried and true.

---

7 O'Dwyer, 'Sweden caught in Swiss referendum controversy'.

It doesn't work *every* time, of course. There are exceptions – rare moments when public opinion reaches such a fever pitch that no amount of money can help. In March 2013, Swiss voters, enraged at news of exorbitant executive bonuses being paid out in a time of economic hardship, approved a referendum that banned giving bonuses to executives joining or leaving companies (thus putting an end to 'golden parachutes'), despite Economiesuisse, the Swiss employers' association, spending 8 million francs (nearly US$9 million) campaigning against the initiative.

Situations like this, however, remain exceptions to a general trend. Overall, money can be used to tip the balance of referendum outcomes, which means that even if wealthy interests lose some referenda, they can still use their resources to win more often than they otherwise would have. This is part and parcel of 'representative' (or 'symbolic') democracy's main dilemma: that it focuses on very few people (elected politicians) and events (occasional referenda). In our modern democracies, all decisions need to pass through these very narrow spaces, and this bottleneck creates the perfect environment for financial influences to momentarily open their pocketbooks and flood the political landscape with misinformation, excessive PR efforts and vague fears and doubts to the detriment of their opponents.

Why regulation fails

So if referenda won't solve our problems, what will?

Perhaps the most common call to action over the past decade has been the movement to demand adequate regulation of political financing. Take the money out of politics.

It sounds like a good idea, but it is doomed to fail for the very same reason that political financing is a problem in the first place: it is possible to influence elections and referenda, and the rewards for success are high. Regulation seeks to place a barrier between the possibility of influencing elections and the rewards for doing so. This barrier, however, is completely artificial and therefore it is weak. The temptation to spend to win remains in place and over time serves to undermine restrictive rules, much as a bridge or dam is gradually undermined by the currents pushing against it. This is amply demonstrated wherever campaign finance regulation already exists.

Campaign finance regulation: a Sisyphean task

No matter how low donation limits are set, donating to a political party will always remain a luxury that most people cannot afford. This is reflected in donor behaviour. In 2010, 165,000 people donated to a Canadian federal party – just 0.7 per cent of registered voters – despite the fact that political donations in Canada are severely limited by law to $1,100 per annum. This means that even very stringent donor controls like Canada's still leave campaign finance in the hands of the wealthiest 1 per cent, because even at this restricted level they are the only people who can comfortably afford to make donations. To wealthy individuals $100 or even $1,000 may not feel like a great deal of money to part with, but for most people making such a donation would be a significant sacrifice – one which they are, as the figures show, mainly unwilling to make.

This, however, is only the beginning of the problem. Within the donating elite, the very wealthiest individuals and corporations have the most to gain from rolling back finance limitations, because without regulation they would be free to outspend their only moderately wealthy counterparts to greater effect. Dropping electoral finance barriers is thus most attractive to precisely those entities that are already most able to exploit a regulated electoral finance system and to the parties and candidates whom they support. After all, as soon as the regulation is dropped, these wealthy individuals and corporations will be free to reward the party or candidate who repeals the laws with even more money. Since it benefits exactly those individuals who are in a position to make the rules, eroding campaign finance regulations is never a very difficult task.

This is exactly what transpired ahead of the 2015 UK national election. In the UK, candidate and party spending had previously been capped at £26 million per party. However, the Conservatives had raised about £70 million since the last election, far more than any of their opponents, and therefore they stood to gain the most from increasing spending caps. The Conservatives therefore used their position in government to increase the spending limit to £32 million just months before the election – a move which paid off in electoral victory for the party and a sympathetic ear in government for its financial backers.

A similar trend is under way in other nations, too. Campaign finance regulation may be undermined in different ways in accordance with the legal culture of the country concerned, but the end effect is always the same.

For example, in the United States wealthy citizens have worn down campaign finance regulation through a series of court cases that are ultimately heard before the USA's highly politicized Supreme Court, a venue where adequate resources for counsel determine not only whether a case is successful, but also whether it is even admitted for consideration. In *Citizens United* v. *Federal Election Commission* the Supreme Court decided that any restriction on corporate funding of independent political broadcasts infringed on the constitutionally protected right to free expression, thus paving the way for unlimited spending by so-called Super PACs. This trend continued with *McCutcheon* v. *Federal Election Commission* in 2014, which struck down the limit on contributions to federal candidates over each two-year election cycle. Thanks to these controversial decisions there are no longer any election finance restrictions to speak of in the United States. Companies and other special interests can basically spend as much as they like in their quest to influence election results.

A similar situation is unfolding in Canada. The Conservative Party, currently in power, has historically received the lion's share of private donations. As a result, the government pushed through measures which abolished public reimbursement of campaign expenses (a policy which offsets the importance of private donations) in 2015. It is expected that this will have a serious effect on the Canadian political landscape, particularly on the New Democratic Party, the mainstream party most committed to policies that benefit poor and working-class citizens.

As these examples demonstrate, campaign finance limits are often directly overturned as soon as it is expedient to do so. But even when such rules remain intact, they tend to be easily circumvented. Legislators directly benefit from loopholes that allow them to receive benefits in return for political favours, so while they are the only people legally empowered to close those loopholes, their incentive for doing so is low. As a result, even laws that look strict on paper are often in reality riddled with flaws. To give an example: in 2007 Canada passed a law stipulating that any donation over $200 must be disclosed and banning donations exceeding $1,100 per year to political parties or candidates. However, these rules are easily circumvented by donors making a contribution of under $200 (which falls under the declaration threshold) to each riding that a party is active in, thus donating amounts in the tens of thousands of dollars, well in excess of the $1,100 annual threshold.

Because the richest and most powerful figures in any country always have the most to gain from eliminating limits on political finance, trying to regulate election spending is at best a Sisyphean task – weaker parties have to make a huge effort to push limits through only to see them get rolled back again and again.

Editorial bias as a campaign resource

To add a further twist to this labyrinth of electoral spending, there are many activities which profoundly affect electoral outcomes, but which are nearly impossible to regulate for. One of the most notorious is editorial coverage in newspapers. What this means is that the editors of a newspaper devote their opinion pieces to praising the party that they favour and disparaging its rivals, often while choosing to run news stories that disproportionately portray a party or candidate in a positive or negative light. This type of treatment can be kept up for weeks or months, totalling thousands of articles.

For example, during the 1992 British election campaign, the *Sun* and *Daily Express* (tabloid papers) carried no negative reports about the Conservative Party or positive reports about the Labour Party, while the *Daily Mirror* carried no negative reports about Labour and no positive reports about the Conservatives. More reputable papers such as *The Times* and the *Independent* also strongly favoured one party over the other (the Conservatives received 296 negative stories in *The Independent*, Labour only 99). Within political and media circles, there is no doubt as to whether these tactics work: following the 1992 national election, the *Sun* felt proud enough of its handiwork to run a headline publicly crediting itself with winning the election for the Conservative Party.

Editorial bias provides a quick and easy way to circumvent campaign finance rules. If the parties had purchased equivalent advertising space in the run-up to the 1992 elections, the cost would have been in the millions, and editorial coverage is generally considered to be three times as valuable as comparable advertising space. That means that the exposure provided by the tabloids alone to the British Conservative and Labour parties was worth more than their entire campaign finances. Yet no money changed hands, and if any attempt were ever made to prevent this practice, newspaper editors could simply claim that they are genuinely expressing their opinion and that any attempt at regulation would infringe on the freedom of the press.

Between these loopholes and the ability of rich entities to persistently fight regulation, limiting election finance is a futile enterprise. Big donors and professional politicians already know all the tricks and have every incentive to use them.

Elections: the perfect habitat for manipulation

All of this spending means that our political decision-making processes are subjected to two separate filters. The first filter is the statistical inaccuracy of electoral representation. This produces results that are – from the voter's perspective – more or less random. To put it another way, there is an elastic causality between how the people voted and the representatives and government they end up with that distorts the will of the people. From the perspective of politicians and political parties, however, election results are much more predictable. They can game the system by gerrymandering, focusing their efforts on the right districts and engaging in tactics like vote-splitting to come out on top and produce manufactured majorities for themselves. If this were the only filter that 'the will of the people' was exposed to, we would have to conclude that elections are won by tacticians and that the party or candidate that has the best political tacticians will win.

But elections are also subject to another filter: money. Those with wealth influence the behaviour of voters with expensive campaign advertising and the behaviour of representatives with campaign contributions. The more a party or candidate spends, the more likely they are to win, and the amount of money that needs to be spent to be successful is so high that it precludes most people from ever running for office. If we combine these two filters, we would say that electoral success = tacticians + money and not, e.g., promising to institute popular policies or reflecting citizens' desires.

Over 2,500 years ago, the Athenians had already realized all of this. They believed that elections were more easily won by the rich, powerful, popular and eloquent. And they were right. By creating the bottleneck of elections and occasional referenda, we deliver a focal point for the rich and powerful to concentrate their resources on, and thereby win easy victories. To take advantage of this system isn't just tempting – it's *logical*. Yet we persist in using it while at the same time toothlessly chastising the rich and powerful for exploiting its obvious flaws.

The Athenians took precisely the opposite tack and used mass participation to introduce so many variables into political decision-making that no one could manage to manipulate them all. Since it was nearly impossible to acquire an advantage over other citizens, political participation in Athens was much more egalitarian than it is today. In fact, as we will see in the next chapter, participation in Athens was radically different from participation in democracies today, with some radically different results.

4

Participation:
Bought In or Locked Out?

> we ... consider the man who takes no part in
> public life not as one minding his own business,
> but rather a good for nothing.
>
> Pericles, Funeral Oration

In modern democracies citizens rarely make any decisions themselves. Instead, they elect individuals to make decisions on their behalf, or, to put it another way, they decide who will decide. Not only is the indirect participation provided by elections prone to many flaws and inaccuracies, as we've seen in the earlier chapters, it also serves to effectively exclude the vast majority of people from national decision-making for several years at a time. Those who are elected are, after all, not under any obligation to consult others during their term in office. They may do as they like – indeed, this is the whole point of trying to win election in the first place. The average citizen in a Western country has very few opportunities to influence these politicians. In fact, the typical person votes in national elections only twelve times over the course of their entire lives. In between these twelve moments the ordinary citizen must struggle to reinsert themselves into the political system and somehow make their needs and desires relevant to elected politicians.

One of the ways they do so is by using tactics such as protest and petition to try to influence their representatives between elections. The idea is that if enough people complain about a government policy that government will start to worry about its re-election chances and withdraw the proposal that people find objectionable. Therefore even if the 'wrong' person gets elected, they will still behave in the 'right' way. This chapter is going to show how misleading this idea of inter-electoral participation is.

The struggle to participate in modern democracy

Contacting a representative: Monsanto does it better

One way in which citizens are supposed to seek to influence public decision-making between elections is to contact the Member of Parliament or Congress for their region and convince them to undertake or abstain from a certain action. For example, a citizen might be concerned that the government is considering allowing fracking in their area. Although he or she will be directly affected by the policy in question, they do not have any way to directly participate in making the decision. They therefore have to operate at one remove and attempt to influence their representative to do what they themselves *would have done* if they were in the representative's position. This is often very difficult to achieve. There are many reasons why a visit or letter to a representative might fail to yield any results. The representative:

- might not think that the constituent's problem is important;
- might not have time to deal with it;
- might not like the constituent;
- might forget about the problem;
- might not know how to fix the problem;
- might not be in a position to fix the problem, especially if the constituent is complaining about something that is part of the party's policy.

Whether or not they deal with any of their constituents' concerns is entirely up to the representative. The citizen has no means of forcing the representative to take action, other than the threat of not voting for them in the next election – a threat which the party's tacticians and donors are well able to neutralize by other means. So for the most part, people are relegated to passively hoping that the representative will take their concerns seriously, with absolutely no guarantees that this will actually happen.

As a result of this uncertainty, contacting a representative tends to be the preserve of those who have the time and energy to put into repeated attempts, namely large businesses and NGOs. This monopolization of representatives' time has been going on for so long and in such a predictable fashion that a 1950s study by MIT staff revealed that 40 per cent of American Congressmen's mail had been generated by big business interests coordinating letter campaigns, and much of the rest by NGOs. Congressmen were already so inured to the flood of mail generated by big organizations that they even ironically rated the quality of communications received, commenting that at least Monsanto (then a pesticide producer and now a gene-technology giant) always had their followers neatly type their letters (or, more likely, gave their followers a pre-typed letter to sign). This means that even an activity that seems as grassroots as writing to a representative is usually anything but. Only a deluge of mail on a specific topic generally results in action, and entities that already command significant resources are the most likely to make this happen for themselves. The ability to write to or visit a representative essentially works to privilege exactly those wealthy entities that are already privileged through elections, rather than providing any real participation benefits for the average citizen.

Petition: the lights are on but no one's home

Petitioning is another popular way to try to influence representatives. Nearly everyone has been asked to sign a petition at some point in their lives, and the process has recently been given an update through the possibility of submitting e-petitions, as set up in the United States and the United Kingdom. Government e-petitions allow citizens to set up a petition that others can sign online. If enough signatures are collected within an allotted time, the government is obliged to take a certain action in response to the e-petition. It sounds terrific on paper, but these government actions are merely hollow pro-forma tasks that do not involve any real engagement with the petitioners or their concerns.

Death stars and fundamentalists: the empire talks back

In the United States, if an e-petition garners 25,000 signatures, a White House functionary issues an official response to it. Some of the most popular petitions to date have included declaring the fundamentalist Westboro Baptist Church (notorious for protesting at the funerals of gay soldiers) to be a hate group and – somewhat more light-heartedly – a request for the US government to build a replica of the Death Star from the famous Star Wars films. To date, the White House has issued over 150 responses to e-petitions. None of these responses, however, actually reconsiders government policy in light of the points raised by the petitioners. Instead, responses merely summarize and justify White House policy at a superficial level of detail that is already easily accessible to the general public.

For example, in response to a petition asking the United States not to block Palestine's attempt to become a member of the United Nations, the government mentions its strong belief 'in the legitimate aspirations of the Palestinian people', as well as its 'profound commitment to a just and lasting peace based on a negotiated two-State solution', without ever squarely addressing the issue at stake: what the government's reasons are for vetoing Palestinian membership in a global body that overwhelming supports it.[1] Similarly, two petitions to repeal the Patriot Act (US legislation that has been used to conduct blanket surveillance of most of the developed world) received the same answer, which waffled about 'responsibility', made an implausible implication that the Act had helped in the capture of one would-be terrorist, and claimed that the law was subject to 'rigorous oversight', which we now,

1 'Committed to a just and lasting peace in the Middle East: White House response to [petition to] not veto Palestine's application to become a member of the United Nations', *We the People*, petitions.whitehouse.gov/response/committed-just-and-lasting-peace-middle-east.

thanks to whistle-blower Edward Snowden, know was a bare-faced lie.[2]

These types of answers, devoid as they are of any substantive reasoning, show that American e-petitions are not an opportunity for ordinary Americans to 'have a say' in government. Petitions do not allow them any say at all – they only get to ask a question, following which the government gets to have *another say* which serves to deflate any budding opposition to its policies.

It is as if in Athens a speaker were permitted to address the Assembly stating the policy he was going to implement, one person were allowed to ask a question about this policy, provided that they could obtain the backing of a few hundred fellow citizens, following which the speaker would reiterate his policy and announce that he would continue with it notwithstanding, after which no further discussion would be permitted. It is hard to imagine that anyone would be in a rush to emulate such a system or equate it with empowerment, yet it is exactly what the United States is currently practising with its e-petition policy.

Fuel duty and Hillsborough: hearing without listening

The situation is not any better in the United Kingdom, where if 100,000 signatures are collected, a backbench Member of Parliament (i.e. an MP who by definition does not wield very much power) may take up the cause and bring the matter

---

2   Lisa Monaco, 'Ensuring the safety and security of the nation while protecting constitutional rights and civil liberties: official Department of Justice response to [petition to] repeal the Patriot Act and [petition to] end the Patriot Act', *We the People*, petitions.whitehouse.gov/response/ensuring-safety-and-security-nation-while-protecting-constitutional-rights-and-civil.

forward for debate in the Backbench Business Committee, which may then, in turn, bring the matter forward for debate in the House of Commons during 'backbench time'.

In other words, if 100,000 people sign an e-petition, a backbench MP *might* decide to bring that petition for debate before the Backbench Business Committee and the committee *might* decide to allocate time to discuss the petition *during backbench time* in Parliament. It is an extremely ineffective approach to bringing about change. In fact, the relevance to the average citizen of someone else merely *talking* about their problem remains as obscure as the parliamentary downtime in which this conversation is supposed to occur.

As a result of all of these filters, far from being empowered, the petitioner is relegated to hoping that the outcome will be favourable and to attempting to indirectly influence decision-makers – for example, by seeking to accompany a petition with a press campaign or other actions aimed at coercing representatives into approving or at least considering the petition. This in turn, however, requires that the petitioner have access to significant resources. The case of FairFuel UK is a perfect example of this process at work.

In 2011, the British government was planning to increase duty on fuel, a plan which British transport companies strongly objected to. After an e-petition secured the requisite number of signatures, the Backbench Business Committee considered the issue and decided to bring up the motion in Parliament. However, the government delayed allocating time for the discussion to the point where it seemed likely that the debate would never reach the floor, despite having secured the relevant number of signatures as well as the approval of the Backbench Business Committee.

FairFuel UK, however, was not merely a group of concerned citizens, but rather an umbrella association of banks, insurers, hauliers and companies that provide fuel-related services to other businesses, and which was advised by professional lobbyists and public relations experts. This association of specialized business interests mobilized their members to write to MPs demanding a parliamentary debate, launched an aggressive public relations campaign and held a reception in the parliament buildings to lobby MPs. All of this activity resulted in the fuel increase being debated in Parliament and subsequently rejected. Despite this positive outcome for Fair-Fuel UK, its members remained less than impressed with e-petitions. Their spokesperson stated: 'The Government told us that their ePetitions would make Parliament more responsive to the public. I'm not seeing any response at all and completely understand the unprecedented frustration of thousands of our supporters.'[3]

The case illustrates how difficult it is for even a well-funded and well-organized campaign to ensure that the contents of an e-petition which has attracted the requisite number of signatures will actually culminate in a debate, much less a result.

When those resources aren't available, the results are even more sobering. To take one well-known example: An e-petition which asked that the inquest into the death of a boy named Kevin Williams be fast-tracked received over 100,000 signatures between October 2012 and January 2013.

---

3 '10,000 frustrated FairFuelUK supporters email Parliament over the weekend', 30 October 2011, fairfueluk.com/quentins_blog.php?entry_id=1319993044&title=10000-frustrated-fairfueluk- supporters-email-parliament-over-the-weekend.

Kevin Williams was only fifteen when he, along with ninety-five other people, was crushed to death in an overcrowded enclosure in a soccer stadium in 1989. The event was later christened 'the Hillsborough Disaster' and became emblematic of class struggle in Britain as authority figures attempted to delegitimize victims of the disaster as worthless and undeserving of sympathy. However, it was eventually revealed that, in stark contradiction to initial reports, the main factor in the fatal overcrowding was not a rush of fans into the stadium or their alleged drunkenness, but rather police mismanagement of crowd control procedures. Worse, it came out that police simply presumed victims to be dead on the scene and impeded the access of proper emergency services. It is possible that up to half of the victims would have survived had they received timely medical treatment for their injuries, and there is particular reason to believe that Kevin Williams survived the initial crush for some time. Several witnesses have testified that he lived for between twenty minutes to an hour after he was pulled from the suffocating enclosure, but that he was not given appropriate medical attention during that time.

In the twenty-three years following her son's death, Kevin's mother Anne Williams worked to investigate the circumstances of the Hillsborough Disaster, becoming a much-loved community leader. While these efforts had some success, an inquest into the event was still ongoing when Anne Williams, by now a middle-aged woman, was diagnosed with terminal cancer. In October 2012, a petition was launched asking that the inquest into her son's death be moved forward so that his mother would be able to hear the result before she died. The petition received over 100,000 signatures by January 2013.

The matter, however, was not taken up by a backbencher and Mrs Williams died in April 2013.

This is the kind of 'empowerment' our society truly gives to a mother who worked for twenty-three years just to procure a proper investigation into the death of her own child, and to the people who, touched by her plight, were moved to grant a final act of kindness.

As this example so eloquently demonstrates, the right to petition does not enable citizens to do anything; it only permits them to ask others to do something – those who have already been granted power through the electoral system, namely representatives and government. This has even been acknowledged by the Backbench Business Committee itself, which complained to government that the e-petition website gives citizens a misleadingly positive impression of the e-petition process. In fact, the committee asked that the phrase 'e-petitions is an easy way for you to influence government policy in the UK' be changed to: 'e-petitions are an easy way for you to make sure your concerns are heard by Government and Parliament'.[4] The new wording was intended to reflect that e-petitions do not actually enable petitioners to influence policy.

Petitions may raise the chance of a politician literally *hearing* of a petitioner's concerns, but nothing can force the representative to pay any attention to them. Because representatives and government are already in a position where they are empowered to do whatever they like, they have very

---

4 'Debates on Government e-Petitions: Government response to the Committee's Seventh Report of Session 2010–12 – Procedure Committee' (www.parliament.uk, 22 March 2012), www.publications.parliament.uk/pa/cm201012/cmselect/cmproced/1902/190204.htm.

little incentive to heed petitions, especially those that emanate from weak and disenfranchised members of society.

Demonstration: he who doth protest too much
doth also cruise for bruises

But if petition does not work, we always have protest. In fact, scarcely a day goes by without politicians reminding people how lucky they are to be able to protest and impressing upon them that this very right is what differentiates their country from less fortunate nations. In fact, the right to protest is often felt to constitute the very essence of democracy, second in importance only to elections. But, in truth, as anyone who has been part of a protest movement can testify, it is a very unwieldy tool in the effort to make change happen.

Because citizens cannot directly make national policy decisions, effective protest depends on putting people who can (representatives) between a rock and a hard place. On one side of the representative are those interests that have paid for and masterminded their election campaign (e.g. gas companies that wish to commence fracking activities in their region); on their other side are the local residents whom they are actually supposed to represent (and who may not be happy to allow fracking in their area). When no one protests, the representative tends to work and pass laws in the interests of their sponsors (e.g. permitting fracking, scaling back environmental protection laws) and they can expect to continue to be rewarded for doing so with generous campaign contributions. When they fail to act in the interests of sponsors they can expect, at the very least, for those rewards to dry up.

Faced with a situation like this, the only real option for protesters is to make clear to representatives that failing to fulfil their wishes will be *even worse* for the representative than failing to do what the donors want. Considering the resources at the donors' disposal, as well as the electoral skewing and gerrymandering that makes even voting against a candidate an ineffective means of punishing them, this is a nearly impossible task. In fact, private donors and representatives usually join forces to punish protesters for protesting, making their task even more difficult.

Thus, even the results of long-lasting and successful protests rarely meet the expectations of the protesters, and activists often pay a heavy price for their years of involvement. The Civil Rights Movement in 1960s America was one of the most successful protest movements of all time, but it had to sustain itself for over fifteen years. Hundreds of protesters were beaten and jailed, many were killed. In Germany, the popular protest against nuclear power which began in the 1970s managed to achieve an agreement to phase out nuclear power by 2022 only after the Fukushima disaster of 2011. That means that nearly fifty years of sustained protest by, at times, hundreds of thousands of people produced only phased results which may still be reversed. Anti-globalization protests have been even less effective. The Battle of Seattle, which drew 40,000 people onto the streets of the West Coast American city to protest against World Trade Organization policies in 1999, merely resulted in the WTO moving its meetings to places like Qatar, an absolute monarchy where security is not an issue.

Drama, setbacks and the danger of personal injury are all part of protesting. Considering these trials and tribulations and the meagre end results that protesting often produces, it is quite odd that we consider it to be such a beneficial part of a functioning democracy. In fact, it is absolutely staggering that we are even willing to entertain the idea that someone would have to organize a protest movement spanning what could be the rest of their natural life and entailing the risk of being jailed, beaten or killed in order to have an impact on public policy. It is more amazing still that we call this 'people power' and even glorify the process, as if forcing people to go to such lengths in the effort to participate is something to be proud of.

Far from being *part* of democracy, protest is a reaction to a *lack* of democracy. Nowhere is this more apparent than in the comparison with Athens. The very idea of protest would have made little sense to an Athenian democrat because in Athens, anyone could employ his time far more effectively and directly through seeking to sway voters in the Assembly or by participating in court.

Similar conclusions can be drawn about other forms of modern 'participation'. The passivity of e-petitions, which place decision-making power in the hands of certain select individuals, renders them qualitatively different from the kind of participation which was on offer in Athens. Had either the FairFuel UK or the Kevin Williams inquest campaign been conducted in Athens, the parties concerned need only have raised the issue in Assembly or before the law courts without the need for any prior endorsement, and a decision by the people would have been immediately forthcoming. While the petitioners may not have achieved their objectives, they would have been spared a prolonged battle just to have a decision rendered.

The same can be said for any other form of contact with representatives. Constituents rely on MPs, because they themselves are not permitted to speak in Parliament. By contrast, in Athens no citizen was reduced to a situation so powerless that he had to ask another person to try to influence the Assembly on his behalf. An Athenian might well have encouraged someone whom he thought was a great speaker to endorse a motion, but if that person refused he still had the ability to take the floor himself. There was no element of uncertainty and the effects were immediate. This meant that participating was a rewarding experience in Athens. Today, however, it is all too apt to result only in frustration.

Participation in modern democracy: running to stand still

Since neither petition nor protest nor visits to representatives are likely to have any effect on politics, it should come as no surprise that citizens in modern democracies often feel discouraged. However, despite the long odds of success, the figures show that ordinary citizens are still willing to sacrifice a substantial amount of time and energy in trying to influence public processes. According to the studies:

- 16 per cent of British citizens have contacted a Member of Parliament at least once, while 6 per cent have contacted a government department over what they considered to be an unjust government action;
- residents of Ireland do even better – 16 per cent of them contacted their national representative or county councillor within only a three-year period;
- 34 per cent of Americans initiate contact with a government official in the twelve-month period leading up to

elections, while 29 per cent attend at least one political meeting over the same time frame;

- 8 per cent of British citizens have been on at least one protest, while in August 2012, 6 per cent of Americans said they had been on a protest over the previous twelve months and 17 per cent said that they had signed an online petition;
- in the 1980s, 3.5 per cent of British citizens had canvassed for a political party in the past five years; in Ireland the figure was 4 per cent;
- 7 per cent of Americans stated that they had 'worked or volunteered for a political party or candidate' over the twelve months leading up to the 2012 presidential election.

It may be in vogue to bewail these low numbers as a sign of woeful citizen disinterest, but they actually indicate a population that remains committed to devoting a surprising amount of time and energy to civic engagement, despite the low rewards associated with such activity. Even in Athens, participation rates were not 100 per cent, but more in the range of 10–25 per cent on any given activity. While participation rates are significantly lower in modern democracies than in Athens, they are not as low as one might expect in a society that makes results via any of these methods of 'participation' so difficult to achieve.

While modern democracy claims to value participation, the truth is that our system values going through the motions of participation. Citizens are disempowered and then exhorted to 'take part' via unwieldy processes that demand that they seek to somehow remotely control others.

This is no accident.

If it were possible for citizens to participate effectively between elections, what would be the reward for winning an election? If effective citizen participation between elections really existed, the victorious party would not 'take it all', but rather be forced to negotiate and compromise with irritated citizens throughout their term in office. It's for these reasons that the incentive to create effective participatory avenues for citizens is minimal. It is necessary to keep alternative avenues of participation as indirect and ineffective as elections are in order to preserve the inequality between governors and governed.

If we truly lived in societies governed by the principle of people power, things would be very different. For one thing, meaningful participation would not be viewed as a glorious struggle, but rather a natural, everyday task. This sharp distinction between participation as a struggle or as a basic part of life becomes very apparent when we compare our society to the democracy of ancient Athens. The Athenians did not waste time glorifying the trials and tribulations of political participation, but rather made every effort to get rid of those difficulties and to make participation both easy and enjoyable. These efforts went far beyond even those aspects of Athenian life, such as lottery selection and *isegoria*, that we have discussed so far.

The Athenian view on participation
Non-participants as good-for-nothings

In Athens, there was no government programme to acquiesce to, so Athenians had a choice between either doing the work of government themselves or accepting that it would not get done. Direct participation was thus essential to the well-being of Athenian democracy. According to Aristotle, if one were to factor in jury duty, public office and part-time administration posts, there were approximately 11,000 peacetime government positions in Athens, which had to be filled by, at most, 45,000 citizens. The administrative Council of 500 alone required that one quarter of all citizens serve on it at some point in their lives,[5] and if Aristotle's estimate is correct, at least one quarter of all Athenians were active in public service nearly every day.

Part of this willingness to pitch in on matters of state stemmed from the prevailing view in Athens that citizens had a duty to sacrifice some of their time and energies to take care of public business. Those who refused to pitch in were castigated as 'good for nothing[s]'.[6] But there was more to maintaining constant, direct participation than just social pressure.

Democratic participation: a service well worth paying for

Since Athenian democracy required a large number of citizens to participate in government on a frequent basis, it was necessary to make this frequent participation possible. The richest citizens may have been able to attend the Assembly and courts regularly because they did not need to go to work every day, but what about everyone else? Most Athenians were self-employed and had to work to take care of

---

5 As the name suggests, an administrative body composed of 500 randomly selected citizens. Each citizen was limited to serving on it only twice in his lifetime.
6 Thucydides, *The Peloponnesian War*, 2.40.2.

themselves and their families. The poorer a citizen was, the harder it would be for him to take a day off to debate public matters. The Athenians resolved this difficulty by doing something as extraordinary as it was effective – they paid people to participate in democracy.

Although no one could get rich just showing up to Assembly and courts, they weren't paid token amounts either. Every citizen who attended an Assembly meeting or court sitting earned half a drachma. This was about half what an unskilled labourer could earn in a day (approximately $30 by today's standards). The *archai* (randomly selected officials) were also financially compensated, usually receiving half a drachma or one drachma a day, depending on their duties.

Pay for participation worked wonders for Athenian democracy. According to Socrates, the Assembly was dominated by fullers, shoemakers, carpenters, blacksmiths, farmers, merchants and traders. These individuals may have been more or less well off, but they all worked for a living. In confirmation of Socrates' observation, Isocrates (a famous teacher and contemporary of Socrates) complained that things had been better in the past when 'those who had leisure and sufficient property were in charge of public affairs',[7] indicating that pay for public service had rendered this no longer the case. Most clearly of all, in his description of Athenian democracy, Aristotle wrote: 'all citizens take part in this sort of government because of the predominance of the masses, and they participate and exercise their citizen rights because even the poor are able to have leisure by receiving pay'.[8]

---

7 Isocrates, *Areopagiticus*, 7.54, quoted in M. Markle, 'Jury pay and Assembly pay at Athens', at 102.
8 Aristotle, *Politics*, 1293a3–7, quoted in Markle, op. cit., at 103.

Driving home this point, he continued: 'the power of the Council [i.e. the executive branch] is weakened in democracies of the sort in which the people in assembly deals with everything itself; this usually happens when there is a plentiful supply of pay for those attending the assembly, for having leisure they meet often and themselves make all decisions'.[9]

It is telling that none of the philosophers who lived and worked in the Athenian democracy thought that the direct participation of any but the richest citizens could be sustained without pay.

The idea of paying citizens to participate in making public decisions might seem radical, but consider the following: although the need for participation is very limited in modern democracies, in the few areas where it is indispensable, we pay for people to participate, too.

Not only do we pay representatives and members of government at quite generous rates, the idea that participation should be compensated also lives on as pay for jury duty, perhaps the only form of democratic participation that is unrelentingly considered to *be* a duty. Jury duty today is, of course, not as exciting as it was in Athens, not least because juries do not decide on matters of public policy, and jurors are generally paid less for their time, despite being far fewer in number. Moreover, unlike in Athens, modern jurors cannot choose when to report for jury duty, nor do they know how long a trial will last. Doubtless, this all contributes to the fact that although jury duty is paid for, many people today do not swoon for joy when they receive their summons.

---

9 Aristotle, *Politics*, 1299b, quoted in Markle, op. cit., at 104.

However, the interesting point remains that in modern society, when we need to force participation, we also need to pay for it. Unlike nearly everything else in modern democracies, initial selection for jury duty occurs on a random and egalitarian basis and the only way to maintain this is to compensate citizens so that they can afford to attend. Otherwise, jurors would go hungry, go bankrupt, lose their savings, fall behind on their mortgage payments and, most likely of all, simply refuse to show up.

This is highly significant, because in all other respects the dynamic between pay and participation in modern democracies works in precisely the opposite manner to how it did in Athens. In modern democracies, citizens either need to spend large sums of their own or their sponsors' money in the quest to be elected, or to devote substantial resources to participating in between elections, e.g. in giving up time and income to protest or petition, or spending money on sustained media or other pressure campaigns in the service of their cause. Few people can afford to part with sums of money high enough to make a substantial difference to any of these courses of action. They simply do not have the resources at their disposal to do so. This means that in modern democracies more and more people are cut out of the political life of the nation, effectively silencing their wishes and interests. By contrast, by paying citizens to participate, the Athenians created a situation of increased equality where more and more people could partake in the decisions that affected their lives.

Different but (more) equal:
decision-making in Athens

By permitting pay for participation, the Athenians ensured that no citizen would be prevented from participating on economic grounds. However, despite everything that the Athenians did to enable participation, the playing field was still tilted in favour of the rich. It may seem like nit-picking towards a society that enabled a far superior degree of free and effective citizen decision-making than we have ever experienced, but it is nonetheless an important point, because the fact, that despite all that they did, Athens was *still* skewed in favour of the rich shows just how much effort is needed to even up the political playing field and how very far we are from achieving that goal. It certainly puts our own issues with inequality into perspective to know that even if we did *everything* that the Athenians did, political participation *still* wouldn't be 100 per cent fair.

So, what were the weak points of Athenian participatory equality?

As we know, the Athenians used elections much like our own before they established what they considered to be democracy. When they entered the democratic era, they largely abandoned elections, choosing instead to fill official positions by lottery. However, as previously mentioned, they did not abolish the practice of holding elections completely, reserving them instead for a small number of positions where technical skill was absolutely necessary.

The most important of these elected positions was that of general or *strategos* of the Athenian army. The Athenians, who were nearly always either at war, preparing for war or recovering from war, could simply not afford to make mistakes on the battlefield. In this particular arena, someone needed to have the authority to give orders. Therefore, on the battlefield – and only on the battlefield – Athens' ten elected generals made the decisions.

As this indicates, despite being elected, Athenian generals did not possess nearly as much power as modern politicians do. In fact, they did not even have as much power as modern generals do. Athenian generals were not permitted to make independent decisions except when they were on campaign and had not received any contradictory orders from the Assembly. They did not, for example, decide on the resources that should be devoted to military expenditure or whether or not a campaign should be approved. In other words, when not actually engaged in combat, the generals were still firmly under the Assembly's thumb, and all of the decisions that they did make on the battlefield were subject to democratic review. If the Assembly thought that a general had made a serious mistake, he could find himself ordered to pay an exorbitant fine or even exiled.

This was exactly the fate of one man whom we have to thank for a great deal of what we know about Athenian democracy. This man, Thucydides, is often considered to be one of the first 'real' historians because he wrote an extremely thorough account of the Peloponnesian War which has survived to the present day. The war, fought between Athens and Sparta, was one of the most serious conflicts of the time and engulfed ancient Greece for nearly thirty years. Thucydides was well acquainted with the ins and outs of the war for the very good reason that before he turned to history, he had served as an Athenian general. As such a highly valued person, Thucydides was given the task of preventing the strategically important city of Amphipolis from falling to the Spartans. When Thucydides failed in his mission, he was punished by exile from Athens. Although Thucydides was extremely bitter about this punishment, it turned out to be a good thing for modern historians, since exile gave him the time and distance he needed to write down his observations about the war. While Thucydides was unusual for the length of his exile and his uncanny ability to turn lemons into lemonade by penning one of the most important historical documents of all time, many generals suffered similar setbacks and had to be constantly on their toes to avoid being sacked.

Nonetheless, despite the constant pressure they were under, the generals did enjoy an elevated position within the Assembly. Since warfare was a near-constant activity, a substantial portion of every major Assembly meeting concerned itself with what was euphemistically termed 'foreign policy'. The opinions of the generals – the acknowledged experts on military strategy – naturally carried great weight during these debates.

And this privileged position within the Assembly was more likely to be held by someone who was rich than by someone who was poor. Successful generals had often enjoyed an expensive education that equipped them to exercise this tactical role, and because the generalship was unpaid, the position was not particularly attractive to anyone who needed to earn a living. According to the writer known as the Old Oligarch, a contemporary critic of democracy: 'all those offices, which involve the receipt of money and benefit for one's household, these the common people seek to hold', but they had an ambivalent attitude towards procuring the unpaid elected offices.[10]

The co-relation between wealth and being elected general was by no means absolute – there are examples of men of humble means becoming extremely successful generals – but it was present to the degree that no one doubted that a general was more likely to be rich than poor. Athenian democracy mitigated the influence of wealth on politics, but it was not totally immune to it.

Another extremely important role in democracy was filled by the so-called *rhetors*. In contrast to that of general, the position of *rhetor* was entirely unofficial. Any citizen who spoke in the Assembly was a *rhetor*, or orator, by virtue of speaking, but some citizens spoke so often as to de facto be self-employed as *rhetors*. While even the most talented and committed of these self-designated *rhetors* were unable to carry every resolution they supported, they were nonetheless acknowledged to be extremely influential people within the Assembly simply by virtue of their willingness to sink so much time and effort into their appearances. This could include not only a predilection to spend free time reflecting on matters of state, but also often entailed considerable effort in training one's voice to address a large crowd. Demosthenes, one of the most famous Athenian *rhetors*, could be found on the beach attempting to speak over the crashing waves when he wasn't busy trying to talk around a pebble in his mouth or reciting poetry while out jogging. And the respected statesman Pericles was given to an even weirder habit – he was known to engage in the laborious and expensive process of making notes before he

---

10   Pseudo-Xenophon, *Constitution of the Athenians*, 1.10–12.

gave a speech to help organize his thoughts. For the average person, that sort of commitment was hard to compete with.

And a truly successful *rhetor* often needed to have other attributes, such as the ability to give a thoughtful and entertaining speech. This privileged the rich, because poor and middle-class citizens were far more likely to be instructed in a trade by their close relatives than to study the high arts of philosophy or rhetoric. As a result, they would likely find it more difficult to present a polished and persuasive argument in Assembly or court than someone who had received specialized training. Not only that, to really make a career as a fully fledged *rhetor*, a citizen needed to be able to point back to at least a decent military record. However, as in other ancient societies, a citizen's function in the Athenian army was based on his ability to provide his own equipment. This meant that anyone who could provide himself with a horse was a knight (i.e. in a relatively well-off and flashy position), those who could provide their own armour were hoplites (most of the middle class) and those who could not afford armour or a horse were consigned to the less exalted status of rowers of the fleet. Rowing ships across the Aegean Sea was hard work, but not the stuff of legends, and it was next to impossible to establish a reputation for military prowess when one's job was not so much to vanquish the enemy as to give the vanquisher a lift.

Unsurprisingly, then, initially most important *rhetors* were descended from wealthy, aristocratic families. And although leaders from more humble backgrounds soon emerged, they had humble *backgrounds* only. Virtually every prominent *rhetor* throughout the democracy was relatively affluent, if not at the time of his birth, then certainly by the time he achieved prominence. Those born wealthy were usually politically active and well known by their twenties or early thirties, while those from less distinguished backgrounds were rarely able to achieve anything of note before their mid-forties, since they first had to build their own success.

Despite these drawbacks, it was possible for an Athenian to move up the social scale within his own lifetime, and it was certainly possible for him to address the Assembly without having to move anywhere at all. We know that ordinary citizens were not shy in volunteering to speak and that they sometimes showed up more experienced and well-known *rhetors* with a superior argument. Furthermore, an Athenian did not need to own any property or have any specific accomplishments to entitle him to make decisions in Assembly or the courts or to serve as an official. Wealthy *rhetors* may have done a lot of the talking, but the people in Assembly and courts still did all of the deciding.

As the positions of general and *rhetor* indicate, there were distinctly different roles for political high achievers and 'the average person' in Athenian democracy, but while the relationship between them was not entirely equal, the balance was different to what it is today. In Athens, the relationship between elite *rhetor* or general and 'the people' operated on consent and respect, instead of force and contempt. Wealth certainly had an effect on the level of democratic participation one could afford to engage in, but not an overwhelming one which deprived others of their decision-making power or excluded them from seeking to speak themselves. Wealth was *a* factor, not *the* factor, in political participation.

From ancient duty to modern privilege

Unlike the citizens of Athens, we do not live in a society where citizen participation in politics is a publicly funded activity. Far from it. In fact, to most of us, paying people to participate in politics sounds more like something you might encounter in an experimental work of science-fiction than like anything that could happen in real life. It's hard to swallow that such a society really existed. But this is not because there is anything inherently strange about paying for participation – as we've seen, it worked well in Athens, and even modern democracies pay jurors for their time. Rather, pay-for-participation sounds so eccentric only because of the preconceptions about participation that are built into modern thinking about democracy.

In modern democracies, participation is viewed not as a *duty* to be shouldered, but as a *privilege* to be fought over. In fact, make that observation to nearly anyone living in a modern democracy and chances are that they will accept the idea of competing for political privilege without a second thought. However, as the example of Athens clearly demonstrates, there is no need to view political participation as inherently competitive at every level, and there are good reasons why we shouldn't.

The very competition to participate, to *matter,* in our democracies means that whoever wins that competition wins power. And in the long run, it doesn't matter that that power comes with a four-to-five-year term limit attached. Once a relatively stable power base has been achieved, it can be used to generate wealth for the winner and his or her associates, for example, by passing laws favourable to them – wealth which can be used in the service of winning again. That means that, over time, small advantages become big advantages and big advantages become enormous advantages. It's exactly like a game of Monopoly – whoever gets hold of the most valuable property in the beginning will eventually win the game, because their small advantage will just keep growing. It may take an agonizingly long time for this to play out – indeed, I've long suspected that no one has ever actually finished a game of Monopoly – but in real life, this is exactly what makes this pattern so dangerous. It's creeping.

In electoral democracies, success depends on consolidating power; in Athenian society power was dispersed among the many citizens who performed an essential role in all decisions. This meant that it was harder to capitalize on small advantages; that these small advantages were transient and had to be refought over every day; that in a society where participation was free and easy, there was simply very little to hold on to. Because it was very hard to alter the balance of power in such a system, it was actually very stable.

But unfortunately for us, we are headed in precisely the opposite direction. Unlike the Athenians, we live under a political system that often saddles us with a government we didn't vote for; where the very people who are supposed to be representing us frequently attempt to devalue our votes; where money is the single biggest determining factor in acquiring power and power the single biggest factor in acquiring money; and where it's almost impossible to participate in politics between elections because the cards are stacked against anyone of average means. Far from accepting free and easy participation as a fact of life, the incentive is to grasp and hoard whatever one can, be it little or great.

It's not a pretty picture.

And it gets worse because nations today do not live in a vacuum; they are hooked into an international system of decision-making that exacerbates all of the flaws of modern democracy and transforms the distressing into the intolerable.

5

Modern Democracy and the International System: A Perfect Storm

All animals are equal, but some animals are more equal than others.

George Orwell, *Animal Farm*

Believe it or not, globalization was not a thing during the time of the ancient Athenians. Instead, various ethnic groups were splintered off and functioned as independent nations. These countries traded with each other and sometimes formed alliances, but these were rudimentary links. The Athenians may have interacted with other peoples, but neither they nor anyone else instituted stable and formal processes to govern their relations with other states. Instead, it was self-understood that each state reserved the right to renege on treaties at any time and to interfere with or change what their negotiators may have agreed to. The Athenians' up-and-coming neighbours, the Romans, even had a custom for dealing with this situation: if they did not like the terms of a treaty, they delivered their own negotiator, bound hand and foot, back to the other party with the message that the treaty was void and that this would be a handy person on whom to take out any feelings of disappointment, seeing as they wouldn't be needing him back. As this indicates, diplomacy back then was a bit touch and go, and so when we study ancient civilizations like Athens, we rarely need to look beyond national boundaries to understand why things happened the way they did.

However, in today's world, it is not as easy to separate the national practices of democracy from international affairs. In fact, it's safe to say we cannot fully understand one without the other, because some of the most severe problems with democracy actually stem from the way that national politics interacts with this international sphere. This is because our national representatives are empowered to negotiate treaties on our behalf and to cast votes for us at international institutions. These decisions are then binding on the entire country. Therefore, when a political party wins a national election, it doesn't just win the right to make domestic decisions, it also wins the right to represent the nation internationally and to use the nation's resources to affect international decision-making in a manner conducive to its own policies and interests. Winning a national election can therefore be a springboard to international power which can in turn be exercised within the original state and within other states.

This chapter is going to show exactly how the interplay between national and international structures works to grant huge levels of power to those who can win election while systematically disenfranchising and impoverishing all others.

The United Nations

The international system as we know it was designed during the final days of the Second World War. Its primary purpose is to maintain global stability and to prevent war, and it has four major organizations at its core: the World Trade Organization (WTO); the International Monetary Fund (IMF); the International Bank for Reconstruction and Development (IBRD), usually called 'the World Bank'; and, of course, the United Nations (UN).

The UN is certainly the most well known of these organizations owing to its numerous programmes (e.g. the World Food Programme or the United Nations Children's Fund) that are aimed at helping vulnerable individuals and disadvantaged communities around the world. There is no doubt that these programmes do a great deal of good, but as real as their impact is on many people's lives, they are a sideshow to the UN's main business of regulating world politics and maintaining international peace and security. And while the UN's day-to-day activities are carried out by numerous administrative officials, the most important of whom is the secretary-general, the organization is ultimately run by its member states, which send representatives to speak and vote on their behalf at the UN's two main bodies, the Security Council and the General Assembly.

The Security Council: permanent power for those that can afford it

The Security Council is the most powerful part of the United Nations organization. It is responsible for maintaining international peace and security, or to put it the other way

Figure 5.1 The post-war international system

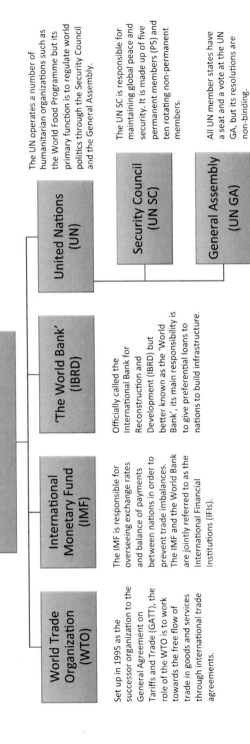

The International Institutions

World Trade Organization (WTO)

Set up in 1995 as the successor organization to the General Agreement on Tariffs and Trade (GATT), the role of the WTO is to work towards the free flow of trade in goods and services through international trade agreements.

International Monetary Fund (IMF)

The IMF is responsible for overseeing exchange rates and balance of payments between nations in order to prevent trade imbalances. The IMF and the World Bank are jointly referred to as the International Financial Institutions (IFIs).

'The World Bank' (IBRD)

Officially called the International Bank for Reconstruction and Development (IBRD) but better known as the 'World Bank', its main responsibility is to give preferential loans to nations to build infrastructure.

United Nations (UN)

The UN operates a number of humanitarian organizations such as the World Food Programme but its primary function is to regulate world politics through the Security Council and the General Assembly.

Security Council (UN SC)

The UN SC is responsible for maintaining global peace and security. It is made up of five permanent members (P5) and ten rotating non-permanent members.

General Assembly (UN GA)

All UN member states have a seat and a vote at the UN GA, but its resolutions are non-binding.

around, it is responsible for preventing war. When the Security Council makes a decision, it issues that decision via a formal document known as a 'resolution'. Not only are the Council's resolutions legally binding on all United Nations members, i.e. on nearly every state in the world, they even override all other obligations that a state may have. As such, Security Council resolutions are a powerful source of international law – they create obligations which states and all of the people and corporate bodies in them must obey. If the Security Council decides that companies may not do business with South Africa then this is the law; if it orders banks to freeze the assets of suspected terrorists, this is the law; if it orders military force to be used against a country, that, too, is the law.

But despite the fact that its resolutions bind everyone, the Security Council's members are few; only fifteen nations have a seat on the Council at any one time. Ten of these nations are non-permanent members that are elected on a rotating basis by all 193 UN members. The five remaining countries are permanent members, who, as the name suggests, hold a seat on the Security Council in perpetuity. These are the five most powerful Second World War victors:[1] the United States of America (USA), the Union of Soviet Socialist Republics (USSR), the United Kingdom (UK), France and China. China's seat was held and exercised by Taiwan until 1971, when the official dogma that the tiny island's pro-Western government was, through unfathomable dark arts, somehow controlling all of mainland China finally gave way to reality and the seat was transferred to delegates from Mao Tse-Tung's

---

[1] The term 'United Nations' was actually first used as another name for the Allied forces during the Second World War.

People's Republic of China. Under somewhat less conten-
tious circumstances, the USSR's seat fell to its successor
state Russia following the end of the Cold War in the early
1990s. In all other respects, the identity of the five permanent members (known as 'the P-5') has remained unaltered
during the seventy years of the Security Council's existence.

Above and beyond simply holding their Security Council
seat in perpetuity, these states also have other privileges.
Unlike the ten non-permanent members, any one of the P-5
can veto a Security Council resolution, meaning that even
if everyone else on the Council votes in favour, a resolution
cannot pass if even one permanent member votes against it.
The representative of any of the P-5 therefore wields a truly
awe-inspiring level of power.

And since power corrupts and absolute power corrupts
absolutely, the veto's history is far from illustrious. It is generally used for three main purposes: to directly protect the
interests of the country exercising it (for example, in 1986 the
USA used its veto to prevent a decision of the International
Court of Justice from being enforced against it); to directly
protect the interests of a client state (for example, the USSR
vetoed sanctions against Iran during the Tehran hostage crisis
of 1979/80, while the USA, UK and France repeatedly vetoed
sanctions on South Africa during apartheid and the occu-
pation of Namibia in the 1980s); and to veto the admission
of members that are viewed as being in another permanent
member's camp (e.g. in 1957 and 1958 the USSR vetoed the
admission of Vietnam when it had a capitalist government,
a favour returned twenty years later when the USA vetoed
Vietnam's admission in 1976 when it had a communist
government). The veto is thus a powerful tool that can be

wielded to mould international relations to the P-5's satisfaction – an option other states simply do not have.

The link between the Security Council and national democracies

Despite their powerful international position, the P-5 are still firmly anchored to the national 'democracy' we have discussed in previous chapters. Whoever holds the seat at the Security Council for the United States, for example, is simply an ambassador who is nominated by the president and confirmed by the Senate. He or she takes instructions directly from the US government. If an ambassador fails to obey the instructions issuing from their government, he or she will quickly be replaced. This ability to recall a representative is often misunderstood as an example of the accountability of international officials to the people of a nation: the people elect a government and the government appoints international ambassadors; the ambassador has to answer to the government, which in turn must answer to the people.

That's the official story.

However, as we now know, the government of a nation is rarely able to win the endorsement of the majority of its people, even at the time of election, and these same people have no effective means to control an elected government at any time. What's more, the politicians who win elections and who determine the actions of their ambassador at the UN invariably spend a great deal of money obtained from large donors in pursuit of victory at the polls.

So, ambassadors do have to answer to the government that appointed them; the problem is that under the electoral system governments are more likely to answer to the vested interests that support them than to the people of a nation as a whole, especially when it comes to making international decisions behind closed doors that most people will never find out about anyway. So, when we say that international representatives are 'accountable' to the institutions of national democracy, we have to remember that in real terms this means they are ultimately accountable to the tacticians and donors who helped get their boss elected – not to the people of a nation, who have very little to do with the electoral process.

This is true in all electoral democracies, each of which has at least some influence on international affairs, but is especially noticeable in the world's most powerful nations. These countries' colossal international influence is inevitably of great interest to some of the winning politicians' donors and friends. In their view, the government should not only implement policies that suit them on a national level, it should use its influence and privileges on an international level to ensure that decisions in their favour are taken there, too. And campaign donors are not necessarily interested in what is best for international peace and security – they are interested in what is best for them.

Nothing illustrates the relationship between national democracy and the Security Council better than the so-called military-industrial complex, a term coined by US president Dwight Eisenhower to describe the mutually reinforcing relationship between big business, politics and weapons manufacturing that began during the Second World War.

Although the P-5, as perpetual members of the UN Security Council, are tasked with maintaining global peace and security, companies based in these nations manufacture 71 per cent of the world's weapons.[2] That's a staggering amount of weaponry to be produced by the five foremost members of an organization dedicated to ensuring global peace, but the explanation for it isn't hard to find.

Armaments companies are often large donors to political campaigns.[3] They may also work closely with government because they fulfil military contracts and share technology with the national armed forces. And like any other private enterprise, arms manufacturers are interested in staying in business, which means there needs to be a demand for their products. From their point of view, the more money governments, militias and rebel groups are willing to spend on armaments, the better. However, for everyone else, the more we spend on weapons, the worse off financially we all are – a state of affairs that worsens considerably when we actually use those weapons to destroy public buildings, utilities infrastructure and cultural artefacts that took years if not decades to build. Since weapons bring humankind nothing but destruction and suffering, there is perhaps no clearer example of a policy that would be in the greatest interest of the greatest number of people than a dramatic reduction in arms production.

However, despite the fact that the Security Council is supposed to be limiting the human and economic resources diverted to producing weapons, despite the fact that it would be entirely possible to do so simply by gradually scaling back

---

2   Most of the rest of the world's armaments originate in Germany and Sweden.
3   For example, defence contractors Lockheed Martin, Raytheon and Boeing each contributed over $2 million to candidate campaigns in the USA between 2012 and 2014.

the P-5's own arms production, and despite the fact that fewer weapons would be better for everyone on earth, there has been no noticeable progress on this point.

At least 7.5 million small arms are produced globally each year along with up to 14 billion bullets, enough to kill each and every man, woman and child on earth, twice over. That sort of output might seem reasonable, if we were expecting an imminent zombie apocalypse, or worldwide outbreak of vampirism, but as things stand, producing such a glut of cheap and easily available lethal weapons is simply asking for trouble.

Worse, the existence of nuclear, chemical and biological weapons has barely been addressed in the nearly seventy years of the Security Council's existence. The Doomsday Clock, which symbolizes the Bulletin of Atomic Scientists' assessment of how close mankind is to ending its own existence, is currently set to three minutes to midnight. That's bad news, because it started out at seven minutes to midnight in 1947. That means that in the opinion of nuclear scientists, under the P-5's watch we have moved *closer* to global self-annihilation. Not only do the P-5 all still have nuclear weapons, Israel, Pakistan, India and North Korea have them now too, and while any state may become destabilized, Pakistan and North Korea are already two of the most unstable and unpredictable nations on earth. The Security Council, in other words, is not doing a very good job of fulfilling its mandate. And it is not doing a good job because it isn't really trying.

Ordinary people may suffer terribly from weapons overproduction, but by contributing to election campaigns, arms producers ensure that P-5 governments will always block the Security Council from interfering with their business model.

As the military-industrial complex shows, far from being an expression of freedom and accountability, electing representatives nationally and then allowing them to represent the state internationally creates a closed circuit between national and international politics that at no point allows for input from ordinary citizens but which can be easily manipulated by those with sufficient resources. It's worth spending some money on a national campaign when the pay-off is a permanent seat at the international table of high politics.

Vote-buying at the UN: carrots,
sticks and the Cirque du Soleil

The veto is, however, only one of many advantages that accrue to political parties that win national elections in powerful states. Not only do elected politicians gain control of the nation's power positions at international institutions, they also gain control of the nation's treasury, tax revenues and natural resources, such as oil and mineral wealth. Winning election, in other words, is essentially a legitimized way to hijack a country's resources. One of the ways politicians leverage these resources is to continue the 'wealth = power and power = wealth' dynamic on an international level by using the nation's assets to bribe and punish other nations into doing what they would like them to do. Governments engage in these tactics at all levels of international relations, including at the Security Council.

Security Council resolutions require nine votes in favour to pass. Thus, it does not suffice for the P-5 to vote in favour of a resolution; they need at least four other states to vote with them. In practice, the P-5 prefer Security Council resolutions to be unanimous, because it lends them an air of greater legitimacy. In order to achieve this, they buy the votes of other nations whenever they truly want a resolution passed. This is mainly done by Western powers, as with three closely aligned members – the USA, the UK and France – always on the Council, it is easier for them to obtain the required numbers of votes in favour.

One of the most publicized examples of this process in action is the UN Security Council vote on Resolution 678, which authorized the use of force to repel the Iraqi invasion of Kuwait in 1990. While the United States favoured military action against Iraq, other nations, including two of the P-5 (Russia and China), were not as enthusiastic. In order to get the resolution passed, the United States thus had to bribe the other Council members with considerable favours, including:

- promising financial aid to Colombia, Côte d'Ivoire, Ethiopia and Zaire (all Security Council members at the time);
- promising the USSR that the Baltic States would be kept out of the 1990 Paris Summit (an international conference aimed at helping former Eastern bloc states to change their political and economic institutions);
- persuading Kuwait and Saudi Arabia to give the USSR hard currency;
- forgiving an Egyptian debt of $14 billion;
- donating military equipment valued at $8 billion to Turkey;
- allowing the World Bank to issue a loan to Iran;
- lifting the sanctions on China that had been imposed after the Tiananmen Square crackdown on protesters, supporting a $114 million World Bank loan to China and resuming normal diplomatic relations.

Perhaps irritated at having to hand out so many carrots, the USA decided that it was high time to apply the stick and make an example of Yemen, the only Security Council member to vote against action in Iraq. Following Yemen's negative vote – a vote which did not have any effect on the ultimate outcome of the resolution – the American delegate approached the Yemeni delegate and bluntly informed him, 'That was the most expensive vote your country has ever cast.' As luck would have it, the Yemeni delegate had not yet switched off his microphone, which picked up this ominous pronounce- ment and broadcast it over the entire Council chamber. Thus, when the United States cut off $70 million in bilateral aid to Yemen and tolerated the expulsion of hundreds of thousands of Yemeni workers from the surrounding Gulf States shortly thereafter, there was no doubt in anyone's mind as to why.

UN delegates are, of course, not always so obliging as to issue their threats into live microphones, but there is little doubt that these tactics are widespread. Like the veto itself, the practice of vote-buying at the Security Council is merely an extension of the national system where money = power and power = money. If a party can win an election, even with a manufactured majority, not only do they go on to control the country they were elected in, they are now also entitled to represent that country on an international level. If that country is endowed with significant resources (as the P-5 are), the winning politicians can use those resources to bribe their way on the international level, too. As in the example of Resolution 678, this national wealth becomes the carrot and stick used to control other nations, effectively thwarting any national democratic practices within those countries. The citizens of powerful nations are often unaware of this carrot-and-stick approach to international decision-making, despite the fact that their tax dollars are paying for it.

The representational structure of national and international systems interlocks in such a manner as to allow politicians to amplify small, and sometimes arbitrary, victories in national elections into near-total global domination. This is why political parties invest so desperately in robocalls, attack ads, gerrymandering and other tactics. Even the tiniest of vote margins in their favour can, if played right, literally deliver them – and their sponsors – the world.

This vote-buying game is not only played by the P-5. It permeates the entire international system from top to bottom, systematically privileging wealth and military power over democracy and equality.

For example, many states actively seek to be elected as a non-permanent member of the Security Council. Not only does a seat on the Council provide a good platform for the state in question to pursue its own goals, it also puts it in a position to receive favours from the P-5 in return for supporting their wishes. In other words, states spend money to get themselves a seat on the Security Council, which puts them in an excellent position to make even more money.

The competition among Western states for Security Council seats is particularly intense. It closely parallels the dominant electoral practices in these politicians' home countries, although in the absence of legal restrictions, they are able to indulge in more direct forms of bribery. For example, in 1998, Canada spent $1.3 million on its campaign for a non-permanent seat on the Security Council. This included the costs of sending out more than a dozen special envoys, including the Speaker of the Senate and several MPs with

ancestral ties to others nations to convince them to vote for
Canada, redesigning Canada's permanent mission to the
UN, and wining and dining UN representatives of various
nations at a *Cirque du Soleil* performance in Manhattan.
During the same campaign one of Canada's hottest rivals,
Greece, took UN representatives and their spouses on two
cruises of the Greek islands.

Ten years later, in 2008, the price of a non-permanent
seat had skyrocketed. That year, Australia announced that it
had set aside $23 million to lobby for a Security Council seat
for 2013/14. The government was explicit on its reasons for
pursuing the seat – it wanted to be able to influence decisions on Afghanistan, Indonesia and East Timor, as well as
the Middle East, 'a strategic region that has become increasingly important for Australia'.[4] Despite the large sums of
money it had set aside for the purpose of buying itself these
voting rights, it was a late start for the Land Down Under. Its
competitors, Finland and Luxembourg, had kicked off their
campaigns for a Security Council seat in 2001 and 2002
respectively. Australia, however, remained hopeful, because
while Finland and Luxembourg donated a greater percentage
of their gross national income to foreign aid, Australia was
simply a much bigger country with a much bigger economy
and could therefore give more in *absolute* terms, while still
giving less in *percentage* terms. Once it had decided it wanted
a Security Council seat, Australia promptly restructured its
development aid programme to give more to African nations
in an effort to secure their votes. This strategy worked and
Australia won the seat.

---

4 Okhovat, 'The United Nations Security Council: its veto power and its
reform', note 247, at 47–8.

As this example demonstrates, international vote-buying systematically disadvantages smaller countries, even affluent ones like Finland and Luxembourg, squeezing them and their citizens out of the decision-making process in much the same way that citizens who vote for losing candidates are squeezed off the national political scene. Instead, rich and powerful nations are able to buy themselves a position where they can become even more rich and even more powerful by manipulating international decision-making in their own interests.

When the stakes are so high, it makes sense to have a seat at the table no matter what the price, and those who are able to pay more for this privilege are more likely to receive one.

Survival of the richest

The way in which the UN Security Council operates squeezes an already very small set of people (national delegates usually chosen after winning an election) into an even smaller set of decision-makers (those who have the resources to reward and punish other national representatives for doing what they want). Vote-buying is detrimental to small and weak states, which are muscled out of the decision-making process by those who can afford to outbid them in the race to obtain voting rights. Even prosperous nations like Luxembourg are simply too small to counteract the efforts of larger nations like Australia. This means that even the elected representatives of these nations are effectively silenced at international decision-making bodies, and thus their citizens often have *no* representation, not even flawed or inaccurate representation, at the Security Council. Instead only a handful of representatives from the world's largest and wealthiest states make all decisions.

And while this handful of 'real' international decision-makers nominally represent their own citizens, the truth is that their constituents are rarely aware of their actions and have no way to effectively control them. Even they have been firmly shoved out of the decision-making circle by an electoral process that is itself often the product of vote-skewing and legalized bribery. In effect, the thoughts, wishes and interests of more than seven billion people are excluded from international decision-making, which resides instead in the hands of little more than a dozen 'representatives', only five of whom can truly act effectively.

When wealth equals power and power equals wealth, as it does here, we enter into a situation where some wealth can be used to acquire more power (e.g. a seat on the Security Council or a favourable resolution), which can be used to acquire more wealth, which can be used to acquire more power, and so on until only a very few entities have any wealth or power at all. The electoral system and international institutions inexorably work to make a few actors very strong and wealthy and all others very weak and poor. There are no counterweights to this process. More 'inclusive' bodies such as the General Assembly work in exactly the same way to create a vast upward spiral of wealth and power for those who already have the most of both.

The General Assembly: the world's most bribable talking shop

Unlike the Security Council, all UN member states have a seat and a vote in the General Assembly, but its resolutions are non-binding, which means that they do not have any legal force. This is no accident – US president Franklin

D. Roosevelt, who was involved in the preparatory work for the UN, dismissed General Assembly meetings as merely somewhere for 'all the small nations ... to blow off steam ...'[5] Because they do not have any legal effect, powerful states do not usually feel a need to intervene in General Assembly votes. However, there are exceptions to this rule: in rare instances General Assembly resolutions can contribute to customary international law (i.e. they develop some legal force, after all), and at other times a vote in the General Assembly may be deemed important to the interests of a major state. In these instances, developed states often turn to buying the votes of their fellow members.

A common exchange is for a developing state to vote in accordance with a developed state's wishes at the General Assembly in exchange for the developed state voting in favour of a loan for the developing state at the International Monetary Fund (IMF) or World Bank. For example, countries that vote along with the USA in votes that the US State Department has determined to be 'key votes' at the UN General Assembly are more likely to have IMF loans approved than countries that vote against the USA. Even switching only one in ten votes to a vote in favour of the USA significantly increases the chances of receiving an IMF loan. This is not an 'even trade' of one vote for another; the United States holds a privileged position at the IMF that gives it a disproportionate influence on loan approval. In trading this approval for General Assembly votes, the USA leverages its powerful position at the IMF to become even more powerful by bribing other states to endorse its interests at the UN, too.

---

5 A. W. Brian Simpson, *Human Rights and the End of Empire: Britain and the Genesis of the European Convention*, at 250.

At other times, states sell their General Assembly votes in return for foreign aid from another country. For example, the average developing country votes in the same direction as France 64 per cent of the time in the General Assembly. But countries that vote only a little more often in France's interests – 73 per cent of the time, as opposed to only 64 per cent of the time – receive on average 96 per cent more French foreign aid. Similar increases in voting in favour of the USA resulted in an increase of USAID by 78 per cent to the country voting in the 'right' way, while voting only a little more often in favour of Japan results in a staggering 345 per cent increase in Japanese foreign aid to the developing country in question.

The numbers speak for themselves, but if any further evidence of vote-buying were needed, a US State Department memo once informed the director of the American Food for Peace program in no uncertain terms that 'at critical moments in the world's history, the US "bought" votes subtly and indirectly to support its stand in the General Assembly. The "buying" is in terms of US assistance to the voting country.'[6]

The mere practice of vote-buying systematically works in favour of wealthier nations because the payments in question are always worth more to the poorer seller than to the wealthier buyer. In fact, the entire vote-buying complex is one big losing strategy, because it works to deepen political and economic inequality on a global scale. In a system where the strong are rewarded, they must inevitably become stronger, while the weak become weaker still.

---

6 Thacker, 'The high politics of IMF lending', at 54.

And the same electoral system that makes it easy for politicians with wealthy sponsors to seize control of a country's resources and use them to dominate others at international institutions also makes it difficult for weak or small states to refuse to participate in the vote-buying market, even though doing so is not in their long-term interests. Most governments in developing nations also need to win elections, and if they lose foreign aid dollars or bilateral investments their economy may suffer in the short term. Since voters are not privy to the international vote-trading market, all they see is a short-term decrease in the country's economic fortunes and the chances that they will vote for the opposition increase. Thus, it is always in the interests of elected politicians to prefer short-term benefits, such as foreign aid payments in return for a vote, to long-term results. After all, the politician who is in power today will not be around when the long term arrives. It is precisely the so-called democratic institution of representative government which creates such a strong incentive for politicians to continue to sell their country's vote, thereby contributing to beggaring their nation in the long run.

Taken together, the entire electoral-representative complex not only fails to meet the standards of democracy, it actually sets up a spiral towards economic and political oligarchy, a spiral which ordinary people around the world are unwittingly paying for either through tax dollars or lost opportunities. The other big international organizations only reinforce this basic dynamic.

The World Bank Group and the International Monetary Fund

For the architects of the post-war institutions, the UN was only one piece in the international framework. After all, the Second World War had been preceded by the long economic hardship of the Great Depression, a circumstance which many saw as a contributing factor to the war. To prevent such global economic crises from occurring again, the UN was to be complemented by two important institutions that would stabilize the global financial system and enable countries to maximize their economic growth. These institutions, the International Monetary Fund (IMF) and the World Bank, grew out of a proposal formulated by English economist John Maynard Keynes, which was called, perhaps with typical British understatedness, 'the Plan'.

We had a plan: Keynes and the IFIs

The Great Depression had been characterized by protectionism, hoarding, and 'beggar-thy-neighbour' economic strategies in which each country short-sightedly grabbed what it could for itself. By contrast, Keynes recognized that when economies become too lopsided, i.e. when some players have too much and others have too little, they simply grind to a halt and collapse in on themselves. After all, it does not matter how productive you are if no one else can afford to buy your wares.

Therefore, Keynes' plan to stabilize the world economy focused on a renewed economic interdependence in which money would be kept circulating, enabling citizens to be productive. Huge loans would be granted to facilitate reconstruction in war-torn Europe, including in enemy states such as Germany. All of these war-ravaged nations would ultimately be integrated into the new global political and economic framework and become important trading partners to the United States, Canada and other nations around the world. In order to implement his ideas effectively, Keynes suggested that the international community create an organization to oversee the new cooperative global economy. In his notes, Keynes called this organization 'the International Clearing Union'.

In Keynes' view, when it came to international finance, it was as detrimental for a nation to have an excessive surplus as it was for it to have an excessive deficit. It really did not matter who was responsible for an imbalanced global economy; once it was imbalanced, the crisis only worsened, and in the end everyone got hurt, whether they had been fiscally responsible or not. Therefore, just because a nation was a creditor nation did not mean that it was any better or less responsible for economic problems than heavily indebted nations were. They had both contributed to the crisis – one through irresponsible borrowing and the other through irresponsible lending. These were but two sides to one coin. In the future, everyone would have to work together to prevent unsustainable levels of debt from accruing and to keep credit and debt flowing freely.

In order to make this happen, every nation would be assigned a quota at the International Clearing Union denoted in an international unit that Keynes referred to as the 'bancor'. The nation's debt and credit levels would be reviewed based upon this quota. If a state's debt were to exceed a quarter of its quota averaged over two years, it would be entitled to devalue its currency to make exports more attractive and prevent capital from leaving the country, and if a state's debt consistently stayed at over 50 per cent of its quota, the Clearing Union could require it to devalue its currency, to control its outward capital transactions, or to give up some of its gold or other liquid reserves. These measures were all aimed at restoring economic balance, not at punishing states for not having enough money or at making their citizens suffer until they got back into line. The entire Plan was directed at *avoiding* exactly such a 'sharp shock' situation. In fact, in order to prevent sudden contractions in a nation's economy, Keynes anticipated that the Clearing Union would give preferential loans (i.e. loans at a lower than commercial interest rate) to allow countries in economic trouble to reduce their consumption gradually. By these means, states would be eased out of financial difficulties, instead of constantly plunging from the black to the red and back again.

So far, so clear, but Keynes was innovative enough not to just focus on debt. Since, according to his thoughts, the global economy worked only when money kept circulating, the Plan also included a number of limitations on states exceeding their quota in *credit*. These states could also be forced to take measures if their credit balance consistently exceeded half their quotas, such as appreciating the local currency, expanding domestic credit, reducing tariffs against imports and giving international development loans. Keynes even suggested that if a state persistently remained in credit surplus over its limit, this surplus might simply be cancelled or compulsorily invested. Once again, these measures were not intended as a punishment, but merely as a recognition of the economic dangers of a state having too much credit.

The merit of Keynes' Plan for achieving a stable and sustainable global economy was obvious to everyone, but it was implemented in somewhat modified form. Instead of creating an International Clearing Union, nations agreed to set up two separate but similar institutions: the IMF and the World Bank (known collectively as 'International Financial Institutions' or 'IFIs'). The World Bank was (and is) mainly responsible for giving preferential loans to nations attempting to build infrastructure, while the IMF was responsible for overseeing exchange rates and balance of payments between nations (i.e. preventing the trade imbalances discussed above). In order to do this, the IMF used (and still uses) an international currency similar to Keynes' bancor, but called the 'special drawing right' or 'SDR'. The IMF also gave (and still gives) loans to allow for structural adjustment, i.e. to prevent a nation whose government has been consistently overspending from experiencing a sharp contraction. However, the IMF and the World Bank left out the most brilliant part of Keynes' plan, the need not just to deter debtors for being in too much debt, but to deter creditors from being in too much credit. To make matters worse, the IFIs, especially the IMF, began to punish indebtedness in ways that didn't make any sense, because they did not allow debtors enough space to adjust their economies to new developments on the ground.

Keynes recognized that if an economic system was going to be a fair meritocracy, it had to be kept in balance and that being too successful could destroy that balance as surely as being too unsuccessful. Once the economic balance was destroyed everyone got hurt, whether or not they had contributed to causing the problem.

To prevent this from happening, any central global financial institution needed to work like a heart in a healthy body, pumping power and money around the system instead of letting it congeal in one spot. If Keynes' plan had been followed, the two most powerful financial organizations in the world would have worked like twin hearts, pumping money out to all parts of the world and keeping the economic circulatory system in top shape. Since, however, the international community chose not to follow Keynes' most important advice and instead to only ever punish debtor nations while continuing to reward creditors, the IMF and World Bank have been working to produce the exact opposite results for the past seventy years. Instead of spreading global wealth around, they have been increasing economic imbalance and deepening global inequality. The predictable result has been a global economic heart attack. During the 'Great Recession' circulation has come to a standstill. And in the long term, the consequences will gradually become much worse.

By only punishing debtors and rewarding creditors, the IMF and the World Bank ensure that the rich get richer and the poor get poorer. And that affects democracy, nationally and internationally. Since wealth can be used to influence elections, the IFIs, by ensuring that wealth remains unevenly distributed, also ensure that the individuals and entities that benefit from these exaggerated wealth inequalities have disproportionate chances of acquiring political power in national elections. It is a vicious cycle that is facilitated not only by IMF and World Bank lending practices, but by the very structure of the two organizations.

Shareholder value: fixed voting at the World Bank and the IMF

The IFIs acquire the capital they need to make loans by assigning each nation a quota of shares that it is obligated to buy based on the strength of its economy. In return, member nations are allotted votes in direct proportion to the number of shares they purchase. Therefore the countries with the strongest economies have the most votes.

On a day-to-day basis, these votes are exercised on behalf of the nation by its representative, who is known as an executive director. There are only twenty-four executive directors at each institution, so most of them are 'shared' between several member states. However, at both the IMF and the World Bank, each of the five countries with the largest number of shares appoints (and controls) its own executive director. Like a permanent seat on the UN Security Council, control of a dedicated executive director is one of the perks that comes with winning election in those nations. Parties that win election in the world's richest nations also win the right to have a big say in IMF and World Bank policy.

At the IMF these countries are:

- the United States (16.75 per cent of all shares);
- Japan (6.23 per cent);
- Germany (5.81 per cent);
- the UK (4.29 per cent);
- and France (4.29 per cent).

The situation at the World Bank is similar. The top five countries there are:

- the USA (15.12 per cent);
- Japan (8.18 per cent);
- China (5.28 per cent);
- Germany (4.59 per cent);
- and the UK and France tied for fifth place (with 4.09 per cent each).

At both the IMF and the World Bank, the remaining nineteen directors are elected in a manner similar to the single transferable vote, and they represent the group of countries that voted for them. The usual pattern is for one or two states with considerable voting power and several less powerful states of the same geographical region or linguistic group to pool their votes for an executive director. For example, in the current grouping at the World Bank, Director Rojas from Venezuela represents Costa Rica, El Salvador, Guatemala, Honduras, Mexico, Nicaragua, Spain and Venezuela, with Spain being the largest shareholding country of the group with 42,951 votes and El Salvador and Honduras being the smallest with 794 and 1,294 shares respectively. Similarly, Director Smith from Canada represents Canada with 59,007 votes, as well as Ireland (7,623 votes) and eleven mainly English-speaking countries of Central America and the Caribbean, the largest shareholder of which is Jamaica with 3,368 votes.

When the IMF and World Bank directors gather to vote on a measure, each director casts as many votes as his constituent nations are entitled to. If an executive director represents a nation that holds 5 per cent of all shares at the World Bank or the IMF, then his vote is worth 5 per cent of that institution's total voting power; if he represents a nation whose voting power is 2 per cent then when he casts a vote that vote is worth 2 per cent of all votes cast, and so forth.

What this means is that the value of each nation's vote varies wildly. Since population also varies considerably from nation to nation, this means that there are gross inequalities in the way in which individual people are represented at these institutions. For example, at the IMF:

- with only 4.44 per cent of the world's population, the USA has 16.75 per cent of total votes;
- Japan has only 1.78 per cent of the world's population but 6.23 per cent of total votes;
- the director for Canada, Ireland and the Caribbean, representing just 0.61 per cent of the world's population, exercises 4.03 per cent of total voting power;
- the director for the Indian subcontinent (India, Sri Lanka, Bangladesh and Bhutan), on the other hand, exercises only 2.81 per cent of total voting power despite representing nearly 20 per cent of member nations' population;
- likewise, the group of predominantly English-speaking African nations enjoys only 3.29 per cent of voting power despite having close to 9 per cent of the world's population;
- the five largest shareholding nations, who each have their own director, between them represent just 9.76 per cent of the population of IMF members, but exercise 37.37 per cent of total voting power.

To compound this inequality, many issues at the World Bank and the IMF are decided via qualified voting. For example, at the IMF a raft of decisions, such as setting the interest rate, various service charges and the rate of remuneration

Percentage of population

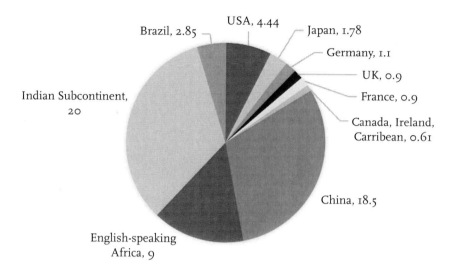

Brazil, 2.85

USA, 4.44

Japan, 1.78

Germany, 1.1

UK, 0.9

France, 0.9

Canada, Ireland, Carribean, 0.61

Indian Subcontinent, 20

China, 18.5

English-speaking Africa, 9

Percentage of votes

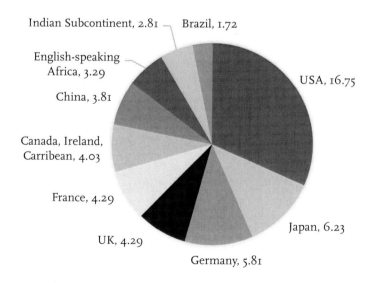

Indian Subcontinent, 2.81

Brazil, 1.72

English-speaking Africa, 3.29

China, 3.81

Canada, Ireland, Carribean, 4.03

France, 4.29

UK, 4.29

USA, 16.75

Japan, 6.23

Germany, 5.81

Figure 5.2 Voting versus population at the IMF

for members who have more money deposited with the IMF than they are obligated to, requires a 70 per cent majority. Thus, the five largest shareholding nations – which hold over 37 per cent of voting power – can collectively veto these, and many other, actions. Moreover, any change to subscription quotas or amendment of the IMF Articles requires an 85 per cent majority, meaning that the USA has a de facto veto on these items. This prevents other countries from simply buying more shares in order to gain more votes, and it has been used by Western leaders to delay having to share power with the leaders of other growing economies. For example, despite being the world's second-largest economy, China is permitted only 3.81 per cent of total shares at the IMF (putting it below the top five), while Brazil, which has an economy comparable in size to those of the UK and France, is allotted only 1.72 per cent of shares (putting it in four-teenth place, behind Saudi Arabia, Belgium and Italy).

This means that when it comes to voting at the IMF and the World Bank even the nominal representation of many nations is squeezed into insignificance. This is especially true of the world's poorest and smallest nations. Owing to their nearly non-existent voting power, even their most basic interests are likely to be ignored. At the same time, the power of representatives from the top shareholding nations is magnified – not only does winning election give these few representatives a great deal of power over national deci-sion-making, it also grants them a disproportionate level of control over international finance.

When we look at this situation the problem seems obvious; rich countries get to have more of a say at the IFIs than poor countries, so it is not surprising that the IFIs often pay more attention to rich countries' interests. Working on this basis, it is easy to construe what goes on at the IFIs as a battle between rich people in developed nations and poor people in undeveloped nations. However, we also have to remember that most people in all nations, including Western nations, have already been squeezed out of their own national political process by elections. A country's executive director is not under the control of the people of a nation, but rather under the control of the government, and that government may or may not be the party that most people voted for in the last election. Even if it is, there is no way to ensure that its actions at the IFIs meet with the approval of most of its citizens, because in the absence of direct and effective participation, there is no way for the people of a nation to influence their director's behaviour between elections. How their director votes at the IMF or the World Bank is therefore in no way indicative of the preferences or interests of most citizens, including the citizens of the developed nations that control these institutions. The IMF and the World Bank thus do not so much act in the interests of the populations of rich countries as in the interests of a certain subset of people within those countries who manage to stay relevant to those politicians by helping them win elections.

The IFIs are thus under the control of a handful of people who cut their own citizens out of decision-making via the national process of election and then cut other elected leaders out via skewed voting privileges on the international level. This means that the handful of people still involved in these decisions have nearly unlimited power to do what they like. And what they like is to make themselves richer and therefore more likely to retain both wealth and power –

nationally and internationally – far into the future. Thus, under their control, the IFIs do not work as the hearts of the global economy pumping out money to its farther reaches and bringing economic vitality to regions in need. Instead, under the guidance of these supposed 'representatives', the IFIs work much as a tornado does, funnelling money up from the bottom and depositing it at the top.

Just as the P-5 ambassadors at the UN work in tandem with arms manufacturers, allowing these interests to reach through national representatives and control international decision-making, the executive directors of the most powerful nations at the World Bank and the IMF work in tandem with the financial interests that contribute to the campaigns or otherwise affect the election chances of the politicians who give them their orders. The goal is to help those in power stay in power by ensuring that they and their allies have the means to manipulate the rules of 'representative' democracy. One way they do this is through conditionality.

Strings attached: profits, dictators and conditionality at the IFIs

Conditionality is the practice of attaching wide-ranging, often business-friendly, conditions to international loans. Both the IMF and the World Bank practise conditionality, but the IMF is the more notorious of the two institutions. This is mainly due to the deep, symbiotic relationship between the IMF and private financiers that can be traced back to poor decisions made in the early years of IMF operations.

Despite their willingness to acknowledge Keynes' general brilliance as an economist, the original IMF members refused to budget sufficient resources to allow the organization to make the necessary structural adjustment loans to countries in trouble. In fact, they endowed the IMF with less than one quarter of the resources Keynes thought necessary for it to fulfil its mission as a lender of last resort. That figure as a percentage of GDP has plummeted even further since. IMF resources were equivalent to 58 per cent of world trade in 1944, 15 per cent in 1965 and just 4 per cent in 2005. By 2012, this had plummeted even further to 1.48 per cent – nowhere near enough money for the IMF to ever do its job properly.

Because the IMF's members failed to adequately endow it, from the very beginning its staff have been forced to ask others to chip in to loan packages for nations in financial difficulty. Sometimes these third parties are other states, but often they are private banks. The IMF itself usually provides only a fraction of the funding for any given 'IMF loan'. To give a few examples:

- between 1954 and 1960, in 77 per cent of IMF stabilization programmes in Latin America at least 50 per cent of the funding came from other states and private financiers;
- between 1974 and 1979, 60 per cent of external financing for non-OPEC states came from commercial banks;
- at the end of 1980, the twelve largest non-oil-producing borrowers had external debt totalling $199 billion, $120 billion of which was owed to private banks;
- since 1980, there have been 176 cases where commercial creditors have agreed to restructure sovereign debt (97 cases in the 1980s, 56 in the 1990s and 23 between

2000 and 2010). These cases cover most of the developing world, from Albania (in 1995) to Zambia (in 1994), and were worth over $1 trillion ($912 billion in the 1980s, $287 billion in the 1990s and $121 billion in the 2000s).

Since the IMF could not operate on its own, but was forced to rely on private entities to help it out, it quickly went from being a public institution funded solely by states, i.e. tax-paying citizens, to something akin to a public–private partnership, with part of the money provided by private companies and the remainder by taxpayers. This meant that IMF staff and politicians needed to explain themselves more often to private banks that could easily affect their operations than to citizens in creditor nations, who had already been cut out of the decision-making process through elections.

The politicians representing large member states, however, did not completely relinquish the reins of power. If the IMF was relying on private banks to supplement its funds, private banks relied heavily on the IMF and the World Bank to provide them with information about the creditworthiness of the nations they were being asked to invest in. The information these institutions gave to private creditors was often biased towards member states' own interests in a potential borrower nation. As we saw earlier in this chapter, many countries received loan approval from the IMF because they voted in developed country interests at the UN and not because such loans made sense based on their economic needs or credit-worthiness. Thus, the IFI's lending decisions were the result of negotiations between a handful of political appointees and a handful of private financiers, each acting in their own inter-ests. You don't need to be an economic genius like Keynes to realize that that's not a very bright way to run the world's finances.

This flawed interplay between national politics and international institutions generated wildly irresponsible lending behaviour. There are many examples, but perhaps the most classic is Mobutu Sese Seko's rule of Zaire from 1965 to 1997. Zaire had been governed by another politician, Patrice Lumumba, for a short time following its independence from Belgium in 1960. However, Lumumba was assassinated after he turned to the USSR for aid in putting down a rebellion in the country's south-eastern province of Katanga. Western countries had not liked Lumumba, but quickly warmed to Mobutu, who seemed both willing and able to prevent Zaire from ever joining the communist camp in the then ongoing Cold War. They thus gave Mobutu the aid that they had refused Lumumba during his brief time in power, despite the fact that there was never any doubt about the type of leader Mobutu was.

He was a straight-up dictator known to (literally) rend his enemies limb from limb, and he embezzled *billions* of dollars in public funds for his own personal use. Nonetheless, from 1972 onwards, both the IMF and the World Bank gave Mobutu ever-increasing lines of credit, not because Mobutu was using the money to invest wisely in Zaire's economy – he wasn't – but because he was regarded as a key ally in the Cold War. The relationship between Mobutu's politics and international lending behaviour is crystal clear: commercial creditors agreed to restructure the nation's debt seven times between 1976 and 1989, and Zaire received loans in excess of 80 million SDRs (about $120 million) from the IMF every year from 1984, before being abruptly cut off in 1989 when the Cold War ended and Mobutu was suddenly surplus to requirements.

When Mobutu was finally ousted in 1997 after over three decades in power, he left Zaire one of the poorest and most debt-ridden nations in the entire world, despite the fact that it is one of the richest in terms of natural resources. The country is probably better known to most people by its current name – the Democratic Republic of the Congo – a nation frequently in the news for its vicious political strife and the poor living standards of its citizens. Although following Mobutu's departure the citizens of the Congo were heavily indebted with little to show for it, the banks that had loaned money to Mobutu were not going to pay for Congo's problems, and the Western companies that had been enabled to do business in Congo by the Western inter-vention to retain it in the capitalist camp during the Cold War were not going to pay for Congo's problems, so the Congolese people would have to pay. And they did pay up to $300 million each year before finally receiving debt relief in 2010, when it became literally impossible to continue to get repayments out of the country.

With Western citizens who may have objected to contin-ually financing a corrupt and abusive dictator effectively cut out of international decision-making through the barrier of elected representation, but private corporations and banks getting privileged access through their close relationships with the politicians who ran the IFIs, this outcome was pre-programmed.

Mistakes like these left not only the Congo in poor shape – the IMF's reckless lending also left many other countries in debt, but still in need of credit to develop essential infrastructure. Because these developing countries now not only needed a new loan, but also enough money to pay off the interest and capital of the old loan until the fruits of the new loan kicked in, they asked for bigger loans.

Faced with the possibility of having to admit that past lending programmes had been failures, the IMF wanted to go ahead with new loans at all costs. However, since it lacked sufficient funds to do so on its own, it needed private banks and individual states to continue lending, too. In this situation, it did not take private banks very long to figure out that they were in the driver's seat. Consequently, they refused to release funding unless the IMF attached certain conditions to the loans. Thus, while retaining power in name and still referring to these loan packages as 'IMF loans', the IMF as an institution was essentially reduced to acting as a mediator between borrowers and powerful banking syndicates, such as the Paris Club (official, i.e. state, creditors), the London Club (private creditors) and the New York Club (private creditors). Although an enormous amount of power had always lain with the IMF's wealthiest members, the situation now became even more tilted as these same members now doubled as additional bilateral state creditors, able to make their own demands outside of the IMF framework, and were joined at the negotiating table by private banks, usually based in their territory. This was, to put it mildly, a serious departure from Keynes' original plan, but it quickly became an institutionalized procedure. Unsurprisingly, the banks used their privileged access to mould the world into what they considered to be a better place – for them.

The original IMF Agreement had not even contemplated the possibility of placing conditions on loans, but owing to the involvement of supplementary financiers right from the beginning, in 1952 the USA, the largest IMF shareholder and home to many large private banks, vetoed lending until conditions were placed on loans. From this point on, loan conditions were laid down and enforced through so-called 'Stand-by Arrangements', under which the borrower does not receive the loan all at once, but rather in instalments (called 'tranches'). Each tranche is released only when the country fulfils certain conditions. Seventeen years later this policy of conditionality was officially legalized in 1969.

Despite this extreme alteration to the IMF's original mandate, at first the conditions attached to IMF loan packages were only moderately onerous, since the IFIs' irresponsible lending behaviour had not yet had time to snowball. Early conditions mainly concerned fiscal and monetary policy in the narrower sense (e.g. exchange rates) and were few in number; the average loan in the 1970s came with only six conditions attached. However, since the IMF and the World Bank were now effectively public–private partnerships, they began to think more and more like companies trying to maximize short-term profits. To this end, creditors demanded that the IMF and the World Bank force countries to accept loan conditions that served to implement extreme libertarian theories of economics.

The problem with these theories was that they had never been proven.

In fact, the most prosperous countries in the world did not – at the time – apply neoliberal free-market policies of deregulation to themselves. There was, therefore, no reason to believe that these libertarian-oriented loan conditions would be beneficial and every reason to believe that they wouldn't be. Most astonishing of all, however, the neoliberal economic theories *directly contradicted* the entire *raison d'être* of the IMF, which had been created to provide increased regulation and cooperation in the world market, not decreased regulation and increased competition. But the right people liked the sound of neoliberal economic policies, despite them having no basis in reality or proven track record of success, so they soon completely dominated international lending practices. And these new policies worked in some very strange ways.

Neoliberal economics measures how strong an economy is based on how *profitable* it is in purely monetary terms to those few people who have the necessary resources to *invest* on a large scale. This framework would make sense if a nation were a private company, but it does not make any sense if it is, e.g., a nation, because companies and countries fulfil drastically different social functions and have different responsibilities.

When a private company needs to downsize, it can take the kind of drastic measures demanded by neoliberal economics, such as laying people off. Private companies do not need to worry about providing for the basic needs of laid-off workers or about getting them back into a job. They do not need to worry about whether letting an employee go will exacerbate mental health issues or lead to drug use or crime. It is not their responsibility. They can afford to be ham-fisted, because they do not have to live with the consequences.

However, when an entire country follows the neoliberal prescription and takes drastic measures to downsize its economy, such as ceasing to provide education or health-care or water or pensions, the people in that country do have to live with the consequences, and these consequences – drugs, crime, health problems, deskilling of the workforce

– can have a negative long-term economic impact that far outweighs short-term profitability. When running a country, it's only common sense to take its long-term sustainability into consideration, and that often means having a little less today in exchange for a little more tomorrow. However, this stream of thought – treating a country like an entity that may well be around in fifty or a hundred years – is not as profitable to investors in the short term as the neoliberal stream of thought, which treats a country like a company that can be exploited to the maximum extent possible and then simply liquidated or sold off once all its value has been extracted. And because the IMF and the World Bank depend on loan finances from private interests, far from rejecting the absurd logic of libertarianism, they have increasingly used conditionality to make sure that a country's creditors get everything back today – even interest on loans made to corrupt dictators like Mobutu – while leaving nothing for tomorrow. If it is necessary to take control of every aspect of political life in a country to achieve this, the IMF and its partners do so by raising the number and scope of conditions attached to loans.

The average number of conditions attached to loans by the IMF was six in the 1970s, ten in the 1980s and twenty-three in 1999. The World Bank did even worse, averaging thirty-four conditions on adjustment loans from 1980 to 1982, thirty-five conditions from 1983 to 1986 and fifty-six conditions from 1987 to 1990. The nature of the conditions also became more wide ranging, including: 'financial-sector reform, privatization and public enterprise reform, social safety nets, tax and expenditure policies ... labour market policies, pricing and marketing/distribution policies, agricultural policies, environmental policies, and policies to combat corruption and money-laundering'.[7] Sometimes, conditions even explicitly lay out the laws that a country's parliament will have to pass by a given deadline.

Once a country's government agrees to these conditions, it becomes very difficult for that country to refuse to fulfil them, despite the fact that they do not technically constitute binding legal obligations. Contrary to popular belief, the IMF does not draw up a contract or treaty between itself and the borrowing state. Instead IMF officials draft a 'Letter of Intent', which outlines the policies the nation will pursue if it receives a loan. This letter is written *as if* it originated from a member of the borrower state government, who later signs on behalf of the country. The IMF managing director then presents the Letter of Intent to the Executive Board, which gives or withholds loan approval. Only a few IMF and government officials ever give their consent to this arrangement, which is not subject to any parliamentary scrutiny. However, once the Letter is in place, it is hard for a nation to refuse to fulfil its terms, because whenever it fails to do so, the IMF will issue an unfavourable report about how it is 'failing' to meet its conditions and will threaten to withhold future loan tranches. This can affect the state's credit rating on international markets and even cause the entire economy to collapse. This means that countries of millions end up having to run their economy in a manner that was agreed upon by perhaps three or four members of government and three or four IMF officials. For top members of the government and their corporate sponsors, the ability to lock the entire nation into decades of economic austerity without

---

7 Kapur, 'Conditionality and its alternatives', at 37.

the need to even get a law through Parliament is another perk that comes with winning an election and which makes victory such a valuable prize.

This conditionality trick can be used by national governments to push through unpopular reforms even against the will of their own party base. For example, in 1990 the president of Uruguay, Luis Alberto Lacalle, found himself in a situation where both his allied parties and most of his own party would not agree to the economic reforms he wanted to make. In order to push through the reforms he took out a conditioned IMF loan, even though Uruguay did not need it. The Parliament was then forced to vote in many of the laws required to meet the loan's conditions in order to avoid a drop in credit rating that would have seriously harmed the country.

Fellow South American leader, Osvaldo Hurtado, president of Ecuador from 1981 to 1984, did not so much as consult his own Congress when implementing an austerity programme. He later candidly declared: 'You can imagine what would happen if I would have subjected economic policy to debates within the party! No political party would have ever approved of the kind of economic policy I undertook ... I did not want economic policy in the hands of people who would politicize it.'[8]

Hurtado's statement is even more striking in light of the fact that he was not even the elected president of Ecuador; he was the vice-president and became president when his predecessor Jaime Roldós was killed in a plane crash early in his term.

8 Schnably, 'Constitutionalism and democratic government in the inter-American system', 155 at 192 et seq.

Western leaders, of course, have learned to be a little more PR savvy and are rarely caught making such blatant admissions. However, it is well known that on the rare occasions when Western countries have taken out IMF loans, similar tactics are used to silence opposition and push through domestic policies that would have been impossible to implement under any other circumstances. These include the 1974 and 1977 negotiations between Italy and the IMF following on from the oil shock of 1973, where the focus was on keeping wages low and the Communist Party out of government, as well as the widespread privatization of water, airports and other public infrastructure in Ireland and Greece ongoing since those nations' bailouts in 2010.[9]

The cooperation between powerful IMF appointees, top politicians in borrower states and wealthy individuals in lending nations who often fund political campaigns and tend to benefit from austerity programmes creates the 'perfect storm' that allows them to transform even the most marginal electoral victory (or even less, as seen in the case of Hurtado) into total economic control of entire nations for decades to come. By financing the right politician, private lenders gain control not only of the economy of the nation that that politician was elected in but – via conditionality – the economy of dozens of other nations, too. The interplay between national democracy and international institutions makes it very easy for politicians and the super-rich individuals who support them to engage in these activities, and very

---

9 Greece privatized about 530 million euros worth of infrastructure in 2014 and was scheduled to privatize a further 3.5 billion in 2015. Kerin Hope, 'Greece backtracks on privatization', 4 February 2015, www.ft.com/cms/s/0/b3f7a5b0-ac61-11e4-afoe-00144feab7de.html#axzz3Y9ROHF6R.

hard for ordinary people who are completely excluded from decision-making and bereft of effective modes of political participation to stop them.

If that sounds frightening, it's because it is.

The IMF's web is as wide as it is deep – at any one time roughly one quarter of all states are participating in an IMF programme – and the system of neoliberal conditionality benefits very few people. Even most people in Western nations do not reap any substantial rewards from these tactics, as they are not included in the wealth payout from the 'heist' of other nations economies. In fact, during the current economic crisis, citizens in Western nations have become but the latest victims of the IFIs' misguided approach to austerity.

Although the current economic crisis was caused by following neoliberal policies of reckless lending and financial deregulation, banks and other investment groups have remained true to form, refusing to pay the price for their irresponsible actions. Instead, they convinced politicians in Western nations to buy their debt and transfer it into national debt. Since these debts were too high for national economies to manage all at once (meaning they were very high indeed), these countries took out loans from, among others, the IMF. These loans came with classic austerity conditions attached: privatizing natural resources, such as water, cutting back on public expenditure for education and healthcare, increasing job insecurity, lowering wages in the public sector, and raising taxes on middle- and working-class families. These conditions have contributed to a widening income gap in Western nations, with most people in developed countries now getting poorer, while a very small percentage is getting much richer. In fact, with each passing year, the basic economic structure underpinning developed nations resembles more and more those of classic 'developing' nations: a few very rich people, many very poor people and not very many people in between.

This is, of course, bad enough in itself, but by forcibly imposing conditions that cannot lead to any other outcome but these economic extremes between rich and poor, the IFIs are also helping to widen the gap between those who can afford to participate in 'representative democracy' by buying representation and those who cannot.

Privatizing profits, socializing risk: no risk, all gain for private infrastructure

The problem with the IFIs, however, does not stop at conditionality. Considering that the IFIs are controlled by a very few people who have acquired political power by leveraging wealth on a national level, it's not surprising that they use their power at the IFIs to plunder money out of other people's pockets and give it to those who support them. In order to keep winning the elections that allow them to control the national and international apparatus, it is absolutely necessary to continue robbing the poor (who have no effective voice in politics and are therefore unimportant) to feed the rich (whose money talks and who are therefore extremely dangerous and cannot be ignored). One way in which this happens is by politicians exploiting their position at IFIs to benefit private companies.

While in a capitalist society most business is privately owned, certain industries are simply too risky or involve too much initial investment for private businesses to be willing to get involved with them. This tends to be particularly true with regard to infrastructure projects, i.e. the provision of energy, water and public transportation. Before the rush to privatization began in the 1990s, many of the biggest infrastructure projects were carried out by governments, since they could count on a steady source of income and guaranteed longevity, and they did not have to worry too much about monetary rewards. Infrastructure projects fulfilled secondary purposes for them, in that they helped individuals and businesses to be more productive and therefore encouraged long-term growth. Ontario Hydro, Petro-Canada, the British National Health Service and the New York subway system are only a few examples of publicly operated infrastructure projects, while many of the United States' greatest infrastructure projects, such as the Hoover Dam in the Grand Canyon, were built with public funds. All of these projects had enormous economic benefits for private businesses: workers were healthier; they could get to work quickly; and just about everyone had access to cheap and reliable energy.

Neoliberal ideology, however, refuses to acknowledge these obvious economic benefits and insists on measuring whether or not each piece of public infrastructure is profitable in itself. For example, under this view, a public transport network would be measured on whether it turns a profit in any given year, without taking into account the fact that cheap and efficient transportation makes the workforce more flexible, as workers are more willing to consider switching to a workplace that they know they can get to conveniently, and more productive when they do not have to spend hours in traffic each day.

In addition to these glaring oversights, neoliberal ideology teaches, as an article of faith, that a private business is always more efficient than a publicly run enterprise and that all infrastructure should therefore be privately run. However, just because they believe that infrastructure should be privatized does not mean that private investors view these projects as any less risky than they did in the past when they were happy to leave them to governments. Thus, under a logic so twisted that it borders on insanity, these private investors often need to be coaxed into constructing the very infrastructure that they insist is their prerogative to build, by having all business risks eliminated in advance through special government guarantees. This is especially true in countries that are politically or economically unstable. In other words, huge corporations believe that they have two inherent 'rights': to carry out these projects and for the projects to return the type of profit that is normally associated with a high-risk investment, but without the risk. Through mandating privatization, the IMF and the World Bank help the corporations enforce their 'rights' by providing the legal and economic framework that obliges governments to act in the interests of large companies and help them to quickly transfer money from public taxpayers to themselves.

a) The moral hazard of loan guarantees: Enron and Suharto do a deal, Indonesians foot the bill

One way in which the IFIs facilitate this public–private transfer is through the loan guarantee. A loan guarantee is a kind of insurance on an investment project. If a country makes a contract with a private company to build a power plant, the World Bank, for example, will guarantee that this undertaking will neither fail nor be cancelled by the government. In other words, it guarantees that the company will not have to undertake the financial risk normally associated with building a power plant in a politically unstable country. However, if the Bank ever has to pay out the guarantee to the company, the state in question has to reimburse the Bank. Therefore, although the money is being invested by a private enterprise, the state ultimately carries the risk of the project working out and can wind up in debt if it doesn't.

And this is exactly what happens in real life. In the late 1990s, the American energy company Enron agreed to build a power plant in Indonesia. At the time the agreement was made, Indonesia was a military dictatorship under the leadership of General Suharto. However, after Suharto was ousted in 1998, the successor government of Indonesia – which, for all its faults, was at least not a dictatorship – cancelled the agreement. Not only had the agreement been concluded between an acknowledged dictator with a horrendous human rights record and a company that only a few years later self-combusted in one of the greatest corporate fraud scandals in history, the World Bank openly agreed that the new Indonesian government was *right* to cancel the project because it was not economically or politically viable.

One would think, therefore, that Enron would simply have had to swallow the bitter wages of having tried to do business with an unpopular dictator and that this would serve as a lesson to other companies which might get the same greedy idea. Instead, in 2000 the World Bank paid out $15 million to Enron to reimburse it for the power plant cancellation and then refused to issue further coverage for business in Indonesia until Indonesia coughed up the $15 million to the Bank. The mistakes of a corrupt dictatorship and (nearly) equally corrupt multinational firm were thus ultimately paid for by the Indonesian taxpayer. The only people who did not have a say in Indonesia's energy policy were also the only people who ended up paying for mistakes in that policy. As the example demonstrates, there is a sharp division between those entities (private businesses) which make a profit from building infrastructure or whose finances remain neutral and those entities (the population of a nation like Indonesia) whose finances either remain neutral or take a loss. For one side 'neutral' is the best state that can be achieved, for the other side it is the worst. It is not hard to see that under these circumstances one side will inevitably get richer, the other inevitably poorer, and that this outcome is directly linked to whether or not they have any say in public decision-making.

b) Tax breaks and power purchasing agreements:
the story of government-subsidized privatization

Many loans are also made by IFIs to facilitate privatization, often of (previously) public services. Some of these services have proven records of profitability as publicly owned companies, meaning that there is no obvious reason to sell them. However, the country in question will often not only be forced to privatize the infrastructure project but to *subsidize* the privatization by giving the buyer or builder additional incentives. These could include: 'cash contributions during the construction period; subsidies during the operating period (e.g. in the form of non-refundable grants), and a favourable tax regime – including tax holidays, refunding of tax on construction and operating costs'.[10] In other words, in these cases the Bank uses public funds (because the public is

---

10   World Bank Annual Report, 1998, quoted in Kessler, 'Assessing the risks in the private provision of public services', at 251 et seq.

taking out a loan to provide all of this, which it will eventually have to pay back with interest) to give private corporations subsidies and tax breaks in exchange for buying or building a public asset. *This means that people in developing countries are literally paying wealthy companies to do business with them.*

Not only is privatization often subsidized, many privatization deals guarantee profits for private firms. To give but one example:

On the advice of the World Bank, Pakistan decided that from 1992 it would allow private companies to generate electricity. When after two years of waiting no private firms had taken up this offer in the poverty-stricken and politically unstable nation, it produced the (not very succinctly named) Policy Framework and Package of Incentives for Private Sector Power Generation Projects in Pakistan, which offered an entire Christmas list of enticements to private companies, such as:

- guaranteed prices for electricity production;
- regulations to mitigate inflation and exchange-rate fluctuations;
- exemption from corporate income tax, sales tax, customs duties and surcharges on imported equipment;
- permission to issue corporate bonds and shares at discounted prices.

With these considerable sweeteners in place, a private generating plant called Hubcap was finally established. In line with the Policy Framework, the relevant government bodies – the Water and Power Development Authority (WAPDA) and the Karachi Electric Supply Corporation – agreed to purchase power at a fixed price, regardless of how much energy was actually used. The agreement explicitly stated: 'The state-owned WAPDA will purchase power from Hubcap and the power purchase agreement assures a guaranteed revenue equivalent to 60 per cent of gross capacity utilisation, irrespective of the actual take-off from the power station.'[11] This means that Pakistan agreed to pay for a certain amount of electricity, *regardless of how much electricity its citizens and businesses actually used.* It's hard to see why Pakistan could not wastefully commit its own production miscalculations in an environment where it would be paying for them anyway, or how a business model that relies on 'guaranteed profits' could even indirectly ever be associated with the notion of capitalism, yet such a mind-set certainly benefits the builders and operators of the power plant.

This pattern of crony capitalism has been repeated the world over.

A power plant founded by US company AES in Bojanala, Uganda, included a power purchasing agreement (PPA) concluded on the basis of advice that the World Bank had given Uganda (another extremely impoverished and politically unstable nation). The PPA required the government to purchase all generated power at a price fixed in foreign currency so that it would be proof against a devaluation of the Ugandan shilling. Of course, this also meant that in the event of a currency devaluation the price of electricity would rise dramatically for Ugandans. 'An independent review by an Indian consulting firm concluded that not only were capital costs the same as other power plants with twice the

---

11 Ibid., at 259.

generating capacity, but the PPA imposes excessive payment requirements.'[12]

These examples are only a few illustrations of a broader pattern. Similar power purchasing agreements have been concluded in Costa Rica, India, Croatia, the Dominican Republic, Hungary and Indonesia.

This 'business model' is unsustainable, because there cannot possibly be enough liquidity in a nation that *needs* a loan to provide basic infrastructure to repay the loan *with* interest *plus* a profit to the enterprise that has garnered the contract to provide it. To think that such a situation might actually occur is so unrealistic as to qualify as delusional. One might as well believe that electricity is generated by fairy dust, or that national loans are going to be paid back with the pot of gold at the end of the rainbow. And considering that the companies involved are often highly successful enterprises, it's hard to believe that they suffer from any such delusions regarding the long-term impacts of this method of operation. Unrealistic assessments of a country's ability to pay are not based on honest mistakes; they are intentional miscalculations that enable multinationals to take their reward – endless profits – for helping the politicians who control the IFIs get into power.

It is important to always remember that neither politicians nor business leaders are disinterested entities: politicians want power and company owners want money. In fact, they do not just want those things – they *need* them to be successful. By cutting all other people out of the decision-making process, the electoral and international systems

---

12   Ibid.

deliver politicians and big businesses the perfect conditions under which they can give each other what they want. Private companies give politicians power by bankrolling their election campaigns, and politicians return the favour by using their power at the IFIs to shackle the entire population of countries like Pakistan or Uganda to an unrealistic utility bill.

c) Saving the creditors: IMF bailouts

Yet another way of shifting money from taxpayers to private companies is the investor bailout. As previously mentioned, part of the IMF's mandate is to give structural adjustment loans to prevent an indebted economy from contracting too quickly. The purpose of these loans is to offset the need for a sharp reduction in government spending. However, because many countries are already indebted to private banks when they receive such a loan, a proportion of the money is not used to prop up government spending, but rather to pay off the interest or capital on a prior loan received from a private lender. This is so common that IMF loans are often referred to as 'bailouts'.

These bailouts do not really serve to help the debtor country, which is about to default, but rather to rescue its creditors, who will lose their money if it does. This can be seen from the fact that a major factor in the decision to grant a bailout loan is not how much trouble a country is in, but rather who stands to suffer from it: those nations in which foreign investors, particularly American banks, have the largest stake receive the largest bailout loans from the IMF (where the USA is the largest shareholder). One study showed that each increase of $4 billion in US bank exposure led to a 3.4 per cent increase in the chances of a state receiving a loan, and on approved loans it led to an increase in the size of the loan by 1.5 million SDRs.

The bailout component of loans is even sometimes explicitly agreed upon. The IMF stand-by arrangement with Ghana in 1983 specified that the loan be deposited directly in a Bank of Ghana account at the Bank of England: 'the Bank of England would then follow irrevocable instructions that these deposits be directly transferred to the Standard Chartered Bank to repay a short-term bridging loan. In other words, Fund financing was being directly funnelled to a commercial bank creditor, rather than to Ghana itself'.[13]

However, once the bailout is done and the creditors have been safely paid off, someone still needs to pay back the bailout loan plus the interest and this invariably falls to the middle class, working class and poor of the country in question. To give but one example of this process in action: One of the European countries hit hardest by the 2008 crash was Ireland. In 2010, the nation received an 85 billion euro bailout that did not require any of the country's unsecured bondholders to 'take a haircut' (i.e. a reduction in the value of their bonds). This means that Irish taxpayers must pay off the 85 billion euro package, while those who freely chose to invest in the Irish economy will not lose any money as a consequence of making these reckless loans. As a result, working Irish people are now saddled with increases in university tuition and sales tax, cutbacks to public service salaries, new payments for property tax, water charges and an income levy that can reach up to 7 per cent of gross income for upper-middle-class earners. Each year, they hand

---

13 Gould, 'Money talks: supplementary finances and International Monetary Fund conditionality', at 564.

over this hard-earned money (8 billion euros in 2015 alone) to the bondholders and other financiers who have the clout to insert themselves into high politics.

According to free market theory, a capitalist who makes a bad loan must bear the consequences of their actions. When someone else jumps in and gives the debtor the money to pay back their creditor, it does not make much of a difference to the debtor – they either default or pass the money on, but either way they don't actually end up with anything. It is the creditor who is saved from losing a lot of money. Continually bailing out those who make bad loans – as the IMF and World Bank do – creates 'moral hazard' – lenders irresponsibly give loans that they already know the borrower will be unable to repay, because they know that the debtor will get a bailout and they will be able to collect the money in the end.

At the international casino
the house always wins

The IMF, the World Bank and even the UN categorically fail to do the job they were created for. In fact, it is no exaggeration to say that they have become tools used by private financiers to reduce whole nations to a condition not much different to indentured servitude. And while there are other complicating factors, the root of this condition lies in the toxic interplay between the national and international systems that puts all political power in the hands of an infinitesimally tiny fraction of the world's population.

As we have seen, politicians depend on donations to win elections, because the statistical skewing inherent in the representative system can allow them to snatch victory from the jaws of defeat provided that they win the right ridings or win votes in the right proportions. Such 'victories' are often the product of spending money in the right places, and since corporations and extremely wealthy individuals are able to give bigger and better donations than the average individual, politicians must be careful not to anger them if they care about remaining in their jobs.

This includes refraining from angering them through their decisions on an international level.

If a government were to decide to champion measures at the IMF that would have negative consequences for big business (such as ending bank bailouts or refusing to protect energy conglomerates that do business with dictators), they would undoubtedly find themselves short of cooperation and funding from this industry during the next election and might even be subjected to attack ads or other discrediting campaigns. This could end the politician's career, and it is the reason why they choose not to punish such behaviour but rather to collude with it. This is why international policies that are beneficial to trade interests, such as trade liberaliza-tion, proceed at the speed of light, while those that benefit the poor and disenfranchised languish in obscurity. It's all about keeping the right people happy and the right people are the people with money.

Thus, national elections do not just sideline citizens from national decision-making, they also cut them completely out of international decision-making. For four years, the winning politicians, who often do not even reflect the way that most citizens voted, go on to bind those very citizens to interna-tional rules and agreements that only a tiny percentage of the world's population – a nation's top politicians, the diplomats and lawyers who support them, and the corporations which make it their business to involve themselves in these decisions – even know exist. And because so few people are involved in this decision-making, it is very easy for anyone with enough resources to apply pressure to them. This would not be possible in a democracy where the entire nation is informed of and partakes in decision-making. It is no wonder that while Athenians enriched themselves by receiving pay for participation, our system, which has cut the people out of the centre and relegated them to cheerleaders on the periphery, is only making them poorer.

Can citizens combat this influence by learning to play the international game themselves? That is the topic of the next chapter.

6

Non-Governmental Organizations and the Civil Society Chimera

> Appearances are deceptive.
>
> Aesop

If national democracies are increasingly *looking* like oligarchies, the international system is already there. The explicit inequalities in voting rights as well as the use of 'representation' to whittle down those entitled to participate to a minuscule number of powerful politicians and financiers effectively annihilates any residual content of democracy that might have theoretically survived the distorting effects of bribery and vote-skewing already present on the national level.

In this grim picture, only one thing holds out hope for citizen involvement in international politics: non-governmental organizations.

Non-governmental organizations, or 'NGOs', as they are usually called, are associations that pursue an issue of specific interest to their members, and they enjoy a very positive image as 'empowering' movements that work towards improving the collective good. In fact, hardly a day goes by without a news story about the good work that NGOs like World Vision or Oxfam are doing in some part of the world.

So it is hardly surprising that the received wisdom is that giving NGOs better access to international institutions would allow grassroots activists to participate in formulating international law and policy. This, it is argued, would redress not only the problems on the international level, but also the participatory imbalances that exist within national electoral democracies: it wouldn't matter so much if citizens were locked out of national decision-making because NGOs would provide them with a shortcut to the international level. This view is so widespread that the UN, the IMF and the World Bank have all been able to improve their public image by involving NGOs in their work.

The message that is put across through this NGO–IGO cooperation is that if citizens truly care about an international issue – say climate change or human rights – they can join an NGO and gain the ability to participate in international decision-making in an informal but effective manner.

It is a nice thought but, unfortunately, it is based on an oversimplified and over-optimistic conception of the role that NGOs play on the international stage.

There are two key points that are absolutely essential to understanding the real position of NGOs and the purposes they truly fulfil:

- NGOs do not necessarily pursue charitable goals;
- in order to fulfil their mandates, NGOs need to engage in lobbying activities in an arena where economic power plays an enormous role in decision-making.

These two facts – that NGOs are not necessarily charities and that they need to lobby heavily to achieve their goals – are almost never mentioned; not by politicians, not by reporters and not by anyone else, either. And yet these two points explain nearly everything that is wrong with the international system and why it keeps getting worse despite all efforts to the contrary.

The nature of modern NGOs: charity begins in the boardroom

When someone hears the term 'NGO', chances are that they will think of an organization like the Red Cross or the World Wildlife Fund. These organizations are run on a non-profit basis and they generally pursue uncontroversial goals, such as alleviating suffering in conflict or protecting endangered species. Associations like these contribute to the positive image many people hold of NGOs. However, 'NGO' at its most basic just means 'non-governmental organization' and there is no requirement that the goals or methods of NGOs be endorsed by, or be of benefit to, the broader public. As a result, many NGOs that cooperate with international institutions are not necessarily founded for the benefit of all humanity or even of all of the citizens of a particular nation. Although NGOs must fulfil certain criteria in order to be allowed to work with international organizations, none of them addresses this point regarding the basic purpose of the NGO.

For example, to be accredited to work with the UN an NGO must:

- operate established headquarters;
- have a democratically adopted constitution;
- enjoy the authority to speak for its members;
- have a representative structure;
- possess appropriate mechanisms of accountability and democratic and transparent decision-making processes;
- derive its basic resources in the main part from contributions of the national affiliates or other components or from individual members.

You will notice that this list of requirements does *not* stipulate that the organization in question serve any public goal and only requires that its *internal* organization be 'democratic'. And so, an NGO established for the purposes of pursuing private interests and deriving most of its funds from its own members is entirely permissible, so long as its members remember to 'organize democratically' by voting on the president of the organization, for example.

And since there is no requirement to do charitable work to be accredited to the UN, a lot of NGOs don't.

The NGO–industrial complex

Many internationally accredited NGOs are actually either umbrella organizations for corporate interests, privately funded think tanks or a mixture of the two. For example, the American Forest and Paper Association, which has enjoyed roster status at the UN since 1996, is an umbrella organization for American paper product manufacturers. It is joined on the UN's roster list by the Arab Federation for Food Industries and the Association of European Manufacturers of Internal Combustion Engines, to name but two. And specialized industry 'NGOs' like these are small fish compared to the International Chamber of Commerce (ICC), the international business association to which many large companies belong. The ICC has held general consultative status (the highest status an NGO can hold) with the UN since 1946, and it has not been working with the United Nations for so long without having clear ideas about the advantages it is getting. According to its website, membership in the ICC gives businesses 'access to the corridors of power' by placing 'company executives ... in contact with ministers and international officials at the heart of intergovernmental groups such as the G20 and the United Nations', promising that they can thus 'help write the rules that business uses every day to reduce costs and uncertainties in areas from arbitration to banking and commercial contracts'.[1] In other words, for the ICC the benefits of UN accreditation do not include the chance to help the destitute and downtrodden, nor even to 'help make the world a better place' in some nebulous sense, but rather the access to power that allows businesses to write their own laws.

It's fair to say that this is not the picture most people have in mind when they think about civil society activism.

The situation is similar at other big international institutions. For example, the World Trade Organization (WTO) is famous for allowing NGOs to attend its negotiating meetings, thereby giving their delegates the chance to directly lobby national representatives on matters of international trade. However, an NGO can send delegates to a WTO meeting only if it is accredited, and this is rarely the case

---

1 'Benefits of membership', International Chamber of Commerce, www.iccwbo.org/worldwide-membership/benefits/.

for grassroots organizations. In fact, at the WTO's Ministerial Conference in 2011, 40 per cent of all accredited NGOs *directly* represented businesses, e.g. the European Chemical Industry Council, the Canadian Turkey Marketing Agency, and MEDEF (France's association of employers).

And disturbing as this is, corporations give the entire business another turn of the screw by funding *other*, nominally independent, NGOs. After all, the 'non-profit sector' operates according to funding principles that aren't much different to those of political parties. While some NGOs still go collecting on the street, it's the corporate donations, which can total hundreds of thousands or even millions of dollars, that really provide the core of their budgets. For example, CARE International (an aid organization that fights poverty in the developing world) includes on its top donors list: Coca-Cola, Credit Suisse, Starbucks, Google, Goldman Sachs, Nike, J. P. Morgan and Procter & Gamble; while Oxfam (which primarily focuses on providing potable water) has 'strategic partnerships' with Unilever (which generously helps Oxfam incorporate small farmers into Unilever's global supply chain), Nokia, Accenture and KPMG (which gives the organization 'tax advice').

It's more than fair to wonder how much the priorities of these NGOs might be affected by their generous corporate sponsors.

In fact, this revolving door between politics, corporations and NGOs was sensationally revealed in late 2014 when the global children's charity, Save the Children, handed former British prime minister Tony Blair (one of the architects of the Second Iraq War which killed and injured thousands of children) a Global Legacy Award. No surprise perhaps when one considers that Save the Children is funded by Unilever, Procter & Gamble, Barclays Bank, Pfizer, Coca-Cola, Goldman Sachs, KPMG and IKEA to name but a few, and that members of Save the Children's top staff had previously worked for Tony Blair. Some of Save the Children's donors also contribute to political campaigns and most have benefited from lax corporate taxation regimes at the national level, which are, of course, maintained by people like Tony Blair. In consideration of the terrible impact some of Blair's decisions had on children, Save the Children's award to Blair was considered by many to be in particularly poor taste, and the charity's own staff protested vociferously. The award, however, was never revoked.

By funding both their own and other pre-existing non-profit organizations, corporations and financial interests are *exploiting* the possibility of NGO participation at international institutions to trap the entire political system in a classic pincer movement.

It's a simple game: big business already exercises a substantial degree of influence over national election outcomes. The winners of these elections go on to represent the state on an international level, where, in their interactions with other states, they need to pay close attention to the needs of their sponsors if they want to be re-elected. This is the first line that corporations have into the international decision-making process: the knowledge that if their wishes are not considered, they can punish a politician for it later.

However, this still leaves the problem of the corporate-backed politician who is willing to break away from sponsors and potentially double-cross them on an international level. Allowing corporations to form NGOs which are accredited to international organizations cuts down on the chances of this happening by giving corporate sponsors a second line into that decision-making process, a back-up plan, as it were, that allows them to directly oversee international negotiations as they are happening. National representatives are thus caught in a vice between funding from the commercial arm of the enterprise on a national level and lobbying from their 'NGO' arm on an international level. There's simply no escape, even for the rare politician who might want to go rogue.

Of course, not all internationally active NGOs are business-oriented. Governments themselves also often take a hand in setting up and funding the NGOs that will be accredited to attend international meetings where they will allegedly broaden participation and serve to 'challenge' those government policies. For example, the European Centre of Development Policy Management is funded exclusively by European governments, while Kenya's Institute of Economic Affairs has received funding from the Canadian and Swedish International Development Agencies, the European Union, the Center for Private Enterprise, the World Bank, the Dutch and Danish embassies and the British Council. Both organizations attended the 2011 WTO Ministerial Conference, where their 'completely different' perspective was no doubt highly appreciated by the representatives from their sponsor states.

Perhaps the NGO that best incorporates all of the elements of the entire NGO-industrial complex is the Club of Madrid (technically called, with a fitting sense of sophistication, the 'Club de Madrid'). The Club of Madrid, which has enjoyed special consultative status at the UN since 2007, is composed of nearly one hundred former democratic presidents and prime ministers: people, in other words, who managed to climb the electoral system all the way to the top. Bill Clinton (USA), Helmut Kohl (Germany), Carl Bildt (Sweden), Mikhail Gorbachev (Russia), Javier Solana (NATO/EU), Mary Robinson (Ireland) and of course Osvaldo Hurtado and Luis Alberto Lacalle (the erstwhile presidents of Ecuador and Uruguay whom you may remember from their IMF double-dealings in the previous chapter) are all members. Considering this illustrious member list, it's something of a surprise that the Club of Madrid is not funded by its associates, but rather, among others, by the cities of Rotterdam and Madrid, the World Bank, the IMF, the governments of Belgium and Mexico and the International Development Agencies of Australia and Sweden. It also receives sponsorship from Walmart, Microsoft and NATO. So, in short, the Club of Madrid is an organization composed of former heads of state (i.e. some of the most powerful individuals in the world) that accepts material gain from Walmart (one of the world's most profitable corporations that has become synonymous with outsourced manufacturing, underpaying its workforce and heavy PAC contributions to American political campaigns), as well as from NATO (a military alliance that has largely degenerated into a glorified Groupon club for arms purchases) and, of course, from the IMF and the World Bank. To put it even more succinctly, the IMF, the World Bank, NATO and Walmart are footing the bill for former presidents to influence decision-making at the UN, well past their term in office.

Not only is it safe to say that this is not the kind of activity that most people think they are going to get when they endorse 'NGO' participation, it's hard to see how NGOs like the Club of Madrid can offer a 'different perspective' from their own members and sponsors, who are, after all, already very powerful figures within the official system of global governance. The sole point of allowing this sort of participation is that it serves as rather good window-dressing to disguise the truly low levels of 'real' citizen participation.

The public image of NGO participation at an organization like the WTO or the UN is one of grassroots activists challenging representatives to act more responsibly on public interest issues, such as protecting the environment or ending poverty. This is because we often see these activists staging theatrical protests *outside* of these meetings. However, *inside* the meetings the reality of NGO participation looks very different. Here national representatives will mingle with delegates from trade and corporate associations, former heads of state, university professors and functionaries from think tanks and institutes funded by their own governments. This is then packaged for public consumption as a consultation between 'differing' or 'wide-ranging' points of view. While a few token grassroots organizations inevitably manage to gain accreditation to these meetings, their views are effectively drowned out in the flood of corporate and government interests that already control official decision-making processes and which use 'NGO' funding to dominate the unofficial channels as well.

NGOs as foreign policy instruments: AstroTurfing into eastern Europe and Central Asia

In extreme cases, professionally funded NGOs staffed by privileged workers don't just limit themselves to international institutions, but come to dominate the political conversation in developing countries as well. In this scenario, NGOs that receive the bulk of their funding from developed nation governments and institutions become the official 'voice' of that country as portrayed in the sponsoring nation's media. It is a misleading state of affairs when these NGOs do not actually enjoy grassroots support on the ground. This style of public conversation-hijacking by pushing sympathetic NGOs to the foreground is most common in South America and former Eastern Bloc countries.

For example, in Georgia, Moldova and the Ukraine (three relatively impoverished and unstable former Eastern Bloc countries) only one fifth of NGOs agree that their strength comes from their membership base. Similarly, in Kyrgyzstan, between 70 and 100 per cent of the budget of a typical NGO is provided by foreign donors and 'the overwhelming majority' of NGO officials recognize 'that the accountability of an NGO *to the donor* is a top priority'.[2] A study into NGO activity in Georgia, Moldova and Ukraine concluded that:

[t]he elitist nature of NGOs is largely attributable to the fact that their main sources of funding are foreign. Western money allows NGOs to attract talent, but their full-time employees are more comfortable networking with Western embassies and various state agencies than holding town hall consultations and engaging with citizens. For example, following the 2009 electoral revolution in Moldova, NGO leaders met with foreign embassies and donors to consult over priorities, but no

2 Musabaeva, 'Responsibility, transparency and legitimacy of socially-oriented NGOs in Krygyzstan', at 7. Emphasis added.

major public forum or debate was launched to discuss a national reform agenda.[3]

These organizations may well be doing good work (and then again they may not be), but they are hardly grassroots enterprises, and there is no clear dividing line between them and their various donors, who are themselves already powerful actors on the international stage. When foreign governments fund NGOs in developing countries and then insist that developing-country governments acknowledge these NGOs as special stakeholders in the national dialogue, far from enhancing citizen participation, this actually serves to subvert national sovereignty. And once again, it isn't because it is necessarily in the interests of developed nation citizens to do so. When government-funded agencies set up NGOs in foreign countries like Moldova or Ukraine, not only do they tend to pay scant regard to the wishes and needs of ordinary Moldovans or Ukrainians, they rarely act with the blessing of their own citizens, who are often paying for these NGOs to operate.

In fact, private citizens tend to fund different causes to those their governments prioritize. In Ireland, for example, 60 per cent of funding for domestic non-profit organizations was received from the government. Thirty per cent of these funds went to health-related organizations, while international development organizations received 7.7 per cent of state funding, arts, culture and heritage groups received 5.6 per cent and environmental groups 0.6 per cent. The pattern of private donations was, however, quite

3 Lutsevych, 'Briefing Paper, How to finish a revolution: civil society and democracy in Georgia, Moldova and Ukraine', at 5.

different. Twenty-five per cent of these went to international development organizations, with 8.4 per cent going to arts, culture and heritage, and only 8 per cent going to health organizations. Extrapolating from here, the existence of a well-funded NGO active in a certain area is not an indication of the level of grassroots support that the organization or cause truly enjoys, either in the host or donor state. It merely indicates the foreign policy preferences of the government that is funding it.

Real NGOs: an endangered species

There are, of course, genuine NGOs out there – the environmental NGO Greenpeace, for example, does not receive funding from companies or governments – but it is very difficult for these NGOs to act effectively in an atmosphere where they are confronted not only with traditional political power brokers, but also well-financed 'straw-man' NGOs that purport to be following the same goals – just from a more moderate, elite-friendly perspective.

Far from being an empowering avenue of citizen participation, the NGO sector is largely a closed shop, where real grassroots organizations tend to be dismissed as 'radical' – because, compared to establishment-friendly organizations like the Club of Madrid, their ideas generally espouse more thoroughgoing change. It is easy, in this atmosphere, to push genuine NGOs to the fringe of political discussion because their policies are often more disruptive to those who hold power, and also because it is more difficult for grassroots NGOs to organize in the first place.

Cohesive, long-term organization is easier to achieve when a group has sufficient resources to create its own self-sustaining infrastructure, e.g. to pay a chairman and other officers, to rent operating premises, or to train volunteers. It is easy for large corporations and governments to divert a small portion of their budgets to these activities. However, it is very difficult for underprivileged groups, the same groups that are least likely to be able to organize for an election or other activity, to do the same. Giving these sectors of society – the undereducated, the poverty-stricken and the exploited – 'a voice' is the official justification for allowing NGOs access to international institutions, but since these sectors of society are by definition virtually always overworked and underpaid, they often simply do not have the resources to effectively participate in the competitive NGO environment. This is why authentic grassroots NGOs are so difficult to find in the international landscape. NGO participation actually privileges the wealthiest and most well-connected members of society to the detriment of the poor and disenfranchised.

The dark underbelly of NGO lobbying: roundtables, drugs and lots of cash

That there are inherently more rich corporate and government-funded NGOs than grassroots ones is only the beginning of the problem with international NGO participation. Wealth is not only a great benefit in establishing and operating an NGO, it is an asset in achieving that NGO's goals. NGOs of every description – big and small, rich and poor, general and specialized – seek to have their agenda implemented by lobbying representatives to adopt it. Indeed, since they are not part of official decision-making processes, there is no other way for them to affect those decisions but through lobbying. But because the quality and quantity of lobbying activity that an NGO can engage in depends on the resources at its disposal, the entire process of NGO participation privileges wealthy, and thus usually corporate, NGOs. It is these organizations that are best positioned to maintain the type of long-term lobbying campaign that inevitably bears fruit.

The European Roundtable of Industrialists (ERT): reshaping Europe one 'personal contact' at a time

Few readers will be familiar with the European Roundtable of Industrialists. It is, after all, an invitation-only organization. However, despite its low profile, ERT has enjoyed nearly unparalleled success when it comes to affecting political decisions over the past fifty years. In fact, if ERT's own literature is to be believed, we are all living in an ERT world.

That's because the organization, which consists of 'around 50 chief executives and chairmen of major multinational companies of European parentage', credits itself with being one of the major drivers behind European and global economic integration. According to ERT, its '"core business" since the mid-1980s has been securing the development and implementation of the European Single Market programme', with some of its main concerns being 'high costs and low profits, fragmentation of the European market, and excessive interference by governments'. Translated into plain English, this means that its prime mission for the past thirty years has been to establish the European Union and the Eurozone in the interests of increasing profits for its members. Creating a single market out of twenty-eight different countries, few of which share so much as a common language, is no small task. However, one cannot deny that there are tangible indications of progress here, in that the European Union and the single-currency European market were not around in the 1980s, but they definitely exist now. It must be admitted that literally redesigning the political and economic landscape of an entire continent is a staggering achievement, and ERT is not shy about explaining how its gets things done.

At European level, ERT discusses its views with members of the European Commission, the Council of Ministers and the European Parliament, and the organization 'strives' to meet the head of government that holds the EU presidency to discuss priorities every six months. At national level, each member is responsible for pushing ERT's views to his or her own national government and parliament, as well as to business colleagues, contacts in industrialist federations, other 'opinion-formers' and the press. These actions have directly resulted in changes to public policy on a number of occasions.

The publication *ERT Highlights* (produced by ERT) recounts a visit by a fourteen-member ERT delegation to then French prime minister Édouard Balladur 'to help resolve the European position in the talks' to establish the World Trade Organization in 1993. The tête-à-tête with M. Balladur resulted in Europe continuing with the negotiations to establish the WTO. ERT also credits itself with successfully setting the conditions for ten new members to accede to the EU in 2004, as well as ensuring that discussions on new EU accounting standards were not 'dominated by professional accountants', an endeavour which, judging by the current state of European accounting standards, it was also successful in.

ERT attributes much of its success to 'personal contacts' with European Commissioners, as well as 'past, present or [eerily] future' European heads of government.[4] Doubtless, its multiple publications with modest titles such as 'Reshaping Europe', distributed to decision-makers in their tens of thousands, also played a role. For most people, having to take your organization 'out of the shadows', as past chairman Jérôme Monod did with ERT in the 1990s, might signal a faint warning that perhaps not everything about it is totally above board. However, to this day ERT remains blissfully oblivious to concerns about its manner of operations.

The case of ERT demonstrates how a well-funded and coordinated campaign can bombard decision-makers with information conducive to their own interests, often investing as much time and money into developing policy as government officials do themselves. Indeed, such interest groups are sufficiently well resourced as to virtually build a shadow government that seeks to always remain one step ahead of the official government in its conceptual planning and execution, a position which enables it to guide discussion and decisions from a position of superiority.

For these select individuals, an election is never truly lost. If campaign finance and vote-skewing fail, there are always private meetings with their 'personal contacts'. These tactics

---

4 All information on ERT taken from its own publication, *ERT Highlights*, ertdrupal.lin3.nucleus.be/system/files/uploads/2010%20October%20-%20ERT%20Highlights.pdf. Page 81 of the report confirms ERT's success in ensuring that negotiations on accounting reforms were not dominated by professional accountants.

are literally available only to the rich, and they require a level of lobbying so elaborate as to preclude the possibility of other NGOs being able to compete effectively. Grassroots organizations representing refugees, victims of human trafficking or minimum-wage workers, for example, are hardly likely to rub shoulders with heads of government or newspaper editors. The end result is that the agendas pursued by moneyed interests tend to be implemented in leaps and bounds while grassroots NGOs struggle to attain recognition. This means that policy tends to be implemented in a very one-sided fashion – the interests of those who can afford to continually elaborate and distribute their opinions simply drown out all other concerns.

The example of access to HIV/AIDS drugs illustrates how this works in practice.

Big Pharma, the WTO and the war for affordable drugs

In the 1980s and 1990s Western pharmaceutical companies became concerned that commercial enterprises in developing nations were copying their patented medications and selling them at reduced prices, either to their own citizens or citizens of even poorer nations that lacked the capability to produce medicine in-country. Pharma companies wanted this copying stopped, even though in many cases they had no intention of truly capturing these markets by lowering their own prices enough for people in developing countries to actually be able to afford their products. In other words, these companies may not have been intending to sell poor people their medication, but thought no one else should be allowed to do so, either.

Understandably, this proved to be a rather controversial position.

Preventing the manufacture of certain drugs at developing-world prices – particularly the antiretrovirals used to
treat HIV/AIDS, a disease then ravaging many of the world's
poorest nations – would literally condemn hundreds of thousands, if not millions, of people to a premature death. In
order to achieve its goals in the face of these serious coun-
tervailing concerns, the pharmaceutical industry worked
with other corporate interests to launch a major lobbying
campaign aimed at convincing decision-makers to make new
international laws entirely in their favour with no consideration for other interests. This expensive and coordinated
campaign included:

- labelling any unauthorized production of a patented
  product, such as a patented medication, as 'piracy', which
  carried the connotation of a crime, even though, at the
  time, many of these activities were perfectly legal;
- moving the debate on global patent protection from the
  World Intellectual Property Organization to GATT (the
  precursor to the WTO) 'because WIPO too closely iden-
  tified with the interests of the majority of developing
  countries';
- commissioning trade and biotech lobbyist Jacques Gorlin
  to draft a paper for the United States Trade Representative which proposed setting up a new multilateral treaty
  to protect intellectual property rights. This treaty, as envisaged by Gorlin, would include minimum standards of
  protection, as well as mechanisms for dispute settlement,
  and enforcement on patents and other intellectual property. Gorlin's paper became the unofficial blueprint for all
  further activities in the corporate lobbying campaign.

These were, however, but the preparatory steps in the battle to impose their ideas, and their ideas alone, on the rest of the world. The corporate lobbying campaign proceeded to:

- use its positions on the ACTN (the Advisory Committee for Trade Negotiations – a body composed of leaders of industry which consults with the US president on trade matters) to further their goals with regard to international regulation. When ACTN created a Task Force on Intellectual Property Rights many of the heads of those corporations most affected by developing-nation copycat products were on it, including 'Fritz Attaway, Vice President and Counsel of the Motion Picture Association, and Abraham Cohen, president of the International Division of Merck & Company, Inc. (at that time America's largest pharmaceutical corporation)'. The Task Force convinced the US government to include intellectual property in the GATT negotiations, taking the recommendations it presented to ACTN directly from the paper it had commissioned Gorlin to write;
- form the Intellectual Property Committee, a group with the explicit goal of concluding a multilateral treaty on intellectual property protection under the auspices of GATT (the organization responsible for world trade at the time). The Intellectual Property Committee met frequently with the largest industrial and employers' organizations in Europe and Japan (UNICE and Keidanren) over the course of a year and a half to negotiate their consolidated position. They eventually published this position in a trilateral document, calling for 'I) a code of minimum standards for copyrights, patents, trademarks, and appellation of origin

issues; 2) an enforcement mechanism; and 3) a dispute settlement mechanism';

- have US trade laws amended to 'institutionalize their desired link between trade and intellectual property'.

Even all of these time-consuming and expensive activities represented only half the battle in pharma's goal of reaching comprehensive international protection for its products and preventing all patent infringements regardless of other considerations.

Once the venue of negotiations had successfully been moved to GATT, and they had succeeded in reaching agreement on their position points with other partners in developed-world industry, the corporate campaign began to lobby the US Congress and the executive branch, emphasizing 'the centrality of intellectual property-based goods and services to U.S. competitiveness, [and] strategically linking its agenda to a major societal concern'. What is more, the Intellectual Property Committee 'stayed in close contact' with American government negotiators, continually shaping specific proposals and successfully pressing their demands throughout the negotiations (all eight years of them) that led to the establishment of the World Trade Organization. 'As recommended in the 1985 Gorlin paper [which the industry had commissioned and previously lifted their recommendations to the government from], negotiators worked in enclave committees to achieve plurilateral consensus – just as the IPC had done with its European and Japanese counterparts.'

All of this work – which took over a decade to achieve – was crowned by success. A restrictive global intellectual property rights regime that included nearly all of the corporate demands, including blanket patent protection and dispute settlement, was implemented through the WTO's TRIPs agreement. Even Jacques Gorlin, author of the oft-aforementioned paper, was pleased with the outcome, stating, 'we got 95% of what we wanted'.

As soon as these new international laws on intellectual property were in place, the USA proceeded to bring a raft of cases against countries whose patent laws were deemed to be in violation of the TRIPs agreement. Since South Africa had particularly come between the pharma industry's crosshairs for allowing generic copying of HIV/AIDS medication and other drugs, its lobbyists (successfully) pressured the US government to punish the nation by withholding preferential tariff treatment from South African exporters. At the time, nearly 3 per cent of South Africans were already infected with HIV, many of them infants born with the disease. That number would skyrocket to 10 per cent by 1999. But instead of helping, the US government, at the behest of private industry, was collectively punishing *all* South Africans for their insistence on trying to prolong their fellow citizens' lives. Thanks to pharma's relentless campaign, and their ability to sew up international politics, things looked very bleak for South African AIDS victims and for other sufferers around the world.

Fortunately, in this case corporate–government policy did not go unchallenged. A group of NGOs known as the Access Campaign worked towards getting exemptions (known as the ability to issue 'compulsory licences') to TRIPs rules that would benefit HIV/AIDS patients in developing countries by lowering drug prices. However, in doing so, the Access Campaign was compelled to go to great lengths, investing substantial time and effort into their cause. For example, they:

- lobbied the World Health Organization (WHO) until it adopted 'a resolution calling upon member states to ensure equitable access to essential drugs and review options under international trade agreements to safeguard access to these medicines';
- mobilized international donors to purchase essential medicines and to make them available to countries facing the HIV/AIDS crisis;
- held a conference in Amsterdam during the 1999 WTO Ministerial meeting in Seattle to issue a statement calling on 'member states to: ask the WTO to establish a working group on access to medicines; endorse the use of compulsory licensing of patents ... and allow exceptions to patent rights ... for production of medicines for export'.

In addition to pressuring international organizations on these points, the Access Campaign also launched a public relations effort aimed at exposing the lack of connection between blanket patent protection and medical science breakthroughs. To this end, the campaign:

- distributed information that revealed 'the astronomical profits that pharmaceutical companies were earning by selling HIV/AIDS drugs', as well as the fact that some of the drugs in question had actually been developed through public funding, thus discrediting the pharmaceutical industry's claim that high private profits were necessary in order to enable research;

- mobilized support from the students and faculty of Yale University, where one of the drugs in question had been developed and was, at that point, licensed to a major pharmaceutical company for $40 million per annum;
- issued rebuttals to pharma-industry papers that blamed the high price of drugs on corruption.

All these activities were a lot of work, but they also bore fruit. Pharmaceutical companies eventually slashed prices for HIV/AIDS drugs in developing nations and the WTO cases were withdrawn. In addition, the Doha Declaration clarified that nations may issue compulsory licensing in cases of national emergency, such as the HIV/AIDS pandemic.[5]

At first glance the battle between pharma companies and the Access Campaign looks like a fantastic case of successful NGO involvement, with first the pharma industry and then the non-profits gaining the upper hand in the struggle over generic HIV drugs. But although the achievements of the Access Campaign certainly deserve to be appreciated, it wouldn't be completely accurate to describe them as ultimately victorious underdogs.

While both sides – business interests and the Access Campaign – used similar strategies to pursue their agendas, there are still key differences. The Access Campaign focused mainly on circulating information and gaining public support for their positions. They successfully shifted the

---

5 All information on the pharma and Access Campaigns taken from Sell and Prakash, 'Using ideas strategically: the contest between business and NGO networks in Intellectual Property Rights', at 158, and Bond, *Against Global Apartheid: South Africa Meets the World Bank, IMF and International Finance*, at 154 et seq.

generic drugs debate to a partially public dialogue in which the average citizen was invited to play a role in pressuring decision-makers. Business interests, by contrast, focused exclusively on directly pressuring decision-makers with no public involvement.

And in the final analysis, this strategy was far more successful than the Access Campaign's as it resulted in the creation of globe-spanning protection for intellectual property, whereas the Access Campaign merely succeeded in enforcing limited and temporary exemptions from this policy. In other words, the Access Campaign gained an exception – but business interests gained a system. Furthermore, while the majority of WTO cases concerning pharmaceutical patents brought by the USA were indeed withdrawn, this only occurred after the United States had secured considerable concessions from respondent countries.

The entire case demonstrates a key point about NGOs: to achieve any goal at all, NGOs must lobby, and this privileges the well funded, because they have the resources to conduct these activities more efficiently. It is these enormous corporations whose members sit on advisory boards and meet with presidents; it is they who have the clout to sway employers' associations to their agenda. Far from *breaking down* barriers to international participation, NGO participation actually introduces *additional* financial hurdles, since grassroots NGOs are not only forced to confront unsympathetic governments, but also these hostile professionally funded 'pseudo-NGOs'. Sometimes genuine non-profit NGOs are able to overcome those hurdles, but often they are not.

NGOs: a beautiful idea gone rogue

NGO participation is largely self-serve: the more one takes, the more one gets. And that works to the advantage of those best able to take. The world's wealthiest and most exclusive NGOs can afford to stay in continuous contact with key decision-makers, and are not limited to participation in public arenas, where their policies may be openly challenged. At the other end of the spectrum, engaging in these lobbying activities presents the greatest financial challenge for precisely those marginalized groups who are least able to participate effectively in the national electoral process. Essentially it squeezes them out of a debate that is viciously fought between well-funded and well-connected business interests on one side and slightly less well-funded and less well-connected, but nonetheless professionalized, NGOs on the other. As hard as grassroots organizations try, they are unlikely to be effective, and most go to a great deal of effort just to counter the policies of corporate and government interests. Therefore, as good as it may sound on paper, in real life the entire idea of NGO participation in decision-making works directly counter to the idea of democratic equality by ensuring that success depends on the money an organization can throw behind its cause.

It is by no means impossible to influence the opinions of an entire population (as we have seen with elections and referenda), but influencing a small number of individuals behind closed doors is child's play. The truth about NGO involvement in international decision-making is that it is just the final piece in a political structure that systematically excludes the vast majority of people from having any effect at all on their own lives while handing a great deal of power to the few who can afford it.

Representative democracy and the international system: fertile ground for oligarchy

We often say that our political system is 'broken', but this isn't really true. The problem is not that democracy is broken.

The problem is that what we are engaged in is not democracy.

This wouldn't really matter so much, if we were happy with the results we are getting.

But we aren't.

The consequences of our version of democracy are only too obvious: increasing poverty, widespread political disenfranchisement and a strong reinforcing relationship between political and economic power.

The Athenians knew that an electoral system like ours could not deliver the kind of widespread prosperity and political equality that both they and we associate with the word 'democracy'. In fact, for thousands of years, it counted as received wisdom, at least among philosophers, that elections and democracy were not compatible.

So how did it come about that today elections and democracy *are* regarded as synonymous terms? Why do we believe so ardently that elections will deliver the political and economic emancipation we crave, when so far they have delivered only a handful of billionaires and unassailable career politicians?

The truth is that electoral democracy as we know it is a long con, although it was not originally intended to be one. In fact, we could say that most of the problems we are currently experiencing with democracy are not so much the product of conspiracy as of confusion. This stems from the very blueprint our societies chose to govern themselves by in the modern era, a blueprint that originated not in Athens, but from a very different civilization – Rome.

7

How Did Things Get to Be this Way? The Roman Republican System and the Founding Fathers of America

> ... in history you have a record of the infinite
> variety of human experience plainly set out for all
> to see: and in that record you can find for yourself
> and your country both examples and warnings:
> fine things to take as models, base things, rotten
> through and through, to avoid.
>
> Livy, Roman historian

So how did a term like 'democracy', which originally meant 'people power', come to be equated with passive acquiescence in a corporate-funded campaign system that funnels wealth upwards and relegates the vast majority of citizens to the role of yes-men, or, as Aristotle would have said, a condition little better than slavery?

The truth is that our form of government was never intended to give power to the people. At the time modern democracy was established, Athenian *demokratia* was already ancient history. European peoples had been living under an oppressive blend of absolute monarchy and theocratically validated feudalism for a thousand years. Finally, during the Renaissance, technological innovation as well as the rediscovery of ancient philosophy led to more and more people questioning the extent of both secular and religious rule. It is now accepted as common knowledge that the solution these dissatisfied individuals came up with was democracy, but the truth is (as usual) more complicated than that.

The first people to permanently abolish monarchy in the modern Western world were the Founding Fathers of the United States of America, i.e. the statesmen who founded the nation and drafted the American Constitution. These men may have been revolutionaries in the sense that they revolted against British rule, but they did not share the impetuous and idealistic disposition that we associate with the word 'revolutionary' today. For the most part, they were sober and respected pillars of society.

And while they may not have been fond of monarchy, they also categorically disapproved of democracy.

According to James Madison, fourth president of the United States and key architect of the American Constitution: 'democracies have ever been spectacles of turbulence and contention; have ever been found incompatible with personal security or the rights of property; and have in general been as short in their lives as they have been violent in their deaths'.[1]

Alexander Hamilton, the first Secretary of the Treasury, who worked tirelessly to have the Constitution ratified and whose portrait now graces the American $10 bill, agreed,

---

[1] James Madison, Federalist Paper no. 10, in *The Federalist Papers*, at 81.

stating: 'It has been observed that a pure democracy if it were practicable would be the most perfect government. Experience has proved that no position is more false than this. The ancient democracies in which the people themselves deliberated never possessed one good feature of government. Their very character was tyranny; their figure deformity.'[2]

Considering this starting position, it is hardly surprising that the Founding Fathers had no intention of inflicting a 'tyrannical' democracy on themselves. Instead, they set out to create a republic – that is, a system of government that is not ruled by a hereditary monarch. In doing so, they employed the same strategy as I have in this book; they searched for a historical precedent that they could learn from.

But, unlike me, the Founding Fathers found their precedent in the Roman Republic, the civilization that governed southern Europe, North Africa and parts of the Middle East from 509 to 27 BC. Like the Athenians, the Romans had long vanished, but they had left even more extensive records of their nation and government behind them. Thus, the Founding Fathers did not need to invent their new government from the ground up – they could borrow from history. And indeed, the United States borrowed a great deal from this ancient predecessor, from its public architecture (heavy on majestic marble pillars) and national symbol (the eagle) to the Romans' preferred way of selecting leaders – election.

This assiduous re-creation of the Roman way of government produced parallels between ancient Rome and the modern USA that probably go far deeper than even the Founding Fathers could have imagined. Indeed, one of

---

2 Hamilton, Speech on 21 June 1788 Urging Ratification of the Constitution in New York.

the most striking examples of these parallels lies in election itself. Although it pre-dated the founding of the United States of America by nearly two thousand years, if we look at the way the Roman Republic elected its leaders and the outcome of those elections, we can see that that the two societies – ancient republican Rome and modern American 'democracy' – are shockingly similar.

This is important because of the way the Roman Republic ended.

Athenian democracy came to a halt because Athens, along with every other country between Egypt and India, was conquered by the Kings of Macedonia – Philip II and his son Alexander the Great. It was an ending that came from outside of Athenian society and which was unrelated to the practice of democracy or any other internal factors.

But the Roman Republic was never conquered by foreign invaders, despite some close calls. Instead, the Republic imploded from inside, and when it did, it stopped being an electoral republic and started being an empire under the rule of one man only – the Caesar, or 'Emperor'. The Athenian downfall was caused by Alexander, but the Roman downfall was caused by Rome. And if we follow the pattern of that downfall, we can see how closely our society is mimicking it.

Roman politics: déjà vu

Unlike Athenian democracy, the Roman political system is easy to understand, precisely because it mirrors our own so closely. Nearly all public business in the Roman Republic was carried out by elected officials, with the highest offices arranged into a particular hierarchical order known as the *cursus honorum*. The most powerful post on the *cursus honorum* was that of consul. Only two consuls were elected each year and they served in a capacity similar to that of a modern prime minister or president.

The *cursus honorum* was complemented by two further important offices: censor and tribune of the plebs. While less powerful than consul, the post of censor was even more exclusive, since only two censors were elected every five years and only people who had previously been consuls were eligible for this post. The censors were responsible for supervising public morality by enforcing the *mos* (unwritten but nonetheless legally binding rules that obliged every Roman to conform to traditional values) and for conducting the census. The office of tribune of the plebs was less illustrious. These officials – ten in number – were charged with safeguarding the interests of Rome's plebeians, or 'commoners'.

Ascending the *cursus honorum* was of pivotal importance to all affluent or 'well-born' Romans, because doing so increased the level of respect they were due from others. Once a man attained a certain office, e.g. consul, he held that 'rank' for the remainder of his life and was entitled to be treated with deference by anyone who hadn't been able to match his success.

Election did not, however, merely provide social status. It also allowed the elected official to exercise very real power over his fellow citizens. Roman officials could enforce their own decrees, even if they had to use physical force to do so, and they were the only people who could table laws before the Senate and the Plebeian Council.

The Roman Senate is possibly the most famous political body in history. Toga-clad actors have depicted debate in this august forum in countless movies, and Roman official documents tended to sign off 'SPQR' – the Senate and People of Rome. As the phrase indicates, in Roman political thought there was a clear difference between these two entities, the Senate and the people.

The Senate was an extremely exclusive body. Seats were awarded only to the head of each of Rome's richest and most important families (often former officials themselves) and were retained for life. Officially, the Senate was empowered only to 'advise' Rome's most senior officials, the consuls, but because it was composed of an exclusive group of people who commanded great political and economic clout, its members, the Senators, were quite capable of thwarting any law that they disliked. Being 'advised' by the Senate was like being advised by Marlon Brando's 'Godfather' Vito Corleone – it tended to come in the form of an offer you couldn't refuse.

For the most part, the laws themselves were actually passed in the less powerful Plebeian Council, which every Roman commoner could attend. The Plebeian Council was the 'People' part of 'the Senate and People of Rome'. However, even here only sitting officials could table legislation (usually only consuls and plebeian tribunes) and the official who chose to propose a new law was entitled to control public debate about it. Thus, debate took place in a series of meetings known as *contiones* where only the presiding official himself and his prominent supporters and adversaries could speak, and then only at the official's invitation. Any citizen could privately express his view on the matter at hand, but he was never given the opportunity to do so in a public forum, much less take a leading role in proceedings. Unlike the Athenians, Roman citizens did not enjoy *isegoria*. Only those who had acquired sufficient status under the reigning political system could participate in public debate.

Thus, in its essential characteristics, Roman legislative activity closely resembled modern processes. Today, only elected politicians may table legislation or speak in Parliament or the Houses of Congress, and only eminent persons are invited to appear as guests in our *contiones* – television panels and newspaper columns. As in Roman times, anyone is free to voice his opinion privately, but all public debate is restricted to a small and carefully selected group of people, most of whom win the right to participate via election. Both today and in Rome there was a sharp dividing line between those who were elected and those who were not. And interestingly enough, the determining factors in getting elected were much the same in both societies.

Getting elected in Rome: know the right people and don't say the wrong thing

The similarity between Roman political campaigns and modern election campaigns is striking – indeed, the two are almost identical, not just in general approach, but right down to the details.

A Roman seeking election donned a specially whitened toga, called the *toga candida*, and walked the streets with his supporters, shaking hands and making small talk with ordinary citizens before asking for their vote; he avoided taking clear positions on the political issues of the day in the interests of appealing to the broadest range of voters; and he collected endorsements from other influential citizens. These endorsements were called *commendatio* and they were often painted on signs along the roads and on the walls of property owned by the candidate's supporters in a manner similar to the use of advertising billboards today. Citizens with political aspirations also drew attention to themselves and ensured that they stayed 'in the news' by throwing public banquets or other entertainments, even reserving good seats for influential citizens they wished to flatter. These tactics are all still in use today, with modern politicians often embarking on weeks, if not months, of hand-shaking and baby-kissing in the run-up to an election, while attempting not to be pinned down on their policies for fear of alienating needed votes. When it comes to public campaigning, both Roman and modern politicians prefer to focus on the optics of being a likeable and popular person, rather than on the substance of their views. In both civilizations these actions constitute the populist outward veneer of any serious campaign, and it is extraordinary that two societies so far removed in time and the external conditions of life should fall into such a very similar pattern.

But the parallels go deeper still. As today, winning high office in Rome was not just about gaining support, it was also about neutralizing opposition. Certain people were so powerful that any candidate had to avoid angering them if he wanted to stand a chance of winning an election. These included: anyone who had scaled the entire *cursus honorum* and obtained the post of censor; anyone who was even wealthier than usual (the 'billionaires' of the day, such as Marcus Licinius Crassus); popular military commanders like Pompey the Great and Gaius Marius, who could call on their loyal soldiers to follow their instructions at the polls; and political string-pullers such as Cethegus, an expert at blackmail. In modern electoral systems, these positions are filled by party functionaries, captains of industry and media tycoons, who fund candidates, hit-list their opponents and provide disproportionate coverage in their media outlets. The appearances might be a little different, but the basic idea is the same.

And as today, mounting such an election campaign was pretty nearly impossible for a Roman of average means to pull off. Ordinary people could not afford to throw public banquets and were unlikely to rub shoulders with top military commanders like Pompey the Great, so deciding leadership via election divided Roman society between those who could afford to be politically active and those who could not. And that suited the architects of the Roman political system just fine.

Rome's elite did not want everyone to participate equally in government because, much like the Founding Fathers of America, they did not think that everyone had the skills to make sound political decisions. At the same time, however, even rich and powerful Romans wanted every citizen to be able to say that he had a vote, since this was an integral part of the ideology behind republicanism and legitimized the power of officials and Senators. It may sound like a curious bit of ancient doublethink, but while they firmly rejected Athenian democracy, Romans just as firmly believed that the right of each citizen to cast a vote was an essential part of what differentiated them from the detested monarchies they encountered in Egypt and Mesopotamia. In contrast to these absolute systems, Roman political power could only be legitimized by its citizens' positive acquiescence. It was fundamental that the people say 'yes' to rule by the Senate and *cursus honorum* officials.

However, because the Senate and *cursus honorum* officials represented only the upper crust of Roman society, it is highly unlikely that Roman citizens as a whole would have continued to agree to their rule for very long had they truly had a choice. The Romans resolved this difficulty by creating a system which accorded everyone a vote but ensured that they could exercise those votes only in a highly inequitable manner.

Romans elected the *cursus honorum* officials in two different assemblies: the Tribal Assembly and the Centuriate Assembly, each of which was governed by its own curious rules.

The Tribal Assembly, where elections for the less important *cursus honorum* officials took place, was based, as its name indicates, on the Roman institution of the tribe.

All Roman citizens belonged to one of thirty-five tribes and all male Romans had the right to attend the Tribal Assembly, where they participated as a member of that tribe. With the exception of the Senate, participation in all Roman assemblies was a collective affair – each person in attendance cast a vote within his tribe and then the tribe cast one vote in the Assembly, in accordance with the way in which the majority of its members had voted. Which tribe a Roman belonged to was partly determined by their family's official place of domicile, but it was also hereditary, so citizens retained their original tribal membership even if their family moved elsewhere (usually into the city of Rome itself). It's a set of rules that seems neither here nor there at first glance, but these simple regulations actually created and perpetuated a system of deep political inequality that becomes apparent when one considers the context under which they operated.

Most of Rome's richest citizens were wealthy rural landowners and therefore they were officially domiciled not in

Figure 7.1 The Roman tribal assembly

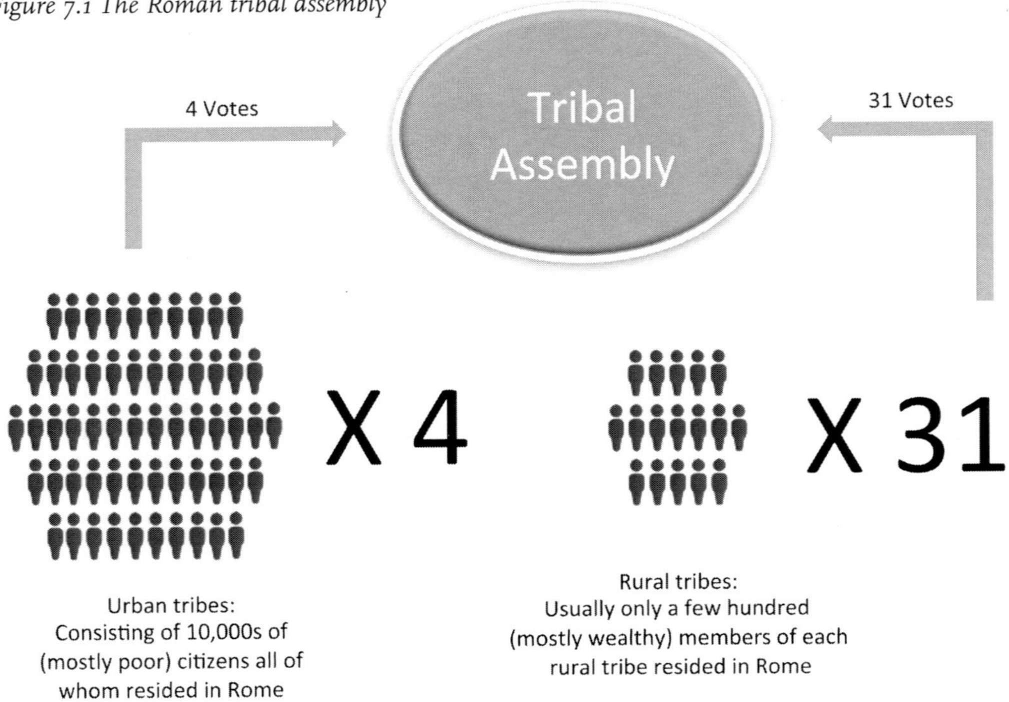

urban Rome but in a rural district, where they had significant holdings. These wealthy individuals were therefore always members of one of the rural tribes. This was advantageous, because Rome had thirty-one rural tribes but only four urban ones, and while the chances of a poor rural farmer travelling to Rome to vote on a regular basis were almost non-existent, wealthy landlords spent most of the year in Rome in a convenient position to exercise this privilege. Thus, some rural tribes had only a few hundred members resident in Rome while the urban tribes had tens of thousands. When an urban voter cast his vote within the tribe, it was diluted by thousands of others, whereas rural voters usually had a real impact on their tribe's final vote.

Needless to say, the thirty-one rural tribes that were usually stacked with Rome's wealthiest citizens had more in common with each other than they did with the four urban tribes. Through this malapportionment, Rome's wealthiest citizens controlled voting in the Tribal Assembly. This bias in favour of the wealthy was not an accident or the result of bad planning. According to the Roman historian Livy, one of Rome's earliest censors had purposely arranged the Tribal Assembly this way by 'cull[ing] out all the market-place mob and cast[ing] them into four tribes, to which he gave the name of "urban"' so that 'the elections might not be in the hands of the basest of the people'.[3] While it might have been more extreme, this type of 'gerrymandering' and malapportionment of the tribes is not much different to modern packing, cracking and other forms of malapportionment in which rural votes are also often nearly always given far more weight than urban ones.

---

3 Livy 9.46.14, quoted in Nicolet at 227.

And as biased as the Tribal Assembly was, the Centuriate Assembly, where election for the highest of the high offices took place, was even worse. In this assembly, citizens were arranged into 193 units, known as *centuriae*. These *centuriae* or 'centuries' were, in turn, organized into six classes based on economic status. The first class had 80 centuries, plus 18 centuries of *equites* (knights). The second, third and fourth classes held 20 centuries each and the fifth class held 30 centuries. The sixth class, composed of all those citizens who did not own significant property (known as the *proletarii* or 'proletariat'), was afforded a single century.

The centuries voted according to rank, i.e. first the knights voted, followed by the remaining centuries of the first class, who were, in turn, followed by the centuries of the second class, and so on. Each century was accorded one vote. As with the tribes, the direction of the century's vote was determined by the direction in which the majority of its members had cast theirs.

And as with the tribes, the number of citizens in each century varied widely. In fact, the first and second property classes, controlling well over 50 per cent of the centuries, made up only 'a very small proportion of Roman citizens'.[4] At the beginning of the Republic, patrician families, who would have comprised most, perhaps all, of the first class, accounted for only about one tenth of the population, and by the end of the Republic the single century of the *proletarii* contained more members than all the senatorial centuries combined. Because the *equites* and the rest of the first class controlled the majority of the *centuriae*, they could often carry

---

4 Staveley, *Greek and Roman Voting and Elections*, at 199.

Figure 7.2 The Roman centuriate assembly

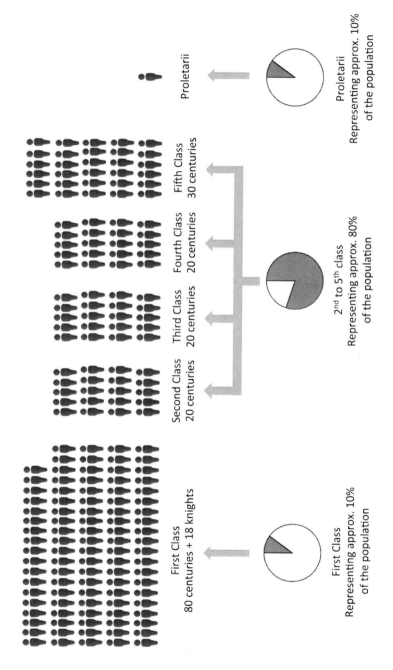

First Class
80 centuries + 18 knights

Second Class
20 centuries

Third Class
20 centuries

Fourth Class
20 centuries

Fifth Class
30 centuries

Proletarii

First Class
Representing approx. 10%
of the population

2nd to 5th class
Representing approx. 80%
of the population

Proletarii
Representing approx. 10%
of the population

a vote without the support of, or with only minimal support from, the lower four classes. In fact, since voting stopped as soon as a majority was reached, usually only the wealthiest citizens even got a chance to cast a vote.

As Livy recorded: '[t]he knights were called upon to vote first, then the eighty centuries of the first class; if there were any disagreement there, which rarely happened, it was provided that the centuries of the second class should be called; and they almost never descended so far as to reach the lowest citizens'.[5]

Cicero, a famous lawyer who lived during the final days of the Republic, justified this system, declaring: 'No one was deprived of the right of suffrage and yet he who had most to gain from the well-being of the State could use his voice to the greatest effect.'[6]

Thus, while everyone could technically vote, in reality only the wealthiest citizens were ever able to do so in any meaningful sense.

The Roman system may sound quite different at first, but bear in mind – modern Western democracies, by and large, did not reject the Roman idea of property-based suffrage. Instead most modern democracies restricted voting rights to those (usually white, male) citizens able to meet property requirements. Only after many years of struggle were these restrictions finally worn away, enabling citizens to cast votes regardless of their income level, gender or ethnicity. However, because an easily manipulable electoral system remained in place – a system essentially hostile to expanded participation – this more inclusive enfranchisement succeeded only in driving property qualifications underground.

5 Livy 1.43.11, quoted in Nicolet at 259.
6 Quoted in Staveley, op. cit., at 128.

Lack of property may be no bar to casting a vote in today's democracies, but property, or wealth, can still be used to win election. The influence of money *before* the ballot box is so pervasive in modern democracies as to create a situation that still largely reflects the Roman experience despite the fact that the present discrimination is more informal. In today's society, the wealthy – like the Roman elite before them – enjoy meaningful participation by virtue of being able to influence political debate and by contributing to candidate campaigns, while all others are restricted to far thinner participation by casting a ballot only, a ballot which, as we have seen in earlier chapters, is often of quite dubious value.

As Cicero would have said – no one is deprived of his right to vote, yet he who has the most to gain can use his voice to the greatest effect.

Competition for power as a Roman way of life

Owing to the high turnover of officials, who were elected every year, as well as the necessity of personally attending the legislative and electoral assemblies that were held approximately sixty days a year, participation in the political and legal system was quite intense for Rome's elite citizens, who genuinely made decisions among themselves on a truly competitive basis. However, the vast majority of citizens could not hope to run for office, rarely had a chance to cast a vote at the Centuriate Assembly and possessed nearly worthless votes in Rome's crowded urban tribes at the Tribal Assembly. Although Rome possessed facilities to accommodate 70,000 voters towards the end of the Republic, only about 17,000 citizens routinely had a chance to cast a vote before a majority was reached and voting stopped. With the total Roman population entitled to vote being 1,700,000, the participation rate for voting in the popular assemblies was thus one in a hundred. The Senate, the most influential political body, held only about three hundred seats, meaning that the participation rate in that body was only 0.0003 per cent of the total Roman voting population. This is exactly on a par with the current participation rate in the American Houses of Congress, but presents a marked contrast to Athenian democracy, where participation rates were better than one in ten at Assembly alone and one quarter of all citizens took some part in government every day. And just as high participation rates affected the political culture of Athens, these much lower participation rates had a profound effect on the political culture and economy of Rome.

Since Rome afforded very little opportunity for ordinary citizens to participate in politics, much less challenge the decisions of an official, whoever held office also held a great deal of power. Therefore, the entire Roman social hierarchy hinged around one event – the election. And the competition to win election only served to consolidate the already very concentrated political power even further in the hands of the few people who had the resources to be successful at it. This gave the competition to hold office a hereditary dimension – those born into privileged circumstances had exponentially higher chances of becoming successful politicians than those who were not.

To give an idea of this inequality, consider the position of the *nove homine*. This term means 'new man', and it is how the Romans referred to a person who was the first in his extended family to attain the rank of consul. Between 264 and 201 BC only eleven *novi homines* became consuls, while between 200 and 134 BC, the consulship remained almost exclusively in the hands of twenty-five families, with only five 'new' family names appearing in the records during this time. In other words, in the space of over sixty years, at two consuls per year, only five men were able to break into this elite circle of politicians and win the highest office in the land.

The Romans were far from ignorant of the fact that their electoral system resulted in these highly inegalitarian outcomes. Like their contemporaries, the Athenians, the Roman elite were well aware that it was much easier for wealthy, well-connected candidates to win elections, but unlike the Athenians they cherished elections for exactly this reason. Elections ensured that only a few select families could maintain a position of extreme wealth and privilege in exchange for showing only a minimum level of accountability to their fellow citizens. Stiff competition, far from being an expression of equality, actually *enabled* the most privileged to permanently exclude others from political life, as it was utterly unrealistic for the average person to 'compete' at the polls with someone born into a very wealthy family.

However, since all citizens had the nominal right to vote and all were free to earn money as they chose, the Roman system gave every citizen one important thing that kept them tied in: hope. It was *possible* to rise through the ranks, although generally only a short way over the course of a lifetime. Nonetheless, being a second-class citizen was certainly preferable to being a third- or fourth-class citizen; attaining any electoral rank, however lowly, was certainly better than none. This cherished hope of even its lowliest citizens to someday climb to the top was absolutely key to Rome's success as a civilization, and in the early years the idea of at least improving one's life circumstances was – much like the American Dream of past centuries – not all that far fetched. However, while the effort to out-compete one's neighbours and gain wealth and influence may have given meaning to Roman life, it was also a very confining ideology, one that eventually yielded grave consequences.

The Roman political and economic system was a ladder extending all the way from the top to the bottom of the social system. As long as Rome was expanding, citizens of all classes spent their time and energy in trying to work their way up that ladder. When the economy began to shrink, they concentrated on trying to maintain their position. The competitive nature of the system kept most Romans so focused on trying to 'win', or at least not to lose, that they were completely distracted from any other considerations. In other words, as we do today, most Romans simply accepted the need to earn the right to participate in political decision-making by winning election, and that the chances of winning were heavily tilted in favour of the rich. For the most part, they did not worry about whether this was a sensible or just way of running society, they merely tried to fix the problem by becoming rich themselves, by trying to climb that ladder and put themselves at the top.

This turned out to be a big mistake.

All sizzle and no steak: the Roman system rots at the core

Rome's entire political system was rigged in favour of the very people who held power. There were, however, still fewer positions of power available than there were elites who wanted to fill them. Even very privileged Romans were thus constantly involved in a game of political 'musical chairs' in which they continually fought the danger of being cut out of the decision-making process and reduced to, quite literally, second-class citizens. Security and success became increasingly ephemeral goods as Roman politicians did not just *want* to win, they *needed* to if they were to have any chance of holding on to their wealth and power. And since they were desperate, they learned to game the system in ways as unscrupulous as they were creative.

Corruption in Rome: from fake taxes to fraudulent festivals

By the time the Republic finally staggered to an end, corruption in Rome extended to all aspects of life.

As early as the second century BC aspiring politicians were openly offering all 100 members of the first-voting century (whose vote was accorded superstitious importance) financial rewards in exchange for their vote, despite harsh legal punishments for such behaviour. Vote-buying in Rome's assemblies had become so commonplace that it was impossible to enforce the laws against it; in just the final thirty years of the Republic, the Romans found it necessary to pass five laws against electoral corruption, a sure sign that there was something seriously wrong. And officials did not just bribe voters, influential voters bribed officials as well. Of all the Roman magistrates, censors were particularly well placed to pay back loyalty at the polls, because – much as the World Bank and IMF do today – they granted mining concessions, as well as public contracts for building aqueducts and roads, and repairing public buildings.

The necessity to continually buy votes, whether directly with cash or indirectly with favours, made running for high office very expensive even by the standards of Rome's affluent citizens. To offset these expenses, most politicians took to enriching themselves wherever they could, often at the expense of the public good. Governorship offered particularly lucrative possibilities here. Most high officials were sent to govern one of Rome's provinces for a year following their term of office, and they often used the opportunity to restore their financial fortunes. The Sicilian governor Verres went down in history for having his assistants invent an entire range of fictitious charges and fees, the proceeds of which went directly into their own and Verres' pockets. While most Roman notables tried to distance themselves from such flagrant examples, the truth is that by the mid-second century BC extortion by governors had become so commonplace that a standing criminal court had to be established in Rome to deal exclusively with this issue.

Not that that helped much: political abuse of the court system was also rampant. While Roman juries, at seventy-five members, were far larger than their modern equivalents, they were still small enough for a very wealthy person to be able to bribe. The Romans frequently resorted to this practice, and when they did, they did not stop at bribing juries to have themselves acquitted – they also bribed to have their enemies convicted. This could be as exhausting as it was frightening – one famous politician had at least forty-four politically motivated charges brought against him during his career. The practice of bribery became so flagrant that a well-known lawyer by the name of Hortensius 'actually had voting tablets of different colours distributed to those whom he had bribed, so as to ensure that he received value for money'.[7] It is not surprising to learn in this context that

---

7 Nicolet, op. cit., at 335.

some Roman texts speak casually of the poor being unable to initiate criminal trials against members of the elite, no matter how grievous the crime.

Even the religious arena was not exempt from political corruption. The yearly calendar as well as festival dates were set by Rome's priests, who were always members of the upper classes and very active in the secular world. Priests could schedule festivals for inconvenient times or declare festivals that had already occurred to have been faulty and demand that they be repeated in order to maximize interference with planned legislation. If this failed to produce results, they could literally shorten the calendar year so as to limit an opponent's time to introduce unwanted legislation.

As the desperation to win at any cost became more extreme, Romans did not hesitate to physically disrupt voting by removing the necessary equipment, such as the ballot urns, or by turning to outright violence by hiring gangs to intimidate voters or prevent them from entering the voting arena. If all else failed, a serious Roman politician would not hesitate to assassinate a political opponent. In fact, during the latter part of the Republic at least one major politician was killed every five to ten years, often together with a number of his more prominent associates.

By the end of the Republic, Roman politicians were so focused on bringing their rivals down that they'd permanently forgotten they were supposed to be running a country. Inevitably, under such circumstances, the crises began to mount.

Competition led to desperation which led to corruption. Corruption, in turn, led to instability. Towards the end of the Republic, all that could be said for certain was that any political battle was likely to be won by whoever had the most wealth and the least scruples. In other words, the political system of election placed an unsustainable level of pressure on the people practising it, and thereby completely undermined itself, becoming a free-for-all where the worst, rather than the best, human tendencies prevailed.

$100 million villas and never-ending debt:
inequality increases and things fall apart

Because Rome's economy and politics were closely intertwined – as our own are today – the political implosion of Rome was accompanied by increasing economic distress. Economic inequality in the Republic was extreme. The average income was only 380 sesterces per year. By contrast, the 'impoverished' aristocrat L. Aemilius Paullus died with a fortune of a mere 1,440,000 sesterces on his hands (about $130 million). Cicero is on record as stating that 100,000 sesterces a year (about $9 million) would permit a gentleman only a very frugal life and that 600,000 per year ($54 million) would be necessary to live in great luxury. He himself paid 3,500,000 sesterces (over $300 million) for a villa in Rome. Wealth discrepancy was thus much greater than in neighbouring Athens. We know that very wealthy Athenians possessed fortunes equivalent to about 150–200 times the average wage of unskilled labour, and that the very, very wealthiest may have possessed estates worth up to 1,200 times the average wage of unskilled labour, but Cicero (by no means the richest of his contemporaries) proposed to spend roughly 250 times the *average* annual wage (of all sectors of society, not just unskilled workers) *each year* just to live 'frugally'.

Unsurprisingly, in this situation of extreme economic disparity, indebtedness of the poor to the rich and the rich

to the richer remained a constant economic strain. Much
of the law of the early Republic focused on alleviating the
debt burden in the interests of balancing the economy: for
example, the *Lex Duillia* (357 BC) halved interest rates, the
Lex Genucia (342 BC) abolished interest on loans and the *Lex
Poetilia* (326 or 313 BC) abolished *nexum* (a form of bond servitude) for debt. In addition, Rome took action to combat the
effects of extreme poverty: the tax burden fell on the wealthy
to the relief of the poor, and everyone was entitled to receive
grain at subsidized prices.

However, because Roman public life still revolved around
competing for power and because wealth and political
power were inextricably linked to each other, none of these
measures could prevent the ever greater concentration of
wealth in the hands of ever fewer individuals.

Rent-seeking activities like moneylending became more
important sources of income for the very rich and increasing
numbers of ordinary people became indebted to the point
of no return, eventually joining the masses of propertyless
proletarii when banks foreclosed on their farms and businesses. The property of defaulters was usually bought up by
the very rich at knockdown prices and added to their own
expansive slave-worked estates and factories.

Although it was in the short-term interests of each
wealthy individual to engage in such activities, which did
bring in higher short-term profits, overall it sent the Roman
economy into another loop on its downward spiral. Middle-
class farmers and artisans were unable to compete with
huge slave-worked enterprises, because slave labour was
always cheaper than free labour. So while the highly efficient slave-worked enterprises produced cheap goods and

59

made huge profits, they also pushed even more middle-class Romans into bankruptcy. In other words, the Roman economy was quite similar to the present-day one in which banking and finance have become the most lucrative industries and multinational corporations bankrupt small businesses by flooding the market with goods produced by developing-world citizens 'employed' under conditions not very different to those experienced by Roman slaves. The effects of this type of economy – the swift erosion of the middle class – are also identical.

In both societies this problem was caused by a system of government that allowed people with political power to reward themselves, sometimes through active means like handing out lucrative contracts (like IMF and World Bank projects, Roman public works were built by private contractors who were invariably very wealthy), but mainly by crushing any attempts at reform that were detrimental to their own short-term material interests.

It seems incredibly selfish, but Rome's elite was so focused on grasping as much power and wealth for themselves in the vicious struggle for survival at the top that it was actually very difficult for them to act differently. In fact, the need to focus all one's energy on snatching short-term advantages while suppressing all other considerations was so strong that the Romans did not turn their economy around, even though *they knew* that their policies were unsustainable. In fact, Rome produced more than a few politicians who attempted to fix the political and economic system before it was too late. Their actions and invariable fate deliver a cautionary tale for our own society.

The Gracchi brothers and land reform:
showdown between the people and Senate of Rome

Tiberius and Gaius Gracchus – known collectively as 'the Gracchi' – were two of Rome's most remarkable politicians. Although the Gracchi brothers were born to an extremely privileged family and were therefore assured of becoming highly successful politicians without ever having to particularly distinguish themselves, Tiberius, the elder of the two brothers, developed a deep interest in the social problems of his day. One problem in particular came to Tiberius' attention again and again: the issue of land distribution.

When the Romans conquered other peoples (which they regularly did) they often acquired new tracts of land. These lands were considered to be public property: after all, they had been obtained through a public body – the Roman army. This property was supposed to be distributed for use among the general public according to a certain formula. However, for centuries the very wealthy had managed to appropriate a proportion of these public lands that far exceeded what they were entitled to under the law. They used this new property to create vast farms and ranches known as *latifundia* that were worked by their slaves. Because slave labour was cheaper than free labour, this practice bankrupted smaller farmers, who were shunted off the land to become members of the urban proletariat, while the rich took over their farms and added them to their *latifundia*. When small farmers were forced off their land, they and their families often came to depend on Roman welfare to survive; that is, they became recipients of the Roman grain dole and a drain on the Roman public purse. To add to these woes, when middle-class farmers lost their property, they also lost their eligibility to enter the army, because they could not afford to purchase weapons or armour. This was not only detrimental to the citizens affected, it was bad for the military capabilities of Rome as a state, and Tiberius decided that it had to stop.

When he was elected as tribune of the plebs in 133 BC, Tiberius proposed a significant land reform through a law known as the *Lex Sempronia Agraria*. The centrepiece of this law was a provision that anyone who occupied an illegally high proportion of public land would have to return it to the state for redistribution to the landless poor. By no means naive, Tiberius offered two measures to the rich to help sweeten this bitter pill. Firstly, although he had obtained the land illegally in the first place, the occupier would be compensated by the state for the property he was obliged to relinquish. Secondly, Tiberius specifically entitled the occupier to retain an additional portion of land for each of his children, a measure which would de facto benefit only the very wealthy and allow them to provide handsomely for their offspring. This was very important, because it meant that the law would not deprive the elite's children of their privileged place in the social hierarchy. They would continue to enjoy the enormous advantages of their birth. The rest of the public land would be distributed to the poor, which meant that they would no longer be poor and that they would also be eligible for taxation and military service again.

Despite the considerable sweeteners offered to the rich and the obvious importance of the law for Rome's well-being, it was virulently opposed by the vast majority of wealthy citizens, who hysterically claimed that Tiberius was seeking to redistribute wealth and incite social revolution. To these super-rich citizens, who had acquired much of their property at public expense, any effort to rebalance Rome's collapsing economy by adequately enforcing its laws was not a necessary medicine, but 'class warfare' in which not the landless poor but wealthy, *latifundia*-operating Senators were the victims.

Instead of respecting Tiberius' rights as a tribune of the plebs, these Senators sought to thwart him in numerous ways, from having their servants steal the voting equipment when Tiberius' land reform bill was set to pass, to persuading another tribune to veto his every action. Tiberius fought back with equally unorthodox methods, having the troublesome tribune deposed (an unprecedented event) and using his own powers to shut down Rome's civic business. Although the forces arrayed against Tiberius were formidable, his proposal was extremely popular among all but the very richest members of society. It even enjoyed some support from Senators who were prepared to admit the necessity of the reforms. Therefore, it is not terribly surprising that Tiberius won this contest of wills with the Senate and succeeded in having the *Lex Sempronia Agraria* passed.

But having finally got his reform package off the ground, Tiberius decided to keep a good thing going. He did the unthinkable – he decided to run for the office of tribune of the plebs for a second consecutive year on an even more ambitious platform of reform. This was a shock to the Senators, who had thought that they had weathered the worst Tiberius could throw at them. Unwilling to stomach further reforms, the Senate ordered the consuls to kill Tiberius. Such an order represented an unheard-of departure from Roman custom and morals. The Roman Constitution absolutely forbade the use of any physical force against a tribune of the plebs, and this rule was considered one of the most important tenets of the entire Roman civilization.

The consuls of the time, showing considerably more class than the rest of the Senate, chose to obey the law and refused to carry out the Senate's orders. At which point the anti-Tiberius Senators took matters into their own hands. They armed themselves, their slaves and their vassals, and marched off to confront the man who had caused them so much misery. Tiberius, who was holding a meeting of the Plebeian Council at the time, was warned of these developments by a sympathetic Senator. Tiberius' supporters quickly armed themselves as best they could with clubs and staves. However, they were no match for the organized Senators, and in the ensuing brawl Tiberius and several hundred of his supporters were beaten to death – Tiberius himself allegedly meeting his end at the hands of a Senator wielding a bench leg. Such was the unreasoning rage of Rome's wealthiest Senators that, not content with Tiberius' death, they again violated custom by throwing his body into the river, and then launching a purge of his surviving supporters, executing many more.

This onslaught of violence achieved its goal: Tiberius' efforts at reform were halted.

But where one brother failed, another would try again. Gaius Gracchus was nine years younger than Tiberius. However, before long he too embarked upon a successful career, much to the chagrin of the Senate, and was, like his brother before him, also elected tribune of the plebs on a reformist platform no less necessary or popular than his brother's had been. According to legend, Gaius' candidacy for the tribuneship was opposed by every wealthy citizen, but so many ordinary people from all over Italy made the effort to travel to Rome to vote in his favour that they booked out every hotel in the city and succeeded in having him elected.

Following his election, Gaius proposed several laws which the Senate – predictably – found incendiary, including granting land to colonist settlers, clothing poor soldiers at public expense, increasing voting rights for Latins and Italians, and lowering the price of grain for the poor. These reforms enjoyed such broad support that despite the skewed voting arrangements in the assemblies, Gaius succeeded in having all of them passed. However, relations between Gaius and the Senate steadily deteriorated, especially when he was re-elected tribune and proposed more new laws, including building new colonies and completely enfranchising the Latins, a group of people who held a form of second-class citizenship. Perhaps Gaius' most revolutionary suggestion was that the centuries be called to vote by lot rather than the pre-ordained wealthiest-to-poorest order.

As a consequence of his vigour in pursuing these ambitious reforms, the Senate redoubled its efforts to undermine Gaius, and he failed in his bid to be elected tribune of the plebs for a third consecutive year. Following his removal from politics, wealthy Senators managed to have several of his laws overturned. To add insult to injury, during a public assembly convened by the Senate-friendly consul Opiumus, one of Opiumus' servants went out of his way to provoke a group of Gaius' followers as he passed them. The exchange between the two sides quickly escalated and a member of Gaius' party killed the servant. This was the mistake that Rome's elite had been waiting for.

The Senate immediately invested Opiumus with extraordinary powers to deal with Gaius under the pretext that the manslaughter committed by one of Gaius' associates in the midst of an argument proved Gaius to be a dangerous and violent man. In the ensuing debacle, Opiumus proved to be cut from different cloth than the consuls who had refused to kill the first of the Gracchi over a decade earlier. When Gaius' followers attempted to reconcile with him, he subjected them to an almost military-grade assault, even employing a body of Cretan archers to rain arrows down on them. The attack succeeded in killing most of the supporters who were with Gaius at the time. Gaius survived the attack, but ordered his slave to kill him so as to prevent him being taken alive. Following Gaius' death, Opiumus rounded up 3,000 of his sympathizers who had not been present and summarily executed them.

The utter destruction of the Gracchi and all who supported them was a major turning point in Roman history as Rome's elite, which had set up the political system, refused to respect the outcomes of that system when they ran counter to their own selfish wishes. The Gracchi's laws were sensible and necessary for the long-term well-being of the nation; the fact that they could have these reforms passed in the heavily stacked Roman assemblies attests to their overwhelming popularity with all but the richest of the rich. Without the Senate's repeated interference, these laws would have been implemented in compliance with Rome's normal legal procedures. However, Rome's elite were so tied in to the demanding over-competitive structure of power acquisition that the thought of giving up even the tiniest of advantages quite literally drove them mad and compelled them to thwart the change that was so obviously needed.

The Gracchan effort at reform was a turning point, but Rome failed to turn.

And because the Republic failed to develop, it collapsed into a dictatorship.

The end of the republic: a bang, a whimper and a brand-new Emperor

The deaths of the Gracchi signalled the end the gentleman's agreement between Rome's elite. Electoral competition became even more vicious and politicians no longer scrupled to whip their supporters into a state of hysteria to further their own chances at the polls. Rational discourse was all but abandoned, embarking on political reform became virtually equivalent to suicide, and leading Romans encouraged their followers to adopt personality cults with themselves at the centre. Soon no one was in control of the nation, which was racked by civil war and endless strife. Eventually, when Julius Caesar was assassinated half a century after the demise of the Gracchi, his heir, Octavian, managed to seize power in a Republic worn out by turmoil and remould it into an empire with himself at the helm. We know him today as the Emperor Augustus. He was followed by more emperors for 500 years. The Roman Republic never returned.

Forgotten fathers: anti-federalists, republicans and the battle for the US Constitution

Notwithstanding its unhappy demise, the political system of Republican Rome was copied by the Founding Fathers of the

United States, down to the architecture, the eagle and the name of its highest political body – the Senate. And they did so despite the fact that when it was first created, its potential negative consequences were already understood.

Contrary to popular opinion, the United States and its political institutions were not created in an atmosphere of tranquil consensus, but rather in the midst of a fierce debate between two groups of American political thinkers. One group, known as the Federalists, favoured a more centralized government that would operate on the basis of national elections covering four-year periods, while another group, known as the Anti-Federalists, favoured a more diffuse system in which more power would reside in the individual states, whose representatives would be elected for shorter intervals.

The Federalists proposed to create a twenty-six-member Senate and a sixty-five-member House of Representatives to legislate for national issues. At the time, shortly after the American Revolution, there were, of course, only thirteen sparsely populated states, so this meant that there would be one national representative for every 30,000 citizens, a much higher ratio than there is today. Nonetheless, Anti-Federalists objected to the Federalist plan, pointing out that the Rhode Island Assembly alone had 70 members, while the Virginia House of Delegates had 150 and the House of Representatives in Massachusetts 400. In other words, most states had more representatives at state level than the Federalists proposed to have at national level. These state representatives also rotated much more frequently, sometimes as often as every six months.

According to the Anti-Federalists, the Federalist plans did not include sufficient representation at the national level to accurately reflect the preferences of the people. With so few seats available, 'only prominent lawyers, or military heroes or the most prosperous merchants in a state could possibly be known by enough people to get elected'.[8] Even George Mason, a Founding Father himself, admitted that the new national representation would offer 'not the Substance, but the Shadow only of Representation'.[9] This was no good to the Anti-Federalists because, like the Athenians before them, they were concerned with equality and thought that democracy depended upon participation by the *average* person. According to the prominent Anti-Federalist Melancton Smith, representatives should be 'a true picture of the people; possess the knowledge of their circumstances and their wants; sympathize in all their distresses and be disposed to seek their true interests', while the Anti-Federalist writer 'The Federal Farmer' stated: 'a fair representation, therefore, should be so regulated, that every order of men in the community, according to the common course of elections, can have a share in it'[10] and that the state legislatures 'are so numerous as almost to be the people themselves'.[11]

The Anti-Federalists were not opposed to prominent or wealthy individuals being elected, but thought enough seats would need to be available to allow a large number of 'average' citizens to be elected, too. By severely limiting the number of national representatives, the Federalist proposal

---

8 Melancton Smith, quoted in Storing, *The Complete Anti-Federalist*, vol. VI.
9 George Mason, 'Objections to the Constitution of Government formed by the Convention', ibid., vol. II, at 11.
10 Smith, ibid., vol. I, cited at 17 and Federal Farmer, Letter II, ibid. vol. II at 230, respectively.
11 Federal Farmer, Letter XII, ibid., vol. II at 300.

would create a situation similar to the one that had existed in Rome, where competition for powerful positions was fierce. On a national level, the middle-class citizens who participated in state assemblies would become small fish in a big pond, unable to compete with the rich and famous for the limited seats available, and once elected only these rich and famous individuals would make all decisions to the exclusion of everyone else. Owing to their privileged position, they would not be able to accurately reflect majority preferences, because they could not possess true knowledge of the circumstances or wants of most people, nor sympathize in their distresses.

The Federalists, our 'Founding Fathers', entirely agreed with the Anti-Federalists about the consequences that restricted representation would have, but they thought that these effects were a good thing. They alleged that democracy was chaotic, lawless and enabled 'lower orders to ruin the great'.[12] Moreover, the 'extended republic [that they intended to create] should not take public opinion in its raw form'. Rather, it was 'to refine and enlarge the public views by passing them through the medium of a chosen body of citizens'.[13] Even George Mason, the Founding Father most sympathetic to Anti-Federalist views, agreed that the president should not be directly elected because 'an act which ought to be performed by those who know most of eminent characters and qualifications' would then 'be performed by those who know least',[14] while Alexander Hamilton stated

---

12 Wolin, 'Fugitive democracy', 31 at 36 et seq.
13 Madison, Federalist Paper no. 10, at 82.
14 Mason, quoted in Fishkin, *Democracy and Deliberation: New Directions for Democratic Reform*, at 93.

that the republican principle 'does not require an unqualified complaisance to every sudden breeze of passion or to every transient impulse which the public may receive from the arts of men who flatter their prejudices to betray their interests'.[15]

Small wonder, then, that:

> The framers sought at every turn to minimize the effect of popular participation, creating multiple layers of government, large election districts, and indirect, staggered elections. The message would be that ordinary people were not the sort to understand the issues of politics. They were competent only to grant or withhold their consent, approve or reject the actions of the elite.[16]

Just like Rome, the American system created a political landscape that could function without a monarch but which did not allow the vast majority of people to exercise any political power. Instead all power was vetted by elected gatekeepers who could be trusted to have acceptable priorities. The fractional level of 'representation' that the Founding Fathers permitted actually served to exclude most citizens from any share in government, just as they, their Anti-Federalist opponents, the Athenians and Romans all knew that it would. Ironically, however, the institutions they created – Congress, the Senate, the president and the Supreme Court – have been emulated the world over, becoming, in the process, synonymous with the term 'democracy'.

---

15 Hamilton, Federalist Paper no. 71, at 432.
16 Nedelsky, *Private Property and the Limits of American Constitutionalism: The Madisonian Framework and Its Legacy*, at 205.

The Founding Fathers were heavily influenced by the British Empire that they had grown to adulthood under, and not nearly so revolutionary as we give them credit for. Educated to the standards of the time, they were also ignorant of many things we know to be fact today. It is likely that some of their antagonistic views on democracy and the dangers of the 'common man' stemmed not only from prejudice, but also from misinformation.

The Founding Fathers knew comparatively little about how democracy was practised in ancient Athens, and what they did know was often acquired from strongly biased sources. Literacy was not very widespread in democratic Athens, and even for those who were literate, writing something as long as a political tract or book would have been a laborious and expensive process. Therefore, most of the political treatises that have surfaced from ancient Athens were written by very wealthy individuals. These individuals had the time and resources to lavish on writing, but they also tended to dislike democracy as a system of government because it had displaced them as the 'natural' rulers of the country. Despite the clear bias in many of these writings, until history began to be systematically studied as an academic discipline, most of these early writers' opinions were not only read out of context, they were also accepted as fact. This prejudiced many earlier thinkers against democracy.

At the same time, preserved writings from the Roman Republic were almost always written by the oligarchs. Unsurprisingly, Rome's richest and most powerful citizens had a very positive view of their government, and relying on these sources led influential Federalist thinkers like James Madison to incorrect conclusions. Madison claimed, for example, that the tribunes of the plebs – the representatives of the people – nearly always triumphed over the Senate and that the Republic ended when they triumphed over it completely. We now know this to be false. The tribunes themselves were often members of Rome's elite and while they tended to be more progressive than other politicians, Rome's history is littered with the corpses of those tribunes who pursued reforms that met with senatorial disapproval. The Gracchi were only two of the most prominent of these. Rome's plebeian tribunes did not triumph in protecting the interests of all non-elite members of society. They failed and they failed badly.

We now know what the Founding Fathers had not quite grasped: that by placing wealth and power in a mutually enhancing relationship, both became concentrated in ever fewer hands, excluding the vast majority of citizens and their interests from any share in the decision-making process. The increasing pressure on Rome's elite to win election at all costs set off a competition so fierce that it triggered decades of political assassination and civil war. Rome decayed *from the inside* and it decayed into an absolute dictatorship.

Because our 'democracies' operate in nearly exactly the same way as the Roman Republic did, it should be no surprise that they suffer exactly the same shortcomings. There are great wealth discrepancies and there is rampant corruption, elections have become the preserve of the rich, and the rich get richer while the poor get poorer. If this is left unchecked, we may well eventually suffer a similar fate to the Roman Republic.

The Anti-Federalists tried to avert this outcome, but their very name suggests the failing that is commonly attributed to their movement – they were 'anti'-Federalists with a stronger idea of what they were against than what they were for. This is one of the key reasons that they lost the battle around American unification.

Our societies today are suffering from a similar problem.

Many of us know what we are *against* – that's fairly easy, not many people are for corruption or extreme income disparities – but we don't know what we are *for*.

It's hard to make real change when you don't have a very clear idea of what you are trying to achieve.

The rest of this book is going to talk about what we could do differently to make our society more democratic and reverse the problems I illustrated in the earlier chapters.

PART II

8

The Way Forward: Digital Democracy

> You never change things by fighting the existing
> reality. To change something, build a new model
> that makes the existing model obsolete.
>
> Buckminster Fuller

The long-term dangers of electoral democracy

The fundamental problem in using an electoral system over
a prolonged period of time is that it concentrates wealth and
power by placing them in a mutually enhancing relationship
– you can always use one to get more of the other. This leads
to deepening inequality, widespread corruption and arbitrary
electoral outcomes that only get worse over time. Eventually,
such systems tend to relapse into more authoritarian styles
of government once wealth and power have become sufficiently concentrated for one person or faction to be able to
seize all of it.

Even if this doesn't occur, a political system like ours
that excludes the vast majority of people from having any
effect on decision-making is hardly going to be capable of

delivering decisions that are in their best interests. There's just no motivation for any such behaviour since 'the people' do not have any effective way of rewarding those who care for them. Much the opposite: those who are given power in representative systems have incentives to reward the private interests that help them. When the entire system incentivizes certain behaviour, that is the behaviour a society will end up having to live with – a few altruistic individuals valiantly swimming against the stream notwithstanding. We saw how this played out in the Roman Republic, where the efforts of well-meaning individuals were unable to turn the tide and avert the consequences inherent in a system where the incentives did not lie in satisfying majority interest.

Why international power cannot fix democracy

To complicate matters, we know that in our societies there is an international dimension to decision-making where popular accountability is even more strained than it was in the Roman Republic and where the incentives to cater to wealth and power are even higher. When it comes to reforming democracy, modern thinkers are faced with a complicated two-tier power game, in which the upper, international, tier is even more warped and corrupted than the lower, national, tier of decision-making.

This international dimension to the problem is the reason why some of the most popular ideas put forward on political reform cannot achieve the results that they seek. This is especially true of those suggestions that are aimed at circumventing the problems with national democracy by transferring more decision-making authority to international bodies. This theoretical 'global democracy' is sometimes envisaged as a World Parliament with citizens voting directly for their global representative. However, the idea may also take other forms, such as creating a web of cooperation between regional parliaments and an international assembly. In some variations these reforms are accompanied by a plan to extend Security Council membership to other powerful states, such as China, Germany or Japan, and to abolish permanent members' vetoes, as well as measures to allow citizens who do not already live under representative democracies to be represented by NGOs at international level. All of these ideas, sometimes referred to collectively as 'cosmopolitan democracy', seem to favour a sort of international enlightened despotism that is heavily focused on safeguarding citizen rights and cutting states and governments, with all of their problems, out of the picture.

It is a tempting but regrettably naive solution.

Like national representatives, global representatives would wield immense power – just even more of it. And that means that they would be subjected to tremendous pressure from special interest groups. We can clearly see this already playing out at the international organizations we do have, where representatives are caught in a vice between domestic corporate sponsors and international lobby groups. And the same is true in the one place where citizens already elect representatives to a supranational parliament – the European Union.

The European Union focuses heavily on the kind of paternalistic rule-giving and rights enforcement favoured by cosmopolitan democrats, but it has also become a focal point for interest groups that are attracted by its ability to set laws for a much larger area than national European parliaments can.

There are already over 30,000 lobbyists resident at the EU's seat in Brussels and the work of the European Roundtable of Industrialists, examined earlier, is a pointed demonstration of what just one such group can manage to achieve. By concentrating political power even further by creating parliaments that cover wider territories with larger populations, we are actually setting up a one-stop shop for powerful organizations to manipulate and corrupt that power.

State governments do not make bad decisions because they are nationalist or because their citizens do not care enough about people in other countries – they make bad decisions because even the smallest state government wields a lot of power over its territory and citizens and that power attracts precisely those sectors of society who *know* that they will never be able to get most people to agree to their policies by any fair means, but nonetheless are not about to give up on having them implemented. This is why the most powerful states tend to make the 'worst' decisions when examined from an altruistic or majority-interest point of view. The more power a government has, the more pressure it will be subjected to from powerful interest groups, precisely because it is in the best place to give them what they want.

It is not because the United States of America is a horrible country or Americans are stupid or uncaring people that its elections are the most out of control in terms of spending and negative campaign strategy – it is because the USA has been the world's only superpower for a long time and because it has a controlling stake in so much of the world's governing apparatus at the IMF, the World Bank and the United Nations. Winning an important election in the USA simply means more than winning in Canada or Germany.

Therefore, this is where private interests have sunk most of their time and effort into corrupting the system. If power is heavily concentrated in one place or person, then seizing control of that place or person makes that power yours.

Just imagine what these special interests would do if they could apply pressure directly on an international level without the inconvenience of having to work at one remove through state representatives.

Cosmopolitan democrats often assume that laws would stop this kind of abuse, but laws are for people who have at least some interest in obeying them, either because the incentive to disobey them is limited or because the punishment or risk for doing so is too great. That is not the case when control of the entire world economy and political system is literally the prize for success, and it is especially not the case when the potential perpetrators of corruption are intelligent and careful people who enjoy a high rate of success at whatever they put their minds to. When rewards are huge and chances of success high, you cannot stop people from breaking laws no matter what the penalty. You can defeat them only by removing the reward.

And you do this not by concentrating political power, but by making it more diffuse.

And thanks to the Athenians, we have some pretty good ideas of how this could be done.

Digital democracy takes off: citizens' budgets and crowdsourced constitutions

We know that over two thousand years ago, the Athenians replaced their electoral system with a sophisticated form of direct democracy, but until recently this knowledge was not very helpful. Unlike in Athens, citizens in most modern states are spread out over such a large area that it is impossible for them to engage in face-to-face communication with each other. Therefore, as we saw in the last chapter, even the Anti-Federalists continued to favour some form of electoral representation after the United States gained independence from Britain in the late eighteenth century. Over the years and decades that have elapsed since that debate, communications technology has improved, but nothing – neither telephone, telegram, radio nor television – could approximate face-to-face communication between citizens as it existed in Athens.

Today things are very different. In fact, it would now be easier to implement direct democracy in a large nation like the United States than it was for the Athenians to practise it over their own limited territories – thanks to the internet.

In fact, the internet has already had a huge impact on traditional representative democracy. In some nations voters no longer have to physically appear at the ballot box in order to cast their vote. Estonia has allowed internet voting in all local, parliamentary and European elections since 2005. In that time, the number of citizens who cast ballots over the internet has steadily increased, with one third of voters casting a ballot online in the national elections of 2015. Likewise, Switzerland has pioneered several projects that make use of internet voting in referenda and elections over the past ten years. Both of these countries are managing a smooth transition to online voting that is secured by personal cards, PINs and question-identifiers. Voters who do not want to use an ID card can register with their mobile phone number and receive PIN codes via SMS.[1]

These national efforts have been directed at using the internet to replace actions that citizens are capable of doing physically, such as voting in referenda or elections.

But what if we used the capabilities provided by the internet for more than that?

What if, instead of just using the internet to make what we've been doing all along a little more convenient, we used it to institute *real* democracy, that is, participatory democracy?

This is not only possible, but already happening.

One example is participatory budgeting. Participatory budgeting allows citizens to vote on how public budget funds are allocated. Originating in Porto Alegre, Brazil, in the late 1980s, the practice of participatory budgeting has spread around the world, including to major metropolises like New York, London and Toronto.

Until recently, participatory budgeting was exercised offline, through traditional paper ballot voting and face-to-face assembly meetings. It has also generally been restricted to discretionary spending, meaning that certain matters. such as debt or pension payments, are not put up for debate. In fact, participatory budgeting is often used purely to allo-cate spending on cultural projects. Despite these limitations, participation is already quite high, showing how eager many citizens are to participate in making the decisions that affect their lives. What is more, far from spending money on bread and games – the outcome so often gloomily predicted by detractors of participatory democracy – citizens tend to vote

[1] Votes are checked against a central register of voters to prevent voter fraud.

in an exemplary manner. Investing in education tends to be the most popular budgetary choice, followed by meeting the needs of children, the elderly and disabled. Environmental projects and road safety are also very popular. Some citizens even advocate saving the money or reimbursing it to taxpayers rather than spending it.

Participatory budgeting has proved to be a deeply empowering project the world over, as citizens take control of local priority-setting and pursue the policies that deliver lasting, long-term benefits for their communities. Municipalities that use participatory budgeting have shown substantial progress on social equality with better access to public goods like education and sanitation.

And it is now going online with citizens not only casting their votes but also making suggestions for projects over the internet. Online participatory budgeting has been used in Cambridge, Massachusetts, the Borough of Windsor and Maidenhead in England, the city of Cologne in Germany and in Paris. In some of these municipalities, online voters decide how millions of dollars will be spent each year – and, whether they know it or not, they are also engaging in a practice that closely resembles the democracy of ancient Athens. The potential to scale up participatory budgeting for national use is already obvious.

Citizens' assemblies provide another avenue for online politics to work. These assemblies are often loosely based (intentionally or not) on the Athenian model. Over the past few decades, randomly selected assemblies have debated and proposed changes to election laws in the provinces of Ontario and British Columbia in Canada, as well as in the Netherlands.

In Ireland, a Constitutional Convention composed of sixty-six randomly selected citizens and thirty-three elected and party members held a series of meetings throughout 2013 and early 2014 to debate constitutional reform. The Convention held meetings with the public and also allowed online suggestions to be submitted. Although it was intended to be limited to fringe issues (getting rid of the long-obsolete law on blasphemy; lowering the voting age), it was allowed to take on topics of its own choosing and the two it chose were reform to the Dáil (the Irish lower house of parliament) and acknowledgment of social, cultural and economic rights. The Convention's work has thus far resulted in two national referenda being held on points raised. However, considering that the Convention made a total of eighteen recommendations for constitutional reform, its success must be taken with a grain of salt. Government politicians have shown themselves extremely reluctant to entertain suggestions for more sweeping reform, much less to put such suggestions to a popular vote.

A similar constitutional reform project was attempted in Iceland. Following the financial crash of 2008, which had serious repercussions for Iceland's economy, the government convened a one-day Assembly of 950 randomly selected individuals to discuss possible changes to the Constitution. The outcomes of this discussion were then refined by a Constitutional Council whose twenty-five members were elected specifically for this purpose. The Council debated for four months, before presenting a bill that would have initiated rewriting the Constitution to the Althingi, the Icelandic parliament.

However, the Council's debate did not occur behind closed doors. It published its findings on a weekly basis and solicited comments and suggestions from the public, primarily over the internet.

Similar to how things unfolded in Ireland, despite the Council's conclusions being widely endorsed by the broader public in a referendum, the move for reform was eventually brought down by political parties working in close cooperation with commercial fishing interests that disapproved of the suggestions to more equitably distribute Iceland's natural resources (such as fishing stocks).

It is obvious, from the way that participatory budgeting and citizens' assemblies are continually undermined by the political establishment, that these measures will not be enough on their own to counter our society's oligarchic nature. However, the broad acceptance of and high participation rates in these online participatory experiments, despite very little publicity, as well as the apparent tendency of ordinary citizens to vote responsibly, show that there is definitely both appetite and potential for greater citizen participation.

The next frontier: online decisions with Loomio and DemocracyOS

Unlike at any other point in history, thanks to the internet it is now possible for a large number of people to discuss and decide on projects in real time without needing to be in the same room, or even the same city. That means that elected representation and centralized power are no longer the only way to govern large countries. It is simply not necessary, for example, for a parliamentary committee on culture to meet in the nation's capital and allocate the arts and culture budget when citizens can do this directly online and, as a bonus, be assured of getting those projects approved that they really want.

This ability to facilitate direct citizen participation on a massive scale comes just in time, because, as we have seen, the electoral system slowly but inexorably concentrates wealth and power and therefore leads to oligarchy.

Political systems that have elections at their centre can work for a while – the Roman system worked relatively well for about four hundred years and its reincarnation in modern Western countries has worked for over two hundred years – but they eventually collapse in on themselves and revert to some form of authoritarian rule. We can see this process well under way today; in many developed countries most of the wealth resides in the hands of only a few families (the Walton family in America owns as much wealth as the bottom 30 per cent of Americans, whereas in Britain the five richest families own more than the bottom 20 per cent) and clans of politicians, such as the Bushes and Clintons in the United States, the Milibands in England or the Trudeaus in Canada, are emerging. Our world is beginning to look a lot like the Roman Republic did right before it collapsed.

So it is very good news that online decision-making might help us to avoid the Romans' fate and move beyond the electoral system – just as the Athenians did – into a form of decision-making that diffuses power and wealth more equitably across society, making it stronger and more resilient to crises. In order to do this, we would have to use the principles of participatory budgeting and citizens' assemblies, but combine them with some aspects of Athenian democracy to roll out online decision-making on a larger scale with more power residing with the people.

And here, there is more good news. The technology to implement wide-ranging online citizen participation already exists: for example, LiquidFeedback, used by the Pirate Party of Germany; Loomio, used by Wellington City Council in New Zealand; and DemocracyOS, used by Buenos Aires in Argentina. These tools allow citizens to communicate directly online with each other to formulate policy and coordinate collective action in a way that loosely resembles a modern version of the Athenian Assembly. Citizens using these online tools do not simply vote. Instead they are invited to discuss topics of interest with other participants who are not anonymous ciphers, but peers clearly identifiable via online profiles. While some discussions may subside without resolution, others may lead to concrete suggestions for a specific community project, e.g. that an abandoned lot be converted into parkland or that a new bus stop be constructed at a certain location. Once firm suggestions are submitted for consideration, users enter a period of online debate. This may last for several days or even weeks, as participants enter their thoughts by text and cast their vote in the appropriate forum. Online software often allows for rich feedback at this stage by allowing participants to enter a reason for their vote and/or to indicate how strongly they feel about the issue at hand.

Thanks to these developments, it should be possible to closely mimic the Athenian Assembly in an online national forum within the next few years. In this scenario, citizens would not necessarily be restricted to debating via text alone, but could hold live Assembly sessions at pre-agreed times. During these sessions, volunteer speakers could give their

thoughts live to camera and be seen and heard by participants in real time in a similar fashion to a Skype conference
call. This speakers' debate could be accompanied by a simultaneous general debate among all participants in a text-only
sidebar. Thus, an online direct democracy would resemble
nothing more complicated than an engaging symbiosis of
Skype and Twitter technology – with enough computing
power and bandwidth, an entirely possible enterprise.
Instead of complaining about politicians on Twitter and
Facebook, citizens could use that time and energy to make
decisions themselves. It is a simple, elegant and, above all,
efficient solution. And unless we want to risk a relapse into
authoritarianism, it is inevitable.

And because, as we have seen in earlier chapters, there
are a lot of reasons to move over to a more widespread
online democracy, and the technology that would make such
a change possible exists, it is a good idea to start thinking
about what the challenges of such a move could be.

Many of our problems with politics are deeply rooted in
our social and economic system, so creating a real democracy requires a deeper change than just moving everything
online. As we have seen, the Athenians did not simply
create a meeting place for citizens to debate and vote; they
buttressed that system with laws and practices that allowed
democracy to flourish and to continually reinvent itself.

So if we truly want a modern direct democracy to work, we
have to think about how we can create a society for it to operate
in. The rest of this book is going to do just that, fleshing out
the steps I think are necessary to create an online participatory democracy, as a system of government that doesn't just
look good on paper, but also does good in real life.

9

Disinformed is Disenfranchised: Why Taming Mass Media is a Necessary Step towards Democracy

The conscious and intelligent manipulation of the organized habits and opinions of the masses is an important element in democratic society. Those who manipulate this unseen mechanism of society constitute an invisible government which is the true ruling power of our country.

Edward Bernays, nephew of psychiatrist Sigmund Freud and father of the modern public relations industry

The medium and the message: how communication methods affect decision-making

When citizens only vote 'yes' or 'no' on pre-approved questions, political outcomes remain very easy for a small group of gatekeepers to manipulate. We've seen this process in action in the Roman Republic, where no law could be passed without affirmation from the people gathered in their tribes, and we have seen it in our own modern referenda, where money and power play no less of a role in securing the desired outcome on each political question put to the people.

To escape this manipulation, in a true participatory democracy citizens need to be able not just to vote in pre-approved ways on pre-approved issues, but to take a hand in deciding what measures are voted on and why. In short, somehow citizens need to be put in a position where they can truly deliberate with one another and come up with their own suggestions for future action. The Athenians, after all, spent most of their time in Assembly not voting, but brainstorming and debating motions.

Direct peer-to-peer deliberation has other advantages for democracy, too. When people discuss political issues directly with one another, they often come to a higher level of consensus regarding the action to be taken, and develop greater empathy for diverging opinions than when they are merely asked to cast a vote on the issue. There is also reason to believe that when citizens engage in direct discussion and problem-solving with each other, they are able to make better decisions because the process harnesses each individual's expertise in the service of the community.

Unfortunately for us, however, facilitating a free and open debate among citizens is much harder to achieve in a modern society than it was in ancient Athens. This is, ironically, mainly due to the very thing that opens up the possibility of exercising direct democracy in large and populous modern states – the radical changes in the way we communicate.

The Mytilenean Debate: hard facts
and slow times in the Assembly

In ancient Athens, writing was an expensive and time-consuming process, even for those few citizens who were truly literate, and, of course, television, radio and other communications technology did not exist. You could not, in Athens, phone someone up and ask them to bring home a jug of milk any more than you could radio port headquarters from a ship to let them know when to expect your arrival. So, for lack of alternatives, during Athens' democratic period virtually all communication occurred face to face. This meant that the opportunities for addressing large numbers of people were limited. Although Athenians could communicate their views and ideas to mid-sized crowds at banquets, house parties and in the marketplace, the only real possibility for reaching a genuinely mass audience lay in the democratically convened Assembly, and this brought its own inherent limitations with it.

Within the confines of the Assembly, debate proceeded in what we would now consider to be a very minimalist fashion. A speaker, or *rhetor*, mounted the speaker's platform, he spoke and he got back down. Of course, the most popular *rhetors* were usually trained speakers and the audience certainly appreciated their skill, but no special ceremony or fanfare encouraged the assembled citizens to take any speaker's opinion seriously. He had to manufacture his own gravitas using nothing more than well-crafted sentences, his tone of voice and a few hand gestures. Moreover, no speaker had the stage to himself for long. Since the Athenians enjoyed *isegoria* – the right to speak publicly in an official setting and to be heard on equal terms to all others – as soon as one speaker sat down, someone else could pop up and criticize or question everything he had just said. This made it very difficult for a *rhetor* to construct his own narrative of events or to invent or twist facts without being called out on his behaviour.

The Athenians were also subject to long periods of political downtime between Assemblies when they had a chance to reflect on what had been said. It was not unheard of for an Assembly to reverse a decision if enough people reconsidered their position or felt that the issue had not yet been fully hashed out. In fact, such a reversal occurred during 'the Mytilene Debate', one of the Assembly's most famous discussions.

Mytilene, a small Greek state, had abruptly decided to transfer its allegiance from Athens to Sparta during a lengthy war between the two ancient superpowers. However, the Athenians proved to be quicker on the uptake than their rivals; before Sparta could take advantage of Mytilene's betrayal, Athens dispatched a fleet of warships to Mytilene and successfully brought it under their own control. Their military objective accomplished, most of the Athenian force returned home to participate in an Assembly decision on how the garrison left at Mytilene should deal with the vanquished.

During the debate, a citizen named Cleon proposed killing all Mytilenean men and selling the women and children into slavery. Hair-raising as it sounds today, this was a fairly standard punishment for rebellious cities in the ancient world and it would have been rather odd if no one had mentioned this crude if effective solution to the issue of Mytilene. However, an obscure individual named Diodotus strongly objected to Cleon's proposal. While Cleon believed that failing to severely punish Mytilene would encourage other states to revolt, Diodotus argued that punishing Mytilene too harshly would mean that no insurrectionary states would ever surrender to the Athenians in future and that this would ultimately prove the more wasteful course of action.

The assembled Athenians were furious at the Mytileneans, who they felt had double-crossed them at an extremely vulnerable moment. The war with Sparta wasn't going very well and Mytilene's backstabbing was perceived as a serious threat. Some of the people at Assembly had just rowed all the way to Mytilene and back with their hearts in their throats and could hardly be said to be in the best of moods. Unsurprisingly, therefore, Cleon carried his motion and the Assembly ordered the execution of Mytilene's male population. However, the Athenians soon realized that they had let their emotions get the better of them and that the matter needed to be reconsidered. Thus, a second Assembly meeting was called for the next day. In this second Assembly the Athenians proved more willing to listen to Diodotus' arguments. Cleon's proposal was overturned and replaced by a more moderate motion to merely execute the rebellion's ringleaders.

The Athenians were by no means more intelligent or more considerate people than we are today. As the example of the Mytileneans indicates, they lived in a rougher and more unforgiving time. But it was also a time when anyone seeking to influence public opinion did not have very effective tools for doing so at his disposal, and where the fitful stop and start of all formal political communications put a damper on emotional decision-making. The very primitiveness of Athenian communication provided more fertile ground for reasonable and weighed discourse to hold sway.

Modern mass communication is far more sophisticated, far more constant and carries far more authority than one person simply speaking in front of a crowd with only their oratory skills to aid them could ever hope to have. Unlike even the most successful Athenian *rhetors*, who were just flesh-and-blood people existing in much the same manner as everyone else, the world of television, magazines, radio and the internet does not exist in real life. It is an irrational, dreamlike world, and the figures who populate it are larger than life. We even refer to people who frequently appear in mass media as 'stars' or 'idols'. Athenian *rhetors* like Cleon and Diodotus were very much embedded in their society, but modern media stars – the voices we listen to – are purposely cordoned off from everyday life in modernity, lest their image be disturbed.

Moreover, mass media forms a closed circuit with itself. It tells us what happened, how it happened, why it happened and what to think about it. This service was neither necessary nor possible in Athens, where people knew what happened and how it happened from their own personal experiences or those of their friends and neighbours. Why events happened and what to think about them were also largely digested in the marketplace. The *rhetor*'s main task lay in convincing others to take a certain course of action based on a set of widely accepted facts. An Athenian *rhetor*, in other words, had a far narrower sphere of influence, and this shows in the kind of results he could achieve as compared to the capabilities of mass media. An Athenian who excelled at changing people's opinion was a very good *rhetor*, but modern mass media can change people's perception of reality.

The doors of perception: mass media
as gatekeeper and dreamweaver

Studies have shown that mass media can distort viewers' perceptions, even when this was not intended, and the people concerned do not believe that they have been influenced.

One US university study showed that topics of public interest, such as defence or the nation's energy policy, only 'become high priority political issues for the public ... if they first become high priority news items for the [television] networks'.[1] The study concluded that television news primed the electorate in that it weighted the importance of various topics by giving them more or less news coverage. This kept certain topics at the forefront of citizens' minds and drowned out others. For example, during the course of the study one group of volunteers was given newscasts containing no stories related to defence for four days, and a second group was given a newscast each day which contained a defence story implying that American security forces were in trouble. Before they were shown the newscasts, those assigned to the second group rated defence sixth in a list of priorities for the American government. A day after watching the last newscast, they rated defence as the second-highest priority. The rankings in the control group did not change. The experiment was repeated multiple times with various topics and influenced viewers' opinion on the importance of the targeted topic every time.

The researchers also ran experiments that took a more open-ended approach. Here participants were asked to name

---

1 Iyengar and Kinder, *News that Matters: Television and American Opinion*, at 4.

the three most important issues facing the nation before and after being shown the newscasts that had been doctored to emphasize a particular issue. An average of 37 per cent – not a majority – nominated the target problem as one of the nation's most important prior to the experiment; this rose to 57 per cent – a 'democratic' majority – after the experiment.

And that's not all. Throughout the study, viewers' perceptions of a topic's importance were found to rise and fall in direct proportion to the amount of coverage that newscasts devoted to it. This became obvious when participants were simply asked to name *any* high-priority issue after being shown doctored newscasts. For example, 24 per cent of those shown no news stories relating to energy named it as a high-priority issue, compared to 50 per cent of those shown three out of fifteen newscasts featuring it as an issue, and 65 per cent of those shown six out of fifteen newscasts featuring it. This pattern held in twelve out of thirteen experiments. Most shockingly of all, the subjects accepted that the importance a news network attributed to a topic was correct, *even when this was at odds with their own personal experience.* Mass media coverage can thus cause viewers – and voters – to literally discount their own real-life experience in favour of the vicarious experience provided by television.

This means that all media are tainted by a strong subjective bias – news editors determine what the public views as important simply by picking topics to cover – and it is possible for this bias to go undetected because, unlike face-to-face communication, mass media generates a deep inequality between consumers and providers.

Blurring the line between subjective
impressions and objective realities

Just as elections and their outcomes are vastly different things to professional politicians and ordinary voters, so too is media production a vastly different thing to media professionals and their viewers. Not only does a small circle of news editors effectively decide which topics are important each and every day, media professionals are paid to construct a smooth narrative of events that is not liable to interruption or contradiction. Moreover, they are employed for their ability to attract audiences with simple and entertaining certainty as opposed to tedious soul-searching and endless relativism.

In the service of doing so effectively, journalists and presenters transform subjective impressions into objective realities. A magazine article might read: 'At our interview, Ms X looked stunning in a blue blouse', but is unlikely to say, 'Ms X was wearing a blue blouse and I thought she looked stunning, but then I've always been partial to redheads'. Likewise, a newspaper headline might scream, 'Minister Y makes defiant declaration', not 'Minister Y makes a statement in an entirely normal tone of voice, but "defiant declaration" is alliterative and sounds exciting'. Journalists record their final views or impressions, but they do not inform their audience about what led to those views being formed. Indeed, time and space would not permit them to do so, even if they wanted to. The impressions they deliver are, by necessity, superficial.

And reporters do not just add content, they can also remove it. A reporter might omit a fact from a story for no better reason than that including it will cause them to go over their word count, because their deadline is approaching, or because including it would slow down the pace of their article or disrupt its tone.

Taken together, all of this means that subjective impressions, often based on nothing more than the reporter's own arbitrary preferences combined with the necessity to sound exciting and not to overcomplicate things, are displayed as objective fact. This would not be so harmful in itself if modern mass media were not a highly concentrated and syndicated enterprise.

While there appears to be more 'choice' in media than ever before, content is provided by fewer organizations. In 1983, fifty companies controlled 90 per cent of American media; by 2011 this was down to six. In fact, by 2001 only three companies accounted for 75 per cent of all market share in American newspapers, with the top six companies accounting for 96.5 per cent of the total market. Across the Atlantic in Britain, the situation is almost identical. There, the top three national newspaper companies account for over 75 per cent of total market share, just four companies own 70 per cent of market share in local and regional newspapers, two broadcasters (BBC and ITV) account for over 85 per cent of the total national television market and the four largest commercial radio owners control 77 per cent of commercial radio stations. Similar patterns of concentrated media ownership are standard across western European countries.

Since news conglomerates reuse and syndicate their own content, coverage of a story is often identical across several different media outlets – for example, across several different newspapers and television channels that appear to operate under different brands, but are ultimately owned by the same company. This creates the false impression that there is a high level of agreement across different sectors of society that the coverage is appropriate and that the facts discussed are those that are relevant, when in reality the coverage has originated in the same place. As a result, a narrative or point of view that may literally have started out as one person's opinion – an opinion they themselves may not have even thought very hard about – is presented as a mainstream consensus that is difficult to contest.

As we saw in the study above, the vast majority of viewers do not consider what they see and hear in the media as merely possible interpretations or partial accounts of events. They accept that what media outlets say *is real*, even when their own life experience contradicts it. This is not because people are stupid or gullible, but rather because our brains are hardwired to readily accept as truth information that is presented as the community consensus. In many ways this is a strength for shared learning and building social structures, but when it comes to modern mass media it is a weakness that leaves us vulnerable to manipulation.

Mass media creates our perception of reality, and some actors are not prepared to leave the content of those perceptions to chance.

Using mass media to guide public discourse

Since mass media determines what the important issues and events of the day are, it is very important to people in many professions to receive media coverage and to ensure the coverage is favourable to their interests. This is true of anyone whose business relies on general public opinion rather than word-of-mouth communication, a category that can include celebrities, manufacturers of mass consumption goods and, of course, politicians. All of these actors not only want the media to pay attention to them so that people will not forget that they exist, they want the media to portray them in a manner that is conducive to their own aims. What this means is that modern mass media is not just a powerful tool for influencing public perception, it is a powerful tool that several parties are constantly fighting to control.

And *this*, in turn, means that the information people receive is not just a version of events distorted by media professionals' own random biases and preferences. It is also distorted by whoever currently holds the upper hand in the battle for media domination. This can include politicians, private companies and, of course, media owners themselves. The following looks at the role each of these actors plays and the effects they can have on political debate.

Media ownership

With only a handful of companies controlling national media, politicians cannot afford consistently negative coverage from a large media conglomerate. Politicians, particularly young, aspiring politicians, depend on media organizations to emphasize their attractions and downplay their faults. In turn, media owners depend on politicians to make laws that benefit them. It is not surprising therefore that media owners and politicians should enter into a symbiotic relationship which gives them both what they want: media owners are able to influence future decisions through the politicians who depend on them for favourable coverage and politicians are able to influence election outcomes by getting media owners to back them in return for those future favours.

Perhaps the media owner most notorious for interfering in politics is the Australian-born Rupert Murdoch, owner of NewsCorp, which operates, among others, the *Sun* and *The Times* newspapers in Britain and Fox News in the USA. Murdoch has been a force in politics, particularly British politics, for decades. In fact, no British prime minister has come to power without Murdoch's blessing since 1983.

That's not conjecture – the politicians involved have frankly admitted as much.

In the 1980s prime minister Margaret Thatcher berated another media owner for his dislike of Murdoch: "'Why are you so opposed to Rupert?" the Iron Lady asked. "He is going to get us in [elected].'"[2] Murdoch indeed delivered and Margaret Thatcher remained in power, despite many deeply unpopular policies.[3] In fact, Murdoch also delivered for Thatcher's successor John Major in 1992, reminding the new prime minister to whom he owed his loyalties with a *Sun* headline that openly claimed that the newspaper had won victory for the Conservative Party.

Murdoch, however, quickly wearied of a Tory Party without Thatcher at the helm. Anxious to change NewsCorp's position, Norman Fowler, then chairperson of the British Conservative Party, visited *Sun* editor Kevin McKenzie in an attempt to convince him 'about the virtues of John Major's government' before the 1997 election. But it was too late. NewsCorp had found a new friend in Tony Blair, the leader of the rebranded 'New Labour' Party, which chose to drop

---

2 Fowler, 'In the post-Murdoch era, we must reform media ownership'.
3 Although the Conservative Party received only 42 per cent of the vote in the 1983 election – 2 per cent less than it had in 1979 – its seats in Parliament increased from 53 to 61 per cent.

most of the policies Murdoch had found so objectionable in the 'old' Labour Party. Tony Blair had not only proved his willingness to listen to the media tycoon by travelling to 'the other side of the globe to woo Murdoch executives', once elected 'his government withdrew the longstanding ban on foreign companies fully owning British television stations',[4] a policy which directly benefited NewsCorp.

The link between favourable coverage from NewsCorp and electoral success is so widely accepted among British politicians that when Tony Blair resigned in 2007, his successor Gordon Brown and Conservative candidate David Cameron vied for Murdoch's attention. Brown met with Murdoch on at least fourteen different occasions. Notwithstanding this obviously sincere attempt to win Murdoch's backing, the two had 'a bitter falling out ... [Murdoch] told Brown his papers would not support Brown's Labour party in the 2010 election'.[5] Instead, James Murdoch, Rupert Murdoch's son and manager of much of his business, met with Conservative candidate David Cameron 'over drinks at a pub and told him his company's *Sun* newspaper would support his Conservative party in the next election'.[6] David Cameron, having arguably spent some of mankind's most profitable hours in a drinking establishment, did indeed become prime minister in 2010 after his Conservative Party won a narrow electoral victory.

As we saw previously, the value of free coverage that a media empire like Murdoch's can provide to a party often exceeds the total campaign finances of the party itself by a

---

4 Fowler, op cit..
5 Greene, 'Murdoch denies political influence, Cameron disagrees'.
6 Ibid.

considerable margin. Parties and candidates know that they literally do not possess sufficient resources either to provide themselves with positive advertisement or to effectively counteract negative media attention, but that they can steer coverage by promising to use their powers in the interests of supportive media enterprises once they are in office.

Fowler, who as the former chair of the Conservative Party would certainly know, openly admitted: 'If you have a company that owns almost 40% of British newspapers and a big chunk of a successful television company you can expect nothing less [than for politicians to go to great lengths to gain your support]. In the main politicians are not fools. They can see where media power is and for a very long time it has been with Murdoch.'[7]

News owners like Murdoch get a privileged say in government and ordinary citizens get the information that these media owners and their allied politicians have agreed they should receive. It is a state of affairs hardly conducive to sound democratic decision-making.

Public relations from the Cato Institute to #JeSuisCharlie: fake photos, fake experts and fake facts

Of course, not every news outlet is owned by Rupert Murdoch. Some news conglomerates are owned only by anonymous shareholders with no particular driving force within the company. However, content on these less ideologically driven news outlets is actually even *easier* to influence, for those with the inclination and resources to do so, because of the way in which media enterprises work.

---

7 Fowler, op. cit.

Media outlets, especially newspapers, often procure their content from wire copy providers, such as Reuters and Associated Press. These are companies that employ their own journalists to generate content which is then sold on to newspapers, television stations and other outlets to be used as part of their coverage. But while mass media outlets always *pay* for wire copy, they often fail to admit this to their readers.

A recent study by Cardiff University revealed that five mainstream, mid-market English newspapers (*The Times*, the *Guardian*, the *Independent*, the *Daily Telegraph* and the *Daily Mail*) used almost word-for-word reprints of press releases and wire copy for 60 per cent of their articles, which were then falsely attributed to a staff journalist of the paper and passed off as their work. A further 20 per cent of stories originated as press releases or wire copy to which the journalist had added some of their own material. Only 12 per cent of material was generated by the reporters themselves. This creates the false impression that the news comes from many different sources; for example, if the *Washington Post*, the *Los Angeles Times* and the *Telegraph* all print the same facts, the reader tends to accept that there is overwhelming agreement on those facts, when the truth is that all of the stories derive from a single source – the person who provided the original wire copy story. Getting a story covered by wire agencies can thus be a simple way to set the media agenda for some time, and interested parties do exactly that by providing newswires and media outlets with free content in the form of 'expert commentary', live footage of events and press releases.

Generating and circulating press releases is a relentless activity for many corporate and government entities – by the 1990s, the British government alone was churning out

20,000 of them a year – and they can have a much deeper impact on reporting than an outside observer might be inclined to think. This is because media enterprises often fail to give their reporters sufficient resources to conduct additional research into any information that they receive. One in-depth researcher interviewed a journalist who admitted that his newspaper made an annual profit of £70 million, but forbade its staff from calling the telephone information line to find sources. Travel to the site of events, even to the closest courthouse, was not permitted. Another journalist, who worked at the *Independent*'s bureau in Washington, DC, claimed that, owing to cost-cutting measures, his job consisted of cutting and pasting material from large American newspapers for his own submissions, and that this tactic was so widespread in the industry as to be unofficially known as 'the JCB technique'.[8]

Since they aren't able to verify the information being fed to them, journalists are obliged to merely regurgitate the content of press releases. The University of Cardiff study cited above also revealed that even in cases where a news story relied upon one important fact or statement, journalists failed to check its accuracy 70 per cent of the time. When a company, government or politician sends a press release (or several press releases) to a journalist, they can often expect to see that release reprinted verbatim in a newspaper at some point, or, at the very least, included as one of two 'sides' in a debate in which none of the issues under contention are actually examined. It is an easy and cost-effective way of ensuring more positive coverage, and bombarding reporters

---

8   Davies, *Flat Earth News*, at 103.

with press releases that present an issue in a certain light is now a basic component of everyday public relations.

But PR efforts can also be much more elaborate.

For example, media coverage can also be influenced by funding academic institutions and think tanks. The scholars associated with these institutions then write 'expert opinions' or undertake 'studies' that align with the interests of the institution's chief financial backers. In media appearances these experts will often be introduced with a byline that creates the impression that they are a member of a professional if bland organization such as 'the Institute for Justice'. This encourages viewers to take the expert's opinion seriously, because there is an assumption that an institute is an impartial entity and that academics have a duty to weigh evidence carefully and act in a socially responsible manner.

Unfortunately, this assumption no longer fits reality.

Since austerity measures and tax cutbacks mean that universities – and particularly researchers – are starved of funds, anyone with enough cash can make a very realistic effort at dictating research terms by funding academic think tanks. Some of the biggest funders of academic think tanks in America are businessmen Charles and David Koch. The Kochs' most successful venture in influencing academic output is possibly the Cato Institute, a libertarian think tank that they have poured millions into since founding it in 1977, and whose scholars teach at George Mason University, the University of Chicago, Yale and the London School of Economics, among others.

The Cato Institute and similar think tanks, such as the Heritage Foundation (which does not disclose its donors), provide an intellectual home and funding for scholars who hold corporate-friendly views, placing them at a competitive advantage over their peers. These favoured scholars are more likely to attain lucrative employment at a younger age and more likely to have leisure for publishing and networking. The likelihood that they will become unemployed or forced to take up other work is diminished, and they are simultaneously provided with a name and a home institution that allows them to speak publicly with a great deal of credibility. In fact, the Cato Institute boasts that its scholars are cited in nearly four thousand news articles every year, as well as participating in two thousand news broadcasts and writing hundreds of newspaper op-eds, making it, according to the Institute, the best value for money of any think tank in America. It is a long-game tactic, but the results are impressive, as media outlets devote airtime to 'institute' members and voluntarily repeat their claims without informing their viewers of the full nature of the organization in question.

And governments have not been slow to master the art of shaping public perceptions, either.

In both Canada and the United States, government press conferences allow the politician or (more usually) spokesperson in charge to determine the range and depth of the information discussed by allowing them to select the reporters who are allowed to ask questions. At White House press conferences even senior reporters employed by the most established news organizations are not allowed more than one question and a follow-up, while most of their colleagues are not permitted to ask any questions at all. This restrictive setting is often the only avenue that journalists have for obtaining government information, because governments do not permit any of their other employees to speak directly to the press. As Canadian journalists complain: 'Instead, reporters have to deal with an armada of press officers who know very little or nothing at all about a reporter's topic and who answer tough questions with vague talking points vetted by layers of political staff and delivered by email only.'[9]

An American journalist corroborates: 'the operative assumption at the Pentagon is, we will talk to you if it fits our specific narrow purpose and not if it doesn't'.[10]

Politicians often punish reporters and organizations that attempt to get around these barricades by freezing all inter-action with them. Since media outlets that can be counted on for more favourable reporting continue to be fed infor-mation, this can have a devastating effect on the target – deprived of the ability to cover the big events, they will lose viewers and their profits will nosedive.

Instead of providing healthy criticism, media outlets are expected to unquestioningly pass on the information govern-ments feed them to the public even when they have no way to verify its authenticity. For example, when European officials criticized seal-hunting in 2009, Canada's cabinet showed their support for local seal hunters by journeying to the Arctic to personally consume seal meat. The event itself was arguably somewhat anticlimactic, since Canada's governor-general had already personally cut out and eaten a raw seal heart earlier in the year, but it was still considered an important component in underlining that the Canadian government had no intention of bowing to international pressure. A photo of the prime minister's 'seal snack', as well as video footage, was duly circulated in Canadian media.

9 'An open letter to Canadian journalists'.
10 Robertson, 'In control'.

While the image creates the impression that it was taken by a photo-journalist present at the event, it (and the accompanying video footage) was actually taken by the prime minister's own press office. Photographers were banned from attending the occasion. It might seem like an innocuous event – 'Who cares whether Stephen Harper really likes seal meat?' one might think – but the point is that Canadians believe they are viewing a spontaneous event that has been confirmed by an independent third party as having really occurred when they are actually viewing a carefully manufactured *appearance* of something occurring. That is an important difference that can have consequences far beyond the popularity of Canada's traditional hunting practices.

For example, a Conservative Party rally ahead of the British general election in 2015, depicting party leader David Cameron speaking in front of several placard-waving supporters, was revealed to be a carefully angled press shoot in which nearly everyone attending the 'rally' was actually *in* the photo. Most importantly, the enormous empty spaces in the venue, which were conspicuously not filled by Cameron supporters, were not in view. The photos presented to the public thus gave a falsely optimistic account of Conservative Party support in the area, using seemingly incontrovertible proof – the photos, which the viewer does not know are carefully stage-managed.

But perhaps the greatest government photo-fake emerged following the deadly attacks on the satirical magazine *Charlie Hebdo* in Paris in early 2015. Following the incident, in which twelve people were killed, a huge public demonstration of solidarity with the magazine was organized in Paris.

Dozens of high-profile world leaders, including German Chancellor Angela Merkel, former French president Nicolas Sarkozy, King Abdullah of Jordan and Israeli prime minister Benjamin Netanyahu flew to Paris, and photos of these top politicians linked arm in arm 'leading' the solidarity demonstration were broadcast around the world.

From a security point of view, such personal leadership was risky to undertake on a public street filled with millions of people in the immediate aftermath of a terrorist attack. So risky, in fact, that the photos weren't really what they seemed. Another set of photos taken from a higher angle soon emerged, showing world leaders posing for the original photos in a separate closed-off side street surrounded only by enough of their own aides and security personnel to give the impression of being at the head of the demonstration. After the photo op, these top politicians simply returned to their own cars to be whisked off the scene – they never participated in the march. Yet dozens of top media organizations unquestioningly published the photos as genuine pictures of world leaders marching in Paris without ever apparently retracting that information.

All of these examples show how easy it is for politicians to stage-manage their own events and then pass them off to the press as genuine interactions between themselves and their constituents. Events that *never actually happened* or which happened very differently are presented as reality simply because it is more favourable to the politician's image to do so.

News organizations run the footage, because otherwise they would have to drop the entire story for lack of information. As a result ordinary people are forced to live in a world filled with false information that is nearly impossible for them to sift through, making real deliberation and sound decision-making hard to come by.

The meaning of mass media for democracy

We are all influenced by what we see and hear on television, radio and in newspapers, and unfortunately much of it is inaccurate, its content controlled by those who have the means to subsidize production. This ability to control information enables these actors to buy election and referendum outcomes without having to resort to outright bribery. We have spoken of parties and candidates spending money to win elections in previous chapters – this is what they spend it on.

The predominance of mass communication is why modern democracy can never truly be like ancient Athenian democracy. Even if we switched over to direct digital democracy with citizens deciding on all matters themselves, that experience would still be accompanied by a controlling and all-pervasive media environment that persistently and intentionally misinforms its citizens.

And under those conditions, how could citizens hope to make informed and well-considered decisions?

The only thing that could possibly alter this would be if internet communication, which is, after all, what will soon make online democracy feasible, could somehow break the stranglehold of mass media over our communications.

Battlefield Internet: how many soldiers does it take to run a Facebook account?

As we said in an earlier chapter, talk is cheap, but gathering an audience to hear that talk is not. This is still true on the internet, which perpetuates the domination of establishment structures over communications.

According to the British House of Lords Committee on Communication, 'traditional news providers ... have been able to transfer dominance of the mainstream media to the internet and in the process attract an even bigger audience'.[11] This is also true of other developed countries. For example, while 8.9 million Australians get their news online, the top ten sites visited are all traditional offline news sources, such as the *Herald Sun* and the *Sydney Morning Herald*. In fact, the top ten Australian news sites are owned by only six companies.

Traditional political spending structures and their results are also mirrored in online communications. In the USA, '[a]ll candidates in the presidential primaries in 2008 invested heavily in online strategies' ranging 'from internet advertising and search engine positioning to Facebook and YouTube to encourage citizens to organise on their behalf'.[12] Utilizing these tools effectively is not free. As in traditional offline campaigns, political candidates use money to dominate online communications with similar effects: Barack Obama spent approximately $16 million on online

---

11 *The Ownership of the News*, Select Committee on Communications, House of Lords (UK), 1st Report of Session 2007–08, 27 June 2008, HL Paper 122-I, from para. 161.
12 Williamson, 'The internet and the British election: politicians get their clicks', at 14–16.

advertising ($600,000 on his Facebook campaign alone), while his rival, Republican Party candidate John McCain spent $3.6 million.

And the cost of online political activity is ratcheting up fast: in 2016, American candidates are expected to spend over $1 billion on online advertising and social media, twenty times what was spent just six years ago in 2010. In Britain, the Conservative Party spent £100,000 *a month* just on its Facebook campaign in the run-up to the 2015 election, and circumvented laws prohibiting paid political advertising on TV by running attack ads on YouTube instead. In the new digital world, cash is still king.

However, proponents of internet communication would argue that while this might be the case, ordinary citizens can also have a voice online that they do not have in traditional mass communication. Anyone, after all, can set up a Facebook page or a Twitter account. You don't *need* to be an American Senator or the prime minister of Britain.

And it is true that by using social media, the ordinary voter can speak online, but the question is who they speak to.

The median active Twitter account has only sixty-one followers; only 4 per cent of Twitter accounts have more than a thousand followers. What is more, the majority of heavily followed Twitter accounts represent people or organizations that are already famous or powerful within the traditional offline media landscape and who can use their resources to procure a commensurate online presence. When an 'ordinary' person tweets they mutter from the peanut gallery to the friends they would have spoken to in real life anyway; when Fox News tweets, its voice resonates to 5 million followers. For the purposes of democratic participation, it does not matter how much a citizen speaks on the internet if there is no one to hear him, but this is precisely what most people do, broadcasting into an endless silence, like a lone Athenian rambling to an empty Assembly. They have spoken, but they have not been heard. They have 'free speech' but they do not have *isegoria* – the right to speak equally in a public forum – and free speech doesn't accomplish much without a free audience to go with it. Like so much else in our thin version of democracy, it is action without result.

In addition to this passive reinforcement of traditional communications structures, there are also ways to actively control online conversation. For example, governments and companies operating under fake identities can infiltrate public forums in order to skew debate. In doing so, they often use special persona management software to generate profiles and online history for fake identities. These programmes can allow a single operator to use up to seventy different identities, creating the false impression that their views are widely shared. This can silence opposition or make it appear that any opposition is a minority view. The Bivings Group, a PR company specializing in internet lobbying, explained, 'there are some campaigns where it would be undesirable or even disastrous to let the audience know that your organization is directly involved ... Message boards, chat rooms, and listservs are a great way to anonymously monitor what is being said. Once you are plugged into this world, it is possible to make postings to these outlets that present your position as an uninvolved third party.'[13]

---

13 Reported by Monbiot, 'Reclaim the cyber commons', note 559.

Leaked documents from security company HB Gary Federal revealed that the US Air Force has asked companies to bid to supply it with persona management software. The British seem to have gone one farther, creating a new brigade (Brigade 77, also known as the Security Assistance Group) to engage in 'shaping behaviour through the use of dynamic narratives' online and with the media.[14] The brigade, which began work in April 2015, has 1,500 members; a mix of regular soldiers, reserves and civilians with experience in mainstream media and social media. The brigade's prime purpose is to 'control the narrative' about conflicts that Britain is interested in. In addition to ISIS, it seems to have its sights set on countering Russian public television and radio services that broadcast English-language programmes over Europe and North America. Russian and Western media channels do not always see eye to eye in their interpretation of events, and apparently the British government has decided to help its side along.

Although most analysis of Brigade 77 focuses on the possibility of it operating its own Facebook and Twitter accounts, it does not take 1,500 personnel to send out the occasional birthday greeting or 140-character tweet. Most people, after all, manage on their own. The British Army's 2014 booklet seems to envision somewhat more ambitious outcomes for its integrated media engagement.

According to the booklet, the army's new SAG unit will contribute to blurring the lines between soldier and non-combatant, as well as between economic, political and military concerns. It will work to influence 'longer term attitudes and behaviour', because the 'desire to achieve

---

14 Sengupta, 'New British Army unit "Brigade 77" to use Facebook and Twitter in psychological warfare'.

success by changing the perceptions of adversaries and populations is as old as warfare itself'. The unit leadership will understand that 'military operations mainly seek to contribute to gaining political or economic advantage' and the brigade will be composed of several earlier British Army units, including the Media Operations Groups and the Psychological Operations Groups.[15]

And as if this weren't enough to worry about, governments and companies can always simply pay or train volunteers to dominate online commenting and ratings sites. The Chinese government allegedly pays 50 cents for every post that criticizes dissidents or disturbs the debate of a point that the government would rather not have debated (the so-called '50-cent party'), while Astroturf groups like American Majority seek to affect consumption patterns by visiting entertainment sites like Amazon and systematically downgrading products they disapprove of while upgrading products they do approve of. This is done in assembly-line fashion solely on the basis of whether the product in question is deemed to conform with their values. The person rating the product may not have actually read or viewed it themselves. As one member of American Majority described it: 'when you type in "Movies on Healthcare", I don't want Michael Moore's to come up, so I always give it bad ratings. I spend about 30 minutes a day, just click, click, click, click. ... If there's a place to comment, a place to rate, a place to share information, you have to do it. That's how you control the online dialogue ...'[16]

---

15 Aitken, 'Mastering a new kind of warfare'.
16 *Astro-Turf Wars* (director: Taki Oldham), astroturfwars.org, cited by Monbiot, 'These Astroturf libertarians are the real threat to internet democracy'.

These are not the actions of individual concerned citizens, but coordinated, well-funded campaigns. Over 75 per cent of the funding for American Majority comes from the Sam Adams Alliance. In 2008, the year in which American Majority was founded, 88 per cent of the Alliance's money came from a single donation of $3.7 million. This means that even something as innocuous as online commenting on entertainment products is skewed by financial interests instead of representing a relatively accurate reflection of general public opinion.

Considering the extent to which it is already being manipulated, there is not much hope for internet communication to provide a genuine avenue for the kind of peer-to-peer debate that is necessary for a democracy. If anything, the internet thus far has served to underline and further entrench the narrow scope of media activity in modern societies. Therefore, we have to accept that the problems mass communication creates for democratic debate are going to stay with us for the foreseeable future. And this means, in turn, that we need to find a way to reduce their impact on democratic decision-making to the greatest extent possible.

Reclaiming the narrative by funding massive participation instead of mass media

Because we will all continue to live in an environment saturated with mass misinformation for the foreseeable future, we cannot afford to think of digital democracy merely as a system in which citizens hold a long series of online votes. In that scenario, the vast majority of citizens would inevitably cast their vote on the basis of the twisted and biased information they have received, and that would be disastrous. Indeed, when I talk to people about digital democracy or participatory democracy, the first concern they tend to bring up is the alleged ignorance of their fellow citizens, whom they do not trust to vote in a responsible manner. And although these fears are often a little exaggerated – in the participatory experiments run so far people tend to vote in a surprisingly responsible fashion – as we've seen in this chapter, when it comes to communication and information, there is still a lot to be worried about.

In order to work against the influence of mass media and other channels of misinformation, in a digital democracy it would be necessary for citizens not just to vote on proposals using online software, but to debate any motions with each other online immediately before voting. Moreover, attending such a debate would need to be compulsory for anyone wishing to vote, and – in the interests of preventing trolling and fake account activity – it could not be anonymous. Online debate prior to online voting would enable people to raise points and views and share information that is normally not heard in major media communications. It would also force participants to confront opposing views and seek to resolve different perceptions of what the facts surrounding the issue at hand are. It's a far from perfect solution, but it would give us a start on mimicking the type of communication that was present in Athens within an enclosed buffer zone where citizens participate on equal terms and have a chance to share their own relevant experiences and expertise.

Of course, sitting through hours of debate is hard work – but the Athenians recognized this and therefore they paid people to do it. A modern democracy that truly wants to enable participation from all sectors of society would also need to take account of this and pay citizens for participating in the debate that will precede their vote.

Is pay-for-participation possible?

Pay-for-participation can sound like something out of a science-fiction novel, but the Athenians did it, and we do it too for jury duty, the one form of equal democratic participation that lives on in modern societies. For most people any opportunity to earn extra money is welcome, especially when – unlike in the current configuration for jury duty – they are free to choose whether or not to take advantage of it. The question is thus not whether people would generally be averse to receiving money for an activity (political debate) that many of them now engage in at least occasionally for free, but rather whether pay-for-participation would be economically feasible. Can we *afford* to pay people to debate and decide in such numbers? I decided to find out.

In investigating whether pay for participation would be feasible, I started with the country I was born in: Canada. There are approximately twenty-four million registered voters in Canada. Assuming that the nation held a public decision-making session at least every two weeks or twenty-six times a year and attendees received $30 (a little less than half the daily minimum wage) for a two-to-three-hour session, this would cost $18.7 billion per year. It is a lot of money, but not more than Canada, a country that has not been attacked since 1812, spends annually on defence. In other words, digital democracy is easily affordable at the mere cost of cutting back spending on a military apparatus that would hardly do Canada any good in the unlikely event of an attack from either of the two nuclear powers it is geographically wedged between. Even such measures, however, would not be necessary, because it is utterly unrealistic to assume that every single eligible Canadian would attend every single Assembly meeting.

The goal of participatory democracy is not 100 per cent participation on every issue, but rather to attain a flexible participation rate that is high enough to reflect the society as a whole. In Athens only about 15 per cent of citizens attended any given Assembly meeting, and there is no reason to believe that attendance would be much higher at a Canadian Assembly. On any given day, many people are busy or ill or uninterested in the topic under debate. Still others are politically apathetic (the Athenians, never ones to mince words, labelled such people *idiotes* – the root of the word 'idiot' – and didn't lose any sleep over them). And unlikely as it is that more than 15 per cent of people would show up at any one meeting, if they did it would be entirely possible to limit Assembly attendance to the first 15 per cent of citizens who register. Reducing participation in a hypothetical Canadian Assembly to around 15 per cent of registered voters shifts the cost down to a very manageable $2.8 billion per year.

This could be easily paid for using pre-existing tax revenues. It's estimated that Canada Revenue loses $8 billion every year to offshore tax evasion. Tax evasion – unlike tax avoidance – is a crime and it is easy and cheap to prevent, because whistle-blowers who work in offshore tax havens are generally willing to part with data that can lead to the recovery of hundreds of millions in tax revenues for a mere million or two, i.e. for far less than it would cost the authorities to mount a traditional investigation. Indeed, the Canadian government has repeatedly been offered information that would allow it to prosecute hundreds of tax evaders. Canada would need to recoup only around 40 per cent of the revenue currently lost through offshore tax evasion to pay for an Athenian-style direct democracy. Recovering the full amount of taxes owed would easily allow Canada to conduct an Athenian-style online Assembly with participation rates of more than 30 per cent (nearly double the participation rates in Athens) or, alternatively, to up the pay rate to $60 per session – nearly a full day's pay at minimum wage – while retaining a 15 per cent participation rate. The only 'price' is needing to enforce the law and punish criminal behaviour, something the government has a duty to do *anyway*.

And Canada isn't the only country able to make this work.

Britain loses at least £5 billion annually to tax evasion, while failing, one way or another, to collect £35 billion in taxes. If Britain recovered all £35 billion of its tax gap, it could pay 15 per cent of its 45 million registered voters £199 (three times the daily minimum wage!) per online debating session, if such sessions were held twenty-six times per year. Just recovering the £5 billion in outright tax evasion would give a payment of £28 a session, about half the daily minimum wage. In Germany, tax evasion losses are estimated at 13 billion euros annually, enough to pay 15 per cent of Germany's 61.8 million eligible voters 54 euros per session.

Not only is simply enforcing *existing* tax law a completely painless way to pay for a participatory online democracy, it would also work towards rebalancing the economy, an important step in stabilizing the political system. Instead of being hoarded in offshore bank accounts, the money 'spent' on direct democracy would go straight into ordinary families' pockets and therefore straight back into the local economy. To take the Canadian figures, a person who attended Assembly twenty-six times a year at a rate of $30 would, besides getting to make direct decisions on policies that affect them, earn $780. That's the price of a new laptop; a year's gym membership; a car repair bill; an extra payment for the retirement plan; or a year's worth of children's clothing. These are exactly the things most people would spend extra money on, and doing so reinvigorates the economy and helps ordinary people secure their own financial future. By helping people help themselves, dependence on government services would be reduced. Pay-for-participation would lead to *smaller* government and *less* government waste.

Direct, digital democracy isn't just fun – it's *free*. Far from requiring sacrifices, it rewards people for their efforts, making high levels of political participation sustainable, even from the most vulnerable members of society, while simultaneously serving to redress severe economic imbalance. Most importantly of all, enabling citizens to debate issues directly between themselves works to mitigate the influence of mass media and the corporations and think tanks that subsidize their content. Pay-for-participation subsidizes citizen-generated content instead, putting citizen deliberation back in the centre of democratic decision-making.

Mass media: the single biggest threat to democracy

In a certain sense Athenian debate was rather dull because there were no bright lights or camera-ready smiles, but in another sense it was terribly exciting, because it was real. Media today might be more exciting on a superficial level, but it is 'fake exciting'. 'Big stories' break for no better reason than that a PR agent was able to have them placed on a wire agency. Politicians clap each other on the back in a friendly photo that is actually a selfie. Experts sit in sharp suits to glare through pince-nez glasses and give the talking points that their think tanks demand. To top it all off, internet conversation is dominated by trolls and celebrities who can afford to hire others to oversee their online presence.

In an environment saturated with mass misinformation, freedom at the ballot box is nearly irrelevant. Manipulation can occur effectively and easily before the voting stage. However, this cycle can be at least partially broken by implementing a financially feasible pay-for-participation model in which citizens participate in online debate with each other immediately prior to voting. When citizens debate online, they are given an opportunity to inform each other and set priorities without mediating filters. This ensures that debate and action will centre around citizens' needs to a greater degree and that direct democracy can be supported by an environment that allows for truly equal debate.

It is not a perfect solution, to be sure: some point out that even in wealthy countries not everyone has access to high-speed internet; others may be concerned about the lack of privacy that unavoidably accompanies a non-anonymous debate. However, notwithstanding these concerns, holding a debate in which a majority of citizens stand a goodly chance of expressing their views or hearing very similar views expressed by someone else without being prevented from doing so by privileged gatekeepers is certainly preferable to going to the polls subjected only to mass misinformation, which is what we are currently doing.

Democracy and Dissent: The Balance between Individual and Community

Laws are like cobwebs: if some light or powerless thing falls into them, they hold it fast, but if a thing of any great size falls into them, it breaks through and escapes.

Solon

In modern Western states, we draw a line between the individual and the community that is, at least on paper, extremely favourable to the individual. When we participate in politics, we tend to do so on an individual basis, and we live under a protective regime of individual rights drawn up by legislators and enforced by professional judges. It is argued that without such a strong protection of individual rights and respect for the individual, we would all degenerate into crazed mob rule in a heartbeat. Life, so the official narrative would have it, is about individual struggle and individual triumph; society owes its existence and progress to the achievements of strong and powerful individuals, not to the community as a whole.

Such views are, however, not necessarily the most conducive to the existence of democracy and, indeed, the Athenians saw things a little differently then we do today. As Aristotle noted, society precedes the individual. No individual, unless he be a beast or a god, can survive for long without some kind of community around him. Therefore, in Athens, as in many ancient societies, when push came to shove, the community was always held to be more important than the individual.

That can sound harsh at first, and the Athenian views on where the balance between individual needs and societal needs should be drawn has been used to inflame fears of democracy for centuries. These fears mainly centre on the idea that 'the people' as a whole are essentially an ignorant mob which, if left to its own devices, will expropriate the rich, deal inhumanely with criminals, and fail to operate with any sense of individuality and personal space. In this view, it is necessary for government to protect 'decent people' from the depredations that the masses would surely perpetrate if they were not constantly kept in check by a strong system of individual rights protection.

This perception is, however, based on a lot of mistaken beliefs.

The truth about individual rights in Athens

Far from living under oppressive mob rule, Athenian citizens enjoyed a broad sphere of political freedom. According to Aristotle this was what democracy was all about, because 'another element [of liberty] is to live as you like. For this, they say, is what being free is about, since its opposite, living not as you like, is the condition of a slave.'[1] Personal freedom was an important ideal in Athens. According to the *rhetor* Pericles, the Athenians were so determined to live and let live that they even tried their best to avoid giving each other dirty looks when it came to private affairs.

Beyond this respect for personal space, the Athenians also enjoyed a set of rights comparable to constitutional rights in many modern states. Athenian citizens could never be made slaves, and they could never be tortured. Only thieves and robbers caught in the act could be executed without trial, and only if they pleaded guilty – a circumstance which, all things considered, one cannot imagine happened very often. All other accused who were taken into custody had a right to trial within thirty days. Laws affecting specified individuals could only be passed if the Assembly voted by a quorum of 6,000 with a ballot to permit such a law, and private property was protected from seizure by the state through a promise made each year by the chief *archon* when he took office. These were very similar standards of treatment to those enjoyed by citizens of Western nations today. If anything, the situation was perhaps somewhat better – after all, in recent years execution without trial by drone strike and torture in far-flung rendition sites have become increasingly common occurrences.

In addition to these protective rights, the Athenian democrats made what was, for the time, an unusually strong effort to legislate for the more vulnerable members of their society. In fact, critics of democracy frequently complained about the Athenians' deplorably soft attitude to their slaves. According to the Old Oligarch, under democracy, slaves and foreign

---

1 Aristotle, *Politics*, at 258.

residents 'can no longer be distinguished from Athenians in appearance or attire and even have the nerve to talk back to free citizens'; Athenians are 'not permitted to strike them, and a slave will not stand out of the way for you'; and democrats 'allow their slaves to live in the lap of luxury'.[2] Socrates corroborates the Old Oligarch's statements, claiming that the distinction between slave and free citizen was not very noticeable in Athens. Indeed, the democrats introduced legislation that prohibited owners from killing their slaves or subjecting them to prolonged cruelty. A right of sanctuary for slaves was recognized, and if a slave was abused he could demand to be sold to a new master. According to the custom of the time, slaves were sometimes freed as a reward for loyalty and good service, but more often by ransoming themselves with the savings that it was traditional to allow them to accumulate. It may not sound like much, but by ancient standards this sort of 'slave protection' was cutting edge, 'loony left' thinking, and it did not win the Athenian democrats many admirers in neighbouring states.

But on top of these various rights and protections, the absolutely central right in Athens was freedom of speech. This right was subdivided into *parrhesia* (the freedom to say what one liked) and *isegoria* (the freedom to speak in the Assembly). It was not only a negative right protecting liberty to express oneself, but also a positive right to participate in affairs of state through the medium of free speech in a public setting. As such, it went considerably farther than the right to free speech that citizens enjoy in modern 'democracies', which is limited to an area similar to Athenian *parrhesia*.

2 Pseudo-Xenophon, *Constitution of the Athenians*.

As this indicates, the Athenians had a slightly different idea of rights to the common one today. They certainly didn't see rights as something that protected them from 'the government' – after all, they *were* the government. Instead, they viewed rights as a mixture of protecting citizens from abuse from others and abuse from law enforcement mechanisms, and *crucially*, as protecting the individual's status as a citizen entitled to participate in society.

Far from being a crazed mob, the Athenian democrats had enormous respect both for laws and the process of law-making. The fact that their laws went in some ways further and also included participatory rights did not *negate* the fact that the Athenians also valued individual life and private property – it simply placed those values in the context of a larger community.

But despite all of this evidence to the contrary, one example is brought up time and again that supposedly proves that in a society where all people rule equally, the short-sighted and envious common folk will inevitably get out the pitchforks and torches and abuse their power to mistreat their own citizens. This example has nearly attained the status of an urban myth and it is the trial of Socrates.

Fact is stranger than fiction: the extraordinary trial of Socrates

Socrates was, as everyone knows, a famous philosopher who lived in Athens, and a democratic court condemned him to commit suicide by drinking hemlock – an order which Socrates duly complied with.

This is the point where most analysis stops and simply concludes that this is a prime example of everything that is wrong with the kind of democracy that gives ordinary people 'too much power' instead of reserving it to 'qualified' and 'responsible' individuals. It was exactly this sort of event that the Founding Fathers had in mind when they condemned democracy as a 'tyranny' and 'spectacle of turbulence'.

However, anyone who bothers to really read up on Socrates will shortly understand that the issue was more complicated than that.

Hard-core philosophy: Socrates' ideal state

Scholars respect Socrates for his profound insights into human psychology, his iron spine in the face of adversity and his thorough method of academic analysis. But it is probably fair to say that most people today would not be very happy to live in the kind of society that Socrates thought was ideal.

To begin with, Socrates did not believe that people were born equal and he complained that democracy dispensed equality 'to equals and unequals alike'. In Socrates' opinion only superior people (whom he called 'guardians') should be permitted to govern a state. Allowing ordinary people to run the nation through Assembly and courts was simply ridiculous.

This alone was already not a very popular view in democratic Athens.

But Socrates went farther.

Much farther.

One of Socrates' chief ambitions for his ideal state was the creation of a sophisticated propaganda model to reinforce rule by the superior guardians. To this end, Greek history and mythology would be completely rewritten so that children could be indoctrinated with what he considered to be appropriate values. 'The first thing will be to establish a censorship of the writers of fiction,' Socrates, victim of state oppression, is recorded as saying, 'and let the censors receive any tale of fiction which is good, and reject the bad; and we will desire mothers and nurses to tell their children the authorized ones only.' In addition to this cradle-to-grave propaganda system, the superior men and women who governed the ideal city would be permitted 'to lie for the public good'. In fact, the population would be subjected to an entire culture of falsehoods as to why it was necessary to order their state under guardian rule, even including fake oracular prophecies if necessary. Imagine a leading philosopher today suggesting that the Bible be rewritten to better gloss over Jesus' obsession with poor people, and you will have an idea of the kind of shock value Socrates' statements delivered to the more traditionally devout Athenian.

And from there things got even weirder.

Socrates also believed in an organized eugenics programme, resembling nothing so much as the infamous Nazi *Lebensborn* association, which encouraged persons they considered to be of high genetic 'value' to enter into extramarital relationships for the sake of producing genetically 'pure' children. And, philosophically speaking, Socrates was coming from a similar place. In conformity with his own ideas on rewriting religion, Socrates claimed that Asclepius, the god of healing, 'did not want to lengthen out good-for-nothing lives, or to have weak fathers begetting weaker sons'. Therefore to allow for the breeding of better offspring, Socrates' guardians would live in a polygamous commune where 'the wives of our guardians are to be common [i.e.

shared], and their children are to be common, and no parent is to know his own child, nor any child his parent'. In fact, Socrates advocated a breeding programme for the entire society. Only the guardians would know of the existence of this programme, which they would impose on everyone else by arranging opportunities for copulation according to a set of lots which the guardians would fix in advance.

Oddly, the Athenian democrats were not in a rush to give this 'ideal' society a try.

However, as truly offensive as some of Socrates' teachings were, Athenian society tolerated his presence and continued to allow him to broadcast his views. In fact, many Athenians thought Socrates was so far off-base as to provide terrific entertainment value; the comedic playwright Aristophanes even wrote Socrates into one of his plays for his audience's amusement.

If Socrates had merely continued propagating his views, other Athenians probably would have just continued laughing at him (it says a lot about the kind of reception Socrates tended to get that in his ideal state fits of laughter were to be avoided),[3] but unfortunately someone actually took him up on them. In fact, several young, very wealthy men became ardent admirers of the philosopher. His ideas that the 'best' should rule had a strong appeal, because as rich, well-educated citizens, this obviously meant them. These young men could see an oligarchy already in practice in neighbouring Sparta, where people like themselves made all decisions and the peasants were at their mercy. What Socrates elaborated on seemed to them to be a more extreme, pure version of

---

3 All of Socrates' quotes in this section taken from Plato, *The Republic and Other Works.*

Sparta.[4] And unlike Socrates, these young men didn't just talk about an ideal society. They set out to make one.

The Thirty Tyrants: Athenians laugh out of the other side of their mouths

While they probably had varying motivations for doing so, the fact remains that several of Socrates' students led and participated in one of the most horrific events that occurred over the entire 140-year course of Athenian democracy. This was the oligarchic coup of 404 BC, known as the rule of the Thirty Tyrants or, as historians have described it, 'a murderous right-wing junta'.[5]

And as that suggests, the Thirty Tyrants truly earned their name. Operating with the backing of Sparta, they lost no time in executing the democracy's leading citizens and dismantling the democratic institutions. Those preliminaries accomplished, they then composed a list of 3,000 citizens whom they considered to be 'the best men'. Anyone who wasn't on that list immediately lost all legal rights. They could be killed and their property confiscated by the Thirty at any time. As if that wasn't all terrifying enough, the Tyrants then began to purge the city in a manner that seemed to borrow straight from Socrates' teachings.

Socrates, well aware that most Athenians would never accept the kind of state that he proposed, had suggested kick-starting his ideal civilization by getting a group of like-minded people to expel everyone who was over the

4 Critias, the leader of the coup, was especially close to Socrates, with Plato even penning dialogues purporting to have taken place between the two.
5 Wallace, 'Law, freedom and the concept of citizens' rights in democratic Athens', at 113.

age of ten from a city. This group of like-minded individuals would then train the remaining children according to Socrates' vision.

The Thirty Tyrants performed a version of this, expelling everyone who was not in the 3,000 from the city of Athens. It was a move that seemed to have been lifted straight from Socrates' playbook as a method of shocking a society into submission. Pol Pot would later use a similar strategy to nullify pre-existing society and start again in 'Year Zero' in Cambodia in the 1970s. As scholars have noted:

> The Thirty depended upon violence to seize power, to rid the community of the previous political culture, and to block opposition ... Once the conspirators had seized control of Athens, they had to secure their rule by reshaping the political culture from a democracy in which the citizens participated extensively in the affairs of the city, to a narrow oligarchy, which excluded a large share of the citizens from the political sphere and demanded obedience from the rest. This could not be done without eliminating the opposition and silencing the survivors so that they would accept their new political role as subjects.[6]

All told, the Thirty Tyrants murdered 5 per cent of the Athenian population in less than a year. They also slaughtered an unknown number of non-citizen residents. In one particularly notorious example, in order to pay their Spartan helpers, the Thirty decided that each of them (that is, each of the Thirty Tyrants) should seize one foreign resident. They

---

6 Wolpert, *Remembering Defeat: Civil War and Civic Memory in Ancient Athens*, at 16 and 22.

then executed these foreigners, confiscated their assets and used them to pay the Spartans.

Throughout this terrifying debacle, Socrates stood quietly to one side. He did not join the thousands fleeing Athens and when the Thirty ordered him to arrest a prominent citizen, Leon of Salamis, while Socrates failed to comply, he did not attempt to prevent Leon's arrest or even to warn him. Instead, Socrates simply returned to his own home. It is unlikely that Leon of Salamis, who was executed by the Tyrants without trial, felt much gratitude for this extremely nuanced stand. If it had been left to Socrates, Athenian democracy would have been utterly shattered by the Thirty Tyrants – his students. Fortunately, however, the very nature of Athenian democracy, which encouraged citizens to take matters into their own hands, asserted itself.

The downfall of the Thirty and the prosecution of Socrates

It didn't take the scattered Athenians long to mount a daring and impressive military campaign against the Thirty Tyrants. When it became clear that they would eventually win and reinstall democracy, the Tyrants slaughtered the entire male population of the nearby city of Eleusis and gave up Athens to retreat there. The two sides eventually negotiated a settlement that allowed the Thirty to remain at Eleusis and – importantly for later events – obligated the Athenians to declare an amnesty for all crimes that had been committed in relation to their rule. Socrates did not take the opportunity to move to Eleusis. He remained in Athens, apparently oblivious to the fact that, far from poking fun at him, people now took his views very seriously indeed. After all, as long as the Tyrants remained at Eleusis, there was a real danger that the

Spartans would again collude with them to overthrow the democracy and embark on another reign of terror.

In fact, some citizens felt that Socrates was too dangerous to be left in Athens. Since the amnesty made it impossible to try Socrates for treason on grounds of his involvement with the Thirty, he was officially indicted for 'worshipping strange gods and speaking blasphemy among the young'.[7] After all, Socrates had permitted himself to rewrite Athenian religion in the service of his chilling ideology. However, everyone alive at the time was well versed in the real reasons for the trial and Socrates' defence indicates the true nature of the indictment by repeatedly referring to a widespread perception of him as a person who 'makes the worse seem the better cause'.[8]

Socrates, of course, like any other Athenian, had the opportunity to defend himself in court, but during his speech he refused to engage in any kind of reconciliation with his jurors over his role in the rise of the Thirty Tyrants or to express real remorse over what had happened. This was an extremely gutsy (some would say stubborn) move, considering that the jurors were, of course, Athenian citizens who had all lived through the Tyrants' reign and were acutely aware of Socrates' connections with, and influence on, some of the key participants.

If Socrates had been put on trial today, his case would have been an open-and-shut conviction. Freedom of speech certainly doesn't cover incitement to genocide, sedition or conspiracy – all of which Socrates seems to have engaged in. One need only think of the fate of 'terrorist masterminds'

---

7 Bury, 'The Age of Illumination', in *Cambridge Ancient History*, vol. V at 376, at 390 et seq.
8 Plato, *Apology*, in *The Republic and Other Works*, at 448, 449 and 453.

like Osama bin Laden to note how modern civilization deals with anyone who attacks it or encourages others to do so. However, the Athenian democrats were far stronger believers in the right to free speech and dissent than our governments are today, and Athenian society was deeply split about what should be done with Socrates. Thus, despite everything that had happened, Socrates was convicted by a margin of only thirty votes.

Only after this point did things take a turn for the worse.

In Athens, the jury decided the sentence in a separate process after the verdict was announced. In doing so, the jurors were allowed to choose only between the sentences proposed by the prosecutor and the defendant. They could not decide to hand out a sentence that they had thought up themselves. In Socrates' case the prosecution demanded the death penalty, as was standard procedure in all cases of sufficient magnitude. In such cases, it was also customary for the defendant to propose the next-worst punishment: exile. Athens, like many other ancient societies, didn't have much in the way of jails and so preferred to simply rid itself of disruptive elements. If the criminal agreed to leave voluntarily, this was often considered the least fuss all round. Even murderers were routinely exiled instead of executed, and there was every expectation that this would be Socrates' fate.

Socrates, however, refused to bow to custom and propose exile as his own punishment. Instead, he maintained that he had been so helpful to the Athenian people that his 'penalty' should be to be given free room and board at public expense for the rest of his life. In his speech to the court, Socrates defiantly explained to the jury why he deserved to be rewarded for his services at some length before finally agreeing to propose a fine of 3,000 drachmae in only a few brief sentences. This was a fairly substantial sum (roughly equivalent to $180,000), although not necessarily commensurate with the severity of the case. To add insult to injury, Socrates made clear that he personally was broke and would therefore pay only about 100 drachmae ($6,000) – his friends would pay the rest. Left with only the choice between imposing the death penalty, as proposed by the prosecution, and imposing a moderate fine on Socrates' friends, as proposed by himself, the irritated jurors – many of whom had lost friends, family and fortune to the Thirty Tyrants – opted for the death penalty. In fact, the jurors were so provoked by Socrates' unapologetic attitude that they voted for the death penalty in greater numbers than they had voted to convict him.

Even that rash decision didn't last, however. As usual, once they'd cooled down, the Athenians tried to patch things up. They gave Socrates to understand that it was not too late to just disappear from his cell and go into exile after all. But defiant to the end, and always keen to prove a point at any price, Socrates chose to kill himself by drinking hemlock in accordance with his sentence.

The prosecution of the great philosopher Socrates at the hands of the angry citizenry was thus a little different to how it is usually made out to be. The trial did not occur because Socrates was just so exceptionally brilliant that other people resented his superiority. It happened because he had managed to give his jurors a lesson in practical philosophy that they were never likely to forget.

Prosecution purely for holding offbeat views is something that, as far as we know, never actually occurred in Athens.

In fact, the Athenian democracy tolerated a large volume of dissent from Socrates, Plato and Aristotle (the last of whom wasn't even an Athenian citizen). This is not to say that it would not be necessary to have legal rights or protections in a direct democracy – points we will come to shortly – it is merely to point out that in the one direct democracy that we have to study, 'the people' generally had better things to do with their time than to terrorize individuals. Far from demonstrating the lawlessness of democracy, the trial of Socrates illustrates the vulnerability of democracy to a few determined opponents like the Thirty Tyrants, as well as the need to contextualize individual rights within the society.

Protecting democracy from dissenters

While the case of Socrates is more complicated than it seems at first glance, it's still an important one for us. When we discuss making democracy more direct and more participatory, we tend to focus on protecting individuals from democracy, but what about protecting democracy from individuals? After all, unlike the Athenians, we live in societies with court systems that are separated from the parliament or congress, and no one is suggesting changing that practice in the immediate future. We've also seen that when people are given the chance to vote directly on political matters, as in participatory budgeting in Paris or Cologne or New York, they are, much like the Athenians before them, downright sober in their choices because, like the Athenians before them, they also have other things to do. When we think about democracy, it's really not *most* people we have to worry about, because *most* people never step out of line. It's only ever a *few* people who are dangerous, and they are dangerous precisely for their abilities to undermine democracy and bring the political system under their own control. And it is precisely these *few* people who are most afraid of *most* people, because these *few* people are highly unlikely to like the laws that *most* people would like to see passed.

It's the same stand-off that occurred in Athens between oligarchs and democrats. The democrats – *most people* – thought that the oligarchs were wrong for wanting to impose an elite-only rule that badly abused the majority, and the oligarchs – *a few people* – thought that the democrats were wrong for running a system that gave them few privileges and passing laws which made it harder for them to exert the authority they thought they deserved. The oligarchs truly believed that 'the masses' were a threat – to their own chosen lifestyle. And today, largely because our media and governments are run by modern oligarchs, we've accepted their narrative as reality. The truth is, however, that oligarchs and democrats will always see each other and everything they do as threats.

And in a way they are both right.

The democratic way of life is an existential threat to oligarchs and the oligarchic way of life is an existential threat to democrats. They can't be reconciled. Based on the research presented in this book, I'm inclined to go with the Athenians and hold that the true threat to democracy is not the angry mob or unwashed masses, but the rich and powerful who continually try to undermine it.

So the question we really need to be asking ourselves is how to protect any nascent participatory democracy from those who do not favour democracy at all.

A fragile balance: the economy, the rule of law and democracy

According to Charles Montesquieu, an Enlightenment-era philosopher, who came up with the idea of constitutional checks and balances, laws 'must make each poor citizen comfortable enough to be able to work as the others do and must bring each rich citizen to a middle level such that he needs to work in order to preserve or to acquire'.[9] Jean-Jacques Rousseau came to a similar conclusion, claiming that democracy presupposed 'a large measure of equality in social rank and fortune, without which equality in rights and authority will not last long'.[10] Even Aristotle subscribed to the desirability of general affluence in a democracy, stating that: 'Poverty is the cause of the defects of democracy. That is why measures should be taken to ensure a permanent level of prosperity.'[11]

These philosophers and the Athenian democrats who preceded them accepted that democracy depended on equal participation and that a democratic society had to enable that participation. A situation in which some people were so well off as to be above the law was dangerous. In fact, if democracy was to thrive no one should feel that they would be better off without it. The Athenians did not resolve this problem perfectly, as the rise of the Thirty Tyrants demonstrates, but they did have some success, and they provide something to orient ourselves on in this regard.

---

9 De Secondat, Baron de Montesquieu, *The Spirit of Laws*, vol. 1, at 44–9.
10 Rousseau, *The Social Contract*, at 113 and 140 et seq.
11 Aristotle, op. cit., at 268 et seq.

Democracy and individual wealth: how rich is too rich?

Democratic Athens was a business-friendly and fiscally conservative city that welcomed foreign residents. At the height of the democratic period, the city held the equivalent of a $1 billion reserve fund (not bad for a place with only 330,000 residents), and Athenian coinage was the reserve currency of its time. Furthermore, Athens enforced an 'unusual respect for private property' as compared to other civilizations.[12] The banking system was both sophisticated and profitable and the Athenians had factory production and shipping organization down to a science. In other words, in its basic structure, the Athenian economy wasn't that much different to our own. Athenians were, by and large, not averse to being well off and Athens was home to some extremely wealthy individuals. We even know how many of them there were: 1,200, or 4 per cent of the adult male citizen population. These were Athens' super-rich.

But wealth is a relative concept – you can only know whether you are rich or poor in comparison to the people around you.

So what did it mean to be 'rich' or even 'super-rich' in Athens?

We can get an idea of this from the records that the Athenians left behind.

For example, we know that the *rhetor* Demosthenes sued his guardians to recover an inheritance worth 50,000 drachmae. This means that Demosthenes possessed a personal fortune equivalent to about two hundred times the average annual income of unskilled labour. In modern

---

12 Nafissi, 'Class, embeddedness and the modernity of Ancient Athens', at 393.

terms, this would have been the equivalent of inheriting an estate worth roughly $3 million. Likewise, we know that in the early years of democracy the two most valuable farms in Athens were valued at 12,000 and 15,000 drachmae ($734,000 and $918,000) respectively. During the reign of the Thirty Tyrants, the writer Xenophon recorded some of the estates that the Thirty desired to confiscate, listing the estate of the wealthy Nicias as worth 100 talents (600,000 drachmae, or $36.7 million) and the less affluent, but still noteworthy, Niceratus' as worth 14 talents (or $5.1 million).

From these and similar records, we can extrapolate that the very wealthy in Athens were, relative to the rest of the economy, something equivalent to modern millionaires – they may have possessed $1 million or $5 million or even $30 million in property, usually in the form of land, but they did not possess hundreds of millions or billions.

By contrast, today, the top 1 per cent of wealthy Americans own one third of all wealth in the United States. In Demosthenes' time, $3 million was considered to be a very substantial inheritance and some people may have inherited fortunes worth up to the equivalent of $30 million, or even a little more. But Sam Walton – owner of Walmart (the same Walmart that pays its workers less than subsistence wages and uses the savings to finance the Club of Madrid) – left $60 billion behind him with each of his six heirs inheriting over $10 billion. In fact, the Waltons own more wealth than the bottom 30 per cent of Americans combined and earn about $350 million in dividends each year. And they are by no means alone. The three Mars siblings (of Mars Bar fortune) inherited a total of $20 billion. The situation is similar in Britain, where the five richest families own more than the bottom 20 per cent of the population. To belong to the economic elite today, you need to be far, far richer than any Athenian democrat. In fact, you need to be richer than even the richest Romans were. Cicero may have bought a villa for $300 million, but the rich today can shell out as much as $500 million just for a private jet. According to Branko Milanovic, a former World Bank economist, Carlos Slim, the Mexican businessman born in 1940, could buy the labour of 440,000 average-earning Mexicans, making him fourteen times richer than Marcus Licinius Crassus, the richest Roman alive at the end of the Republic. That means that the current gap between rich and poor is not only much wider than in Athens, it is even wider than it was in Rome, a state that made no bones about being an oligarchy.

This is a deep problem for democracy, because when the gap between rich and poor is so wide, it is extremely easy for the wealthy to buy influence and very difficult to enforce laws against them. We can see this in many areas of life – for example, in the application of tax laws. Internal revenue bureaus often spend a great deal of time and money enforcing tax laws against small businesses, but tend to let the big fish get away with tax evasion. Similarly, the very rich often escape the full consequences of crime, as they are able to mount an effective, expensive defence, whereas poorer people are forced to rely on underfunded legal aid, which is often unable to defend them adequately in court. This creates, in effect, two different societies: those who make the laws – through financing legislators – but who do not need to obey them, and those who do not make the laws, but are compelled to obey them. There is no unified country, but rather two different communities, who are hostile to each other.

And there is no reason to expect that too many of the very rich, who are used to getting their way, would be willing to live in a democracy and abide by the rules of the majority. Some undoubtedly would – as a few did in Athens – but many others would likely focus their substantial resources on simply toppling the system in order to bring back 'the good old days' when they could do as they liked.

That's bad news for democracy, because participation rights and even laws, no matter how ardently defended, simply cannot hold out against extremely rich individuals intent on bending them in their own interests. They only ever need to find the weakest link in the chain to start the vicious cycle of wealth = power and power = wealth rolling again.

This is why it is impossible to contemplate creating a direct or digital democracy without addressing the severe economic imbalance in our society. Democracy can thrive over a long period only if no one is so powerful as to literally be above the society they live in. The Athenians failed to do this perfectly, but since they were at least robust enough to overcome the Thirty Tyrants, their experience offers some useful starting points for what a democracy-compatible economy might look like.

Democratic Athens: Solon, Seisachtheia and the ultimate tax break

It's oddly reassuring to learn that the Athenians also didn't always get things right the first time and that their well-balanced, democracy-supporting economy was actually the product of deep mistakes that the nation had made in the past. In the years preceding democracy, the Athenian economy was one long disaster. As a matter of fact, events in this period bore a striking resemblance not only to the rapid economic changes in the Roman Republic at the time of the Gracchi but to our own financial crisis today. However, while Rome's elite stubbornly refused to change, the Athenians confronted and resolved their economic difficulties. The results were impressive, but it was no easy task.

At the height of the Athenian crisis, many citizens were so far in debt to others – mainly through mortgages – that the economy had literally ceased to function. The high levels of debt meant that Athens, which at the time operated on a political system of restricted representation, was becoming increasingly feudal. Great landowners exercised a degree of patronage over their tenants, and smaller landholders were constantly working just to pay off their debt with no hope of improvement. Recognizing that they were really in serious trouble, those property-owning Athenians who enjoyed the right to vote elected a man named Solon and charged him with resolving the crisis.

Solon took several measures to restart the Athenian economy, but the most serious one was the most effective: Solon cancelled the debt, an event later known as 'the *Seisachtheia*' or shaking off of burdens. After this debt cancellation, the Athenians continued to have differentiated levels of income, but total economic dependence between citizens had been eradicated. This meant that there was a level of freedom in how they contracted with one another, opening the door not only to more equitable economics, but to more equitable politics as well.

Democratic Athens did not forget the lessons learned during the *Seisachtheia*, namely that capitalist economies are tilted in favour of those who already have money and property. Provided they do not make any major mistakes, people who start out rich almost inevitably get richer, and people who start out poor almost inevitably get poorer, no matter how hard they work or how talented they are. When this happens the economy becomes inefficient. Money does not flow to the investments and projects that can use it most productively to create new wealth. Businesses fail, or at least fail to get off the ground, and the economy shrinks, making the poor even poorer and the rich even richer. Therefore, in order to prevent a capitalist economy from crashing, it is necessary to create a financial counter-flow.

One of the methods the Athenians used to achieve this was what seems at first glance to be a very extreme form of progressive taxation. In Athens, not all public revenue was provided by the wealthy – the average Athenian had to pay small import and export duties, market dues and sales tax – but quite a lot of it was. The *eisphora*, a capital levy imposed in times of need, was exacted only from those who owned property worth more than 2,500 drachmae, i.e. all of those citizens whose holdings placed them in the upper middle class and higher, about 30 per cent of the total society.

The Athenians also placed additional burdens on the truly rich. These were known as 'liturgical duties' and consisted of financing specific public projects. One of the most important of these was the duty to act as trierarch – that is, a person who had to bear the costs of outfitting a naval ship. The cost of being trierarch was estimated at about 5,000 drachmae (ca. $300,000) each time one was called to this service. Other liturgical duties included: paying for gymnastic and musical equipment; hosting banquets; financing a chorus at the festivals; and sponsoring a relay team for the torch races.

In other words, in Athens, defence and entertainment basically went on the tab of the super-rich. And as far as those wealthy individuals were concerned, these were not necessarily enjoyable acts of charity, but repetitive, state-mandated legal obligations. The cost of fulfilling liturgical duties was considerable – it is thought that the wealthy spent more than 50 per cent of their income on liturgical duties. While this sounds like a lot, it is important to remember that today most ordinary people have a total tax burden that nearly equals the one that was imposed only on Athens' wealthiest – even low earners pay nearly 30 per cent in income tax and social charges, in addition to sales tax and other consumption taxes on property, fuel and cigarettes – whereas the majority of Athenians never paid any income tax.

In Athens, having to pay tax was a sign of prosperity. To fulfil or over-fulfil liturgical obligations was to be a good citizen, worthy of honour and respect, whereas to avoid such obligations was to be a bad citizen whose commitment to democracy was very questionable. We know this because people who scrupulously fulfilled or over-fulfilled their liturgical obligations spent a lot of time and energy making sure that everyone else knew it. Many wealthy individuals today boast about their charity efforts, but '[n]o one today boasts in a persuasive way of the size of his income tax, and certainly not that he pays three times as much as the collector demands. But it was standard practice in the Athenian courts'.[13]

This exemplifies the different attitude towards public obligations in Athens, where contributing to the community was something to take pride in. Most Athenians did not view the

13 Finley, *The Ancient Economy*, at 151 et seq.

public budget or public welfare as something that was 'not their problem' – the common refrain heard from tax avoiders today. Wealthy Athenians were well aware that the welfare of their economy was absolutely their problem. After all, wealthy and secure countries where they could comfortably make their home didn't grow on trees. Taxpaying Athenians appreciated that their nation was something they were very much a part of and that it was precious enough to be worth a few sacrifices.

It was a wise attitude.

Through the *eisphoria* and liturgical obligations wealth was redistributed from rich to poor (and ultimately back again) in a healthy, mutually beneficial manner. Some of these revenues were used not just to provide public infrastructure, but to care for the more vulnerable members of Athenian society. Cultural activities were subsidized in that the 'poor' were usually allotted 5 drachmae a year from the Theoric Fund (Athens' treasury fund for surplus revenue) to allow them to attend the theatre at festivals. Disabled citizens who possessed less than 200 drachmae in property were given 2 obols a day from the state, an amount sufficient to purchase adequate food for themselves. During their recovery from the oligarchic coup, the Assembly passed a decree providing a small allowance to the orphans whose parents had died in the fighting, obtaining funds for this by simultaneously reducing the pay for cavalry soldiers, who were among Athens' wealthier citizens. Furthermore, the revenues from public property (including the publicly owned gold and silver mines in Thrace, Macedonia and Laurium) were distributed among all citizens, much as a portion of oil revenue is distributed to citizens in some modern Gulf states. This further equalized income while preventing individual citizens from usurping national resources for themselves. And, of course, as we know, Athens paid its citizens for their participation in democracy, meaning that a constant trickle of small payments flowed from the public treasury to Athenians of all income classes who were willing to partake in the business of running the state.

In addition to all of this, Athenian wages were relatively egalitarian and stable. That meant that while some people were becoming wealthier and wealthier every day they worked, it didn't happen to such an extent that it put lower earners and their descendants at a permanent disadvantage. We know this because we still have some of the bookkeeping accounts for the Erechtheum, the famous temple to Athena and Poseidon that sits on the Acropolis.

According to these accounts, the site's labourers received 1 drachma per day while the architect received 37 drachmae for the thirty-six-day month. Since the architect was not required to be on-site full-time, his advantage is slightly larger than appears at first glance; however, his income per hour spent on the job cannot have been much more than two or three times that of the labourers. He who contributed more earned more, but not ridiculously more, and the architect contracted to build the Acropolis must have been very distinguished in his field. It is not unusual for famous architects today to earn millions – a far cry from the wages of the labourers and bricklayers who actually build their projects.

This wage egalitarianism was reflected in the price of essential commodities. The median value of houses sold in Athens in 414 BC (around the same time as the accounting records from the Erechtheum) was 410 drachmae. Housing prices thus represented less than two years' income from unskilled labour. By comparison, the average house price in London (and Athens was the London of its day) is £458,000. The average UK salary is £26,500, meaning that an *average* house in London represents over seventeen years of income for the average worker. Drop that down to unskilled labour, which earns around £7,000–12,000 a year, and the average house price in London is equivalent to forty-five years' income. Not forty-five years of mortgage payments, forty-five years of pre-tax income.

All of this information tells us that the Athenian economy was much more healthy and balanced than our own. It was possible to become very rich and it was possible to become very poor, but it was not possible to drive things to the point where some citizens, to all intents and purposes, owned others and were placed in a situation where they could purchase their political compliance. This level of economic balance is key to how Athenian democracy lasted as long as it did, in as stable a state as it did. The question for us is how we could adapt some of the Athenian economic principles to work in a modern democracy to ensure that everyone is part of that democracy and that no one can use their wealth to place themselves above it.

Rebalancing the economy today

Three of the key causes of serious income inequality in modern-day society are financial speculation, corporate exploitation and (especially in Western countries) accumulated inheritance in a shrinking population. The measures suggested here are aimed at regulating these three core areas.

Levelling the playing field: restricting inheritance

Alexis de Tocqueville, the famous French writer who studied government in the early USA, noted the importance of regulating inheritance in the interests of democracy and equality. During Tocqueville's time, inheritance in America was divided by law among the sons of the deceased instead of passing in its entirety to the first son, as was common in France under the law of primogeniture. Tocqueville observed that in America great fortunes were gradually diminished as they were split among more and more offspring instead of being hoarded and producing substantial financial inequality at birth. Although there is now no law of primogeniture, inheritance is still a significant factor in creating extremely high levels of wealth inequality, owing not least to the fact that today people can make more money faster and usually do not have as many relatives among whom to split their wealth at the end of their lifetime. In fact, the population in many countries, especially in Europe, is decreasing, which means that wealth and inheritances automatically become more concentrated. And that creates serious inequalities – from birth.

The average inheritance received by British citizens from a single beneficiary is just £17,500, while the average American household inherits only $40,000. Even these 'average' numbers are, however, deceiving. Over 70 per cent of people do not receive any inheritance at all (in fact, many of them must meet the costs of end-of-life care for their relatives), while some inherit thousands or hundreds of thousands, and a few individuals inherit millions or billions. This creates deep intergenerational inequality that is nearly impossible to overcome and which stands in sharp contrast to modern ideals of meritocracy and entrepreneurship. No one *earns* an inheritance.

More worryingly, however, enormous inheritances deeply undermine the idea of democratic equality. Those who inherit large fortunes are placed in a politically and economically unassailable position from birth. They are simply not subject to the same living conditions as others, nor are laws or rules as easy to enforce against them, as they can afford expensive lawyers to exploit legal loopholes in their interests or even buy themselves residency rights in other countries to escape the law in their home state. The very practice of permitting unlimited inheritance creates, as Solon would have said, the 'large creatures' that can easily break through law's 'web'.

Nothing could be simpler than addressing this problem by limiting the inheritance that any one person can receive. This limit could even be quite high – $100,000, say, far above what over 90 per cent of all people can ever expect to inherit – and still be effective. Wealthy individuals would be condemned to nothing worse than either spending their money during their own lifetime – some individuals like Bill Gates are already doing just this – or splitting their estate among enough beneficiaries that none of them exceeds the $100,000 limit. Only if a person who has amassed a large fortune fails to take advantage of these options would the law come into effect and the remainder of the estate be confiscated. This portion of the estate could then be auctioned off and the proceeds distributed evenly to all citizens. Auctioning off Sam Walton's estate (worth $60 billion) would have generated $200 for every man, woman and child in America, all of whom would still remain eligible to inherit up to $100,000 each themselves. Like pay-for-participation, this measure would recirculate money into the economy by distributing to those who are likely to spend it. In many cases, this would reduce reliance on public services and ultimately reduce the tax burden.

The only reason this very simple solution is not implemented is a deeply cherished belief that it is some sort of human right to amass as large a fortune as you wish and to continue commanding that fortune after death. The rights of the individual to private property are so deeply venerated that even the grave is no bar to exercising them. But interpreting individual rights so widely does serious harm to the community by creating a two-tier system that is incompatible with democracy. By limiting wealth inequality to the levels that one person can achieve in their own lifetime, we are doing nothing more than conforming to our own ideals of personal merit and entrepreneurial spirit. After all, there is nothing particularly entrepreneurial or meritorious in inheriting one third of all wealth in a nation. Massive, unearned inheritances are an aristocratic foible that Tocqueville would have recognized and as such not worthy of legal protection.

Dismantling the casino: taxing financial speculation

In many parts of the world gambling is banned, purely in the interests of societal prosperity. The dangers of gambling – addiction, financial ruin – are seen to outweigh the individual's right to engage in it, whether or not there is any reason to believe that that particular individual might behave irresponsibly or become addicted. However, there is one form of gambling that is not subject to the same type of regulation even though its negative impact on society is far worse than all of the slot machines and roulette tables in the world combined: financial speculation.

Many very wealthy people buy and sell large amounts of currency on the stock market every day. For example, a speculator might buy 60 million rupees for $1,000,000 and sell them moments later for $1,010,000. This means he makes $10,000 in seconds, nearly as much money as a minimum-wage-earning American makes in a year, and without having to do any actual work. Needless to say, the $10,000 profit isn't generated through magic, but rather extracted from the workers of the target economy. Such transactions are a regular occurrence on the financial markets today. They serve no purpose whatsoever but to enrich the person making the currency bet at the expense of workers in the target economy. In other words, these transactions do no one much good – the speculator after all doesn't *need* the money, and many people are harmed – just like other kinds of gambling.

And in order to combat this practice, in 1972 James Tobin, a distinguished American economist, suggested that currency conversions should be taxed at 1 per cent. Such a tax would halt extreme forms of currency speculation, a significant source of aggravated income inequality in some parts of the world, while also raising public revenues. According to the Bank for International Settlements, turnover in foreign exchange markets is running at $3,200 billion per day, and some sources have estimated that it would be possible to raise as much as $20–30 billion per year with a Tobin Tax as low as 0.005 per cent. These revenues could be distributed evenly ($30 billion would deliver something over $3 annually to every person on earth) or be used to fund global social welfare projects, such as health-related research, access to clean water or developing clean energy, all measures that are not only good for people but good for the economy. Money would once again flow back into the economy instead of being hoarded to one side and a serious source of extreme income inequality would be alleviated.

However, in the forty years that have passed since James Tobin developed his idea, no such tax has been implemented. In other words, lawgivers have decided that the 'right' of individuals to make financial bets without incurring any penalties outweighs the damage that such speculations wreak on target economies. This does not strike the right balance between individual and community needs – at least not one that would allow democracy to thrive – and it isn't the same balance we choose to strike when we legislate against casinos or online gambling. There, the rights of individuals to host or participate in gambling activities are subordinated to the need to protect communities from the dangers of gambling addiction. And that happens despite the fact that your mortgage payments do not increase or your savings get wiped out just because your neighbour engages in a round of blackjack. If we want democracy to succeed, we have to apply the same standards to everyone. The individual's right to make sophisticated financial bets without adequate taxation cannot supersede the rights of others to financial security if we want to create a society capable of sustaining democracy.

Lifting all boats: pegged salaries

Another severe cause of economic inequality is that our legislators have decided that individuals should be allowed to make as much money as they can possibly get on the market.

Capping the maximum amount of what an individual can earn is considered a terrible infringement on personal rights, even when that 'right' goes so far that it endangers a functioning economy and democratic society, replacing them with a two-tiered system of dependency between ordinary workers and the super-rich.

In most small companies, it is unusual for the owner to make more than two or three times what one of their own typical workers earns. In Japan, CEOs of large companies are paid only sixteen times as much as a typical worker, and in 1964 American CEOs earned only twenty-four times as much as the average worker.

Today, however, the average American CEO earns 243 times the pay of a typical worker, while in some industries the pay gap is even greater. At large banks, the highest-paid workers receive 500 times more money than the lowest paid. As if this were not shocking enough, at pharmaceutical company Novartis the highest-paid employees receive 752 times what the lowest paid receive, while at Credit Suisse, the highest-paid workers receive 1,812 times as much money as the lowest paid. Not only does this enable high earners to extract the wealth of a company into their own pay packets and leave a hollowed-out husk of a corporation behind them when they quit, the wage differential at large corporations is so high that high-paid workers cannot even spend their own wages.

This alone can create severe intergenerational inequality. The children of someone on a low wage will not receive the same educational benefits or attention to their healthcare as the children of a family that makes nearly two thousand times as much money every single year, and they will never be able to compete with them later in life. By allowing this situation of severe income inequality to exist, we are essentially deciding that it is more important for adults to make more money than they know what to do with than for children to have roughly equitable opportunities in life. The 'fairness' of allowing everyone to make whatever they can get away with actually leads to deep unfairness. It is also impossible to maintain a democracy in such a state. How can someone be asked to respect institutions such as social welfare when these will never play any role at all in their lives? How can someone be asked to work hard, when they know that their fate is not in their own hands? What is more, how can these two groups of people ever sit down in Assembly and truly understand each other? When economic equality ceases to exist, political equality also becomes a fiction. If we desire people to work together on a roughly equitable basis, they must, in fact, be more or less equal.

This could be done without infringing on Western values of personal merit and differentiated returns simply by tying the salary of the highest-paid employee of a company to the salary of the lowest-paid employee. For example, the highest-paid employee (or proprietor) would not be permitted to earn more than a certain multiple (say thirty or fifty times) the wages paid to the lowest-paid employee. The highest-paid employee would thus be able to increase his salary only by increasing the salaries of his lower-paid workers. This would tie all workers to the economic productivity of the corporation, and increase economic equality, while still allowing for a significant pay gap to reflect personal merit. It preserves the right of workers to make as much money as they can – there is no absolute upper limit – but it strikes a balance with society. The high-paid worker must take the people who contribute to their success up the ladder of prosperity with them. It makes sense, and a 2013 referendum in Switzerland to have a pay ceiling on high earners of twelve times what lowest earners made received a surprising number of votes in favour. Although it earned the scorn of the business and political establishment, the initiative was greeted by many economists as a necessary market correction. As the neoliberal saying is, 'a rising tide lifts all boats' – this measure merely makes sure that the statement is true.

The economy and democracy: chicken and egg

Monetary influence controls so much of the current political landscape that it is highly unlikely that legislators would ever pass these or similar reforms, which primarily affect the top 1 per cent of earners. After all, this 1 per cent is financing political campaigns precisely to make sure this doesn't happen. However, it is important that these or similar measures are high on the list of priorities for creating a more participatory democracy. Those few persons who are far richer than all others are often able to circumvent laws to their own advantage, quickly eroding any egalitarian political organization (e.g. pressuring judges and juries to make decisions in their favour, influencing public opinion through large communications networks, or failing all else simply mounting a coup). All of these things are only possible where severe wealth inequalities exist, and bringing those disparities down to a sustainable level helps to stabilize democracy while creating a more prosperous society.

The old bugbear: tyranny of the majority

Of course, none of this should blind us to the fact that individuals do need protection from abuse in any society. Socrates' trial may, indeed, have been very different to how it is made out to be, pointing more towards the dangers presented by a few oligarchs than those presented by the democratic majority, but even if fears of the tyranny of the majority were not realized in Socrates' case, it is still beyond dispute that any democracy needs to take adequate measures to prevent oppression and bullying. In a participatory democracy, this is especially the case with regard to minorities. In fact, in a society run on the principle of majority rule, serious consideration needs to be given to how best to enable meaningful minority participation.

And here the example of Athens doesn't provide much help. Like most ancient peoples, the Athenians were an extremely homogeneous crowd. Women, foreigners and slaves were completely excluded from public life, so the active citizenry consisted solely of ethnic Athenian males, who shared a common history, culture and religion.

Most societies today are, of course, very different. Not only do women enjoy the same formal entitlements as men, many countries are home to ethnic minorities, who often share a different history, language or religion to that of the ethnic majority. And inevitably, political issues that de facto affect particular groups arise in these highly diverse societies.

For example, domestic violence, sexual crime, prostitution and other forms of sexual commodification, eating disorders, harassment in the workplace and single parenting are not per se gender-defined issues. There are many male victims of sexual violence, as indeed there are many single fathers. But, for cultural and historical reasons, all of these issues *disproportionately* affect women. Similarly, in some countries ethnic minorities are disproportionately victims of police harassment and workplace discrimination. Even certain diseases, such as diabetes, sickle cell anaemia and cystic fibrosis, disproportionately affect certain ethnic groups.

Thus, while far from true in every case, members of certain groups are more *likely* to be personally affected by these particular issues, and this naturally affects how a voter prioritizes a situation, as well as their assessment of what would constitute appropriate action on the matter. Even group members who are not affected by the issue in question might vote with those who are out of feelings of solidarity. However, as long as they are a minority and the rest of society does not share their concerns, they are unlikely to win a vote on the issues that are of particular interest to them.

And this is where the game theory of electoral systems meets the tyranny of the majority that exists in every true democracy.

Because electoral skewing almost always favours majorities, minorities are generally under-represented in electoral systems. However, this can be offset by the fact that politicians often attempt to capture the loyalty of small groups by catering to their interests, because even a marginal group of committed voters can make the difference between electoral victory and defeat. This gives minorities who are organized and patient enough a chance to get their way on issues important to them by applying pressure to a candidate who needs their vote at the right time. It's not particularly effective, but it does sometimes work.

In a more direct democracy without elected politicians, the option of getting things done by going 'straight to the top' this way would diminish. Instead minorities would have to convince their fellow citizens to side with them for more altruistic reasons. If this fails to happen over a long period of time, the consequences for democracy can be dire. Minority voters can become frustrated and lose the incentive to participate. They may try to get their way by other means, or they may simply fade into the position of disenfranchised citizens who become increasingly subjected to exploitation by the majority.

The key to preventing such minority–majority entrenchment is to keep the political landscape in a constant state of flux. Majority rule is bearable only when every minority opinion has the chance of someday becoming the majority opinion, and when the identity of citizens in the minority and the majority is constantly fluctuating from issue to issue. One method of achieving this lies in encouraging the greatest number of citizens to participate in formulating policy through online deliberation and pay-for-participation, as discussed previously, since this means that the identity of participants is constantly ebbing and flowing. Under these circumstances it is difficult to form hardened groups of voters who work together to exclude others.

Another strategy lies in encouraging citizens to consider each issue on its own separate merits and to discard blind loyalties to broad platforms.

One way to do this would be to ensure that motions are always voted on separately, never bundled together and passed as a package. This enables voters to separate the points they support from points they reject and prevents them from being forced to take sides, i.e. to agree to some points that they do not want for the sake of getting others that they do want.

If we were to take the example of women's rights, we can easily imagine a proposal being made that women should receive equal pay for equal work; that the workplace should be free from conduct that is degrading towards women; that women should have the right to affordable birth control; that women should have the right to terminate a pregnancy; that women should have the right to breast-feed in public; and that women should have preferential custody rights in the event of a divorce. If we accepted this proposal as a package, voters would be forced, for example, to accept preferential custody rights for the sake of equal pay. Not only does this give a distorted perception of what voter preferences actually are, it entrenches public opinion into 'for' and 'against' camps that can become increasingly antagonistic as each side tries to coerce its supporters to accept or reject the entire package.

By breaking down each issue, citizens are no longer locked into these 'for' or 'against' positions, but can move more fluidly between them. A citizen could choose to support affordable birth control, but not preferential custody rights. They may find themselves in the majority on some points and in the minority on others. The identity of those in the majority and minority is subject to variation, which means that there is no cohesive group of winners or losers. Not only does this allow for more nuanced policy-making, it increases citizen satisfaction with majority decision-making and makes it more difficult to develop hardened ideological and divisive positions. This, in turn, encourages an atmosphere of dialogue that prevents the kind of entrenched ill-will that can easily lead to a tyranny of the majority.

In some countries where there are already groups that strongly self-identify on the basis of ethnicity, religion or other traits, other measures may need to be taken to ensure minority protection. A particularly promising measure here is cumulative voting. Under this system, each voter receives several votes which they can distribute across proposals as they choose. For example, if a debate results in ten different proposals being put forward at the end of an Assembly, each voter would be allotted ten votes, but *not* necessarily one vote per proposal. They could put all ten votes for or against one proposal and not vote on any of the other nine. Or they could put eight votes on one proposal and two on another. Or any other combination they choose, including placing one vote on each proposal. Cumulative voting allows voters to indicate the strength of their interest in each proposal in an easily quantifiable manner, while still ensuring that everyone has equal voting power.

This enables minority groups to exert influence over issues that are of particular importance to them by allowing them to place a high number of votes on that issue. While this could still be counteracted by a majority vote against the issue in question, cumulative voting serves to prevent the casual interest of the majority from trumping strong minority interests.

Measures like these – which come in addition to the system of human rights and judicial protection that we already enjoy – should help to ensure that, in redrawing the line between individual and community, individuals and minorities remain protected from the tyranny of the majority.

Community and the individual: yin and yang

Creating a more participatory democracy requires rebalancing the needs of the individual and community. To think of democracy purely as a matter of individualism or individual rights might be popular in some circles, but it's based on a skewed idea that society was created for the individual. In a certain light, that is of course true. Society was created for the individual, and individuals develop themselves against the background of the culture and knowledge that any given civilization provides. But the deal isn't all one way. Individuals – unless they be beasts or gods – will always be dependent on some form of community. And if they do not nourish that community in the same way that it nourishes them, it will die or wither away into something different, a more feudal society perhaps, one that is, ironically, not so nourishing for individual needs.

For a participatory or direct democracy to flourish, it's necessary to ensure that everyone is bought into that society, that no one is able to stand above the democracy and ignore its laws to their own benefit. When laws are like a spider's web, trapping the vulnerable but allowing the strong to escape, democracy begins to unravel. The same can be said when some members of society do not need to contribute to the community in order to gain great wealth, or are able to gain a position of leadership purely through loyalty to partisan forces. By refusing to rebalance the needs between individual and community in a way that reflects the changing nature of our political and economic system, and continually insisting that the individual should virtually never be subject to the desires or needs of the community as a whole, we are gradually pulling our own civilization apart. And that will have consequences, because we are not gods – however much some people might like to believe that they are.

Direct Democracy Today:
Cutting the Gordian Knot

It is not because things are difficult that we dare
not venture. It is because we dare not venture that
they are difficult.

Seneca

It is often said that democracy as we know it was invented
in ancient Athens, but I hope I've shown that nothing could
be further from the truth. It may not have been perfect,
but no one can deny that Athenian government was truly
all about '*demo-kratia*' – people power. By contrast our own
'democracy' was purposely modelled after the oligarchic
government of Republican Rome. This system was never
expected to deliver 'people power', so much so that originally
it wasn't even called 'democracy'.

And having embraced this undemocratic system, we are
now reaping its bitter rewards.

Not only do our elections fail to reflect voter preferences, the results are, for all practical purposes, bought by
corporations and wealthy individuals. Things are no better

internationally, where vote-buying predominates and the international financial institutions use their influence to bind entire nations into paying for the bad business decisions of the rich. For the vast majority of people, this political system is not a very good deal, and it is time to seriously ask how long it can go on for.

Do we really want to live in a world where a party that loses the election can end up in government, and then sign the nation into binding treaties for all eternity? Are we really satisfied with a society where the first thing any aspiring politician needs to think about is how to win corporate sponsors over to their campaign? Does anyone actually believe that it is possible for us to make good decisions about our future and our children's future when 70 per cent of the information in mass media is generated from corporate and government press releases that haven't even been fact-checked? And can we feel any pride in ourselves and our society when we've allowed international institutions like the UN and the IMF to be hijacked by predators that grind people in developing countries into the dust for their own short-term gain?

I don't think so.

But despite all of these blatantly horrific shortcomings, proponents of modern democracy never tire of asking citizens to give it one more chance because, so they insist, it is *possible* for this Republican system to function; eternal freedom and prosperity beckon just around the corner if only we give it one more shot.

I hope the research shown here makes absolutely clear that such an outcome is possible only in the same way as it is theoretically *possible* to jump from a ten-storey building and survive. It is *possible*, but it is *improbable*, because there are many flaws inherent in representative democracy, just as there are many dangers inherent in jumping off tall buildings.

Practice elections for long enough and you will always end up, not with democracy, but with oligarchy. Elections tie wealth to political power, creating a strong reinforcing relationship between the two. A little bit of power can be used to get more wealth, which can be used to get more power, which can be used to get more wealth. Power becomes more and more centralized, the people of a nation more and more incapable of affecting its decisions. We saw the consequences of this in the Roman Republic, which first self-destructed and then re-formed into an empire. It's a sobering historical lesson under any circumstances, but becomes much more so after a lucid consideration of present realities.

Despite everything else, we have made huge technological advances over the past century, but technology is a double-edged sword, capable of bringing both freedom and oppression. In thirty or fifty years, will our greatest technical advances serve the few or the many? Will they be used by those in power to crush any nascent threat to their privilege? Or will they be harnessed to disperse power across nations, to support 'people power'?

We are now standing at a crossroads.

On the one hand, we live in a society that still uses an outdated and oligarchic political system to allot power to virtually predestined 'winners'; a system that is bowing under the weight of decades and centuries of stagnant corruption; a system in which governments appropriate powers to themselves that Roman Senators could barely have dreamed of; in which politicians can buy themselves victory and punish whole countries that do not do as they like; in which corporations play all sides of the political game – campaign donors, media owners and NGO consultants – writing their own laws at will; in which we are embarked on a downward spiral of deepening wealth and political inequality in which fewer and fewer citizens can affect their government or even their own lives.

On the other hand, technology has put us in touch with each other as never before, giving us a degree of hope for real democracy that hasn't existed since the time of Aristotle. And in order to develop real democracy, it is not even necessary to fight the current system.

We simply need to create a parallel politics that encourages real democracy. Indeed, when one is locked into a self-perpetuating system, which is what the electoral-representative system is, this is the *only* approach that really has any chance of success.

And the good news is that creating such a parallel system is much easier than one might think, because real democracy never completely disappeared. From credit unions that pay dividends to shareholders, to work co-ops with egalitarian decision-making and pay, to the participatory budgeting of Porto Alegre and Paris, real democracy has always been there, accompanying our daily lives. If we want to replace our current corrupt politics with something better, we need only to strengthen and multiply these practices until they become so widespread and so natural for citizens to use that existing representative 'democracy' will lose the little legitimacy it has left and simply fade away.

And, once again, the Athenians provide a historical example of just such a development. Democracy did not come easy in Athens. No one waved a magic wand and caused the

Assembly, courts and *cleroteria* to appear out of thin air. On the contrary: it took the Athenians nearly a century to move from a situation of near-feudalism and economic crisis to prosperity and equal decision-making. They encountered many hurdles along the way. In fact, looking at Athenian history, there are certainly many points where an observer would think that this civilization would *never* have developed democracy. The only reason they did is that they never gave up striving for something better, no matter how dark things looked. They always believed in themselves and they always pushed forward. And as a result, they threw off the shackles of the electoral system and gained true people power.

And what took the Athenians a hundred years is, for us, only a click away.

We need only to put our weight behind the tools that already exist. When participatory budgeting is common-place from the smallest hamlet to the greatest metropolises, when local councillors and MPs across the globe use tools like DemocracyOS and Loomio to consult their constituents, and when secure e-voting is in place from Moscow to Mumbai and from Tokyo to Tennessee, not only will no one think twice about whether or not citizens deserve to make their own decisions, no one will be able to stop them from doing so.

Bibliography

In writing a book of this sort, one relies on a great deal of research by other writers and academics. While – for the sake of the reader's sanity – it was not possible to retain the original 800 footnotes in this book, I have been able to include a rough bibliography here. Most of the sources cited provided raw data that I interpreted in light of the questions considered in this book, but some were also invaluable for the insights they provided in understanding the ramifications of the data. While I do not always agree with the authors' interpretation, their insight into the meaning of these events has always been useful and the credit for it belongs to them not me.

In particular, these include: Martin Ostwald (on what it meant to be a citizen in Athens), M. M. Markle (on pay for participation), C. Nicolet (on what it meant to be a citizen in Rome), Raphael Sealey (on the Athenian legal system), Mogens Herman Hansen (on the Assembly), M. I. Finley (on the ancient economy), Ofer Eldar and David Malone (on vote-buying at the international institutions), Joseph Stiglitz (on the workings of the IMF and the World Bank), Tim Kessler (on specific privatization projects in developing countries), and Nick Davies (on media manipulation).

Chapter 1 – Democracy in Athens

BOOKS

Alan Sommerstein, *Aristophanes: Lysistrata and Other Plays*, 2nd edn, Penguin Books, 2002

Aristotle, *Politics*, 3rd edn, Clarendon Press, 1968

A. R. W. Harrison, *The Law of Athens*, vol. II, 2nd edn, Bristol Classical Press, 1998

C. Nicolet, *The World of the Citizen in Republican Rome*, Batsford Academic and Educational, 1980

E. S. Staveley, *Greek and Roman Voting and Elections*, Thames and Hudson, 1972

Martin Ostwald, *From Popular Sovereignty to the Sovereignty of Law: Law, Society and Politics in Fifth-Century Athens*, University of California Press, 1986

Peter Krentz, *The Thirty at Athens*, Cornell University Press, 1982

ARTICLES

Mogens Herman Hansen (1978), 'Nomos and Psephisma in fourth-century Athens', *GRBS*, 19, 315

Mogens Herman Hansen (1979), 'Did the Athenian ecclesia legislate after 403/2 B.C.?', *GRBS*, 20, 27

Mogens Herman Hansen (1981), 'Initiative and decision: the separation of powers in fourth-century Athens', *GRBS*, 22, 345

T. J. Morgan (1999), 'Literate education in classical Athens', *Classical Quarterly*, 49, 46

The following contributions to P. J. Rhodes (ed.), *Athenian Democracy*, Edinburgh University Press, 2004:
- M. I. Finley, 'Athenian demagogues'
- Mogens Herman Hansen, 'How did the Athenian Ecclesia vote?'
- Raphael Sealey, 'Ephialtes, Eisangelia and the Council'
- Sterling Dow, 'Aristotle, the Kleroteria, and the courts'

The following contributions to the *Cambridge Ancient History*:
- E. M. Walker, 'The Periclean democracy', vol. V
- Marcus Tod, 'The economic background of the fifth century', vol. V
- Martin Ostwald, 'The reform of the Athenian state by Cleisthenes', 2nd edn, vol. IV

- P. J. Rhodes, 'The polis and the alternatives', 2nd edn, vol. VI
- W. S. Ferguson, 'The fall of the Athenian Empire', vol. V

The following contributions to Josiah Ober and Charles Hedrick (eds), *Demokratia: A Conversation on Democracies, Ancient and Modern*, Princeton University Press, 1996:
- Kurt Raaflaub, 'Equalities and inequalities in Athenian democracy'
- Martin Ostwald, 'Shares and rights: "citizenship" Greek style and American style'
- Paul Cartledge, 'Comparatively equal'
- Robert W. Wallace, 'Law, freedom and the concept of citizens' rights in democratic Athens'

Chapter 2 – The myth of representation

REGARDING STATS, FUNCTIONS AND PROBLEMS OF FPTP

Arend Lijphart, *Patterns of Democracy: Government Forms and Performance in Thirty-Six Countries*, Yale University Press, 1999

Arend Lijphart, *Patterns of Democracy: Government Forms and Performance in Thirty-Six Countries*, 2nd edn, Yale University Press, 2012

Feargal McGuinness, Richard Cracknell, Martin Davies and Mark Taylor, 'UK election statistics: 1918–2012', Research Paper 12/43 (7 August 2012), House of Commons Library

Ray Argyle, *Turning Points: The Campaigns that Changed Canada*, White Knight Publications, 2004

Stuart Weir, 'Primary control and auxiliary precautions: a comparative study of democratic institutions in six nations', in D. Beetham (ed.), *Defining and Measuring Democracy*, SAGE, 1994

The following contributions to Arend Lijphart and Bernard Grofman (eds), *Choosing an Electoral System: Issues and Alternatives*, Praeger Publishers, 1984:
- Richard Rose, 'Electoral systems: a question of degree or of principle?'
- William Irvine, 'Additional member electoral systems'

There were two British national elections in 1974, hence this year figures twice in the statistics.

Beasts and Gods

Although absolute manufactured majorities occur in about one out of every five elections in Britain, they are sometimes short lived. The 1929 government lasted only two and a half years and the 1974 government lasted only eight months. The 1951 government, however, served out its full term, meaning that UK citizens spent about eight years out of ninety living under absolute manufactured majorities, nearly one tenth of their lives. The situation is similar in Canada. The 1957 election resulted in a manufactured minority government. The government called elections a year later and became the majority at that point. The 1896 election was a majority that served out its full term.

REGARDING STATS, FUNCTIONS AND PROBLEMS OF STV

The following contributions to Shaun Bowler and Bernard Grofman (eds), *Elections in Australia, Ireland and Malta under the Single Transferable Vote*, University of Michigan Press, 2000:
- Colin Hughes, 'STV in Australia'
- David Farell and Ian McAllister, 'Through a glass darkly: understanding the world of STV'
- Michael Laver, 'STV and the politics of coalition'
- Nicolaus Tideman and Daniel Richardson, 'A comparison of improved STV methods'

The following contributions to Arend Lijphart and Bernard Grofman (eds), *Choosing an Electoral System: Issues and Alternatives*, Praeger Publishers, 1984:
- Steven Brams and Peter Fishburn, 'Some logical defects of the Single Transferable Vote'
- William Riker, 'Electoral systems and constitutional constraints'

REGARDING STATS, FUNCTIONS AND PROBLEMS OF PERSONALIZED PROPORTIONAL VOTING

Dietmar Hipp, 'Überhangmandate: Wie die Stimme zur Gegenstimme wird', *Der Spiegel*, 2 July 2008, www.spiegel.de/politik/deutschland/ueberhangmandate-wie-die-stimme-zur-gegenstimme-wird-a-563558-5.html

Stuart Weir, 'Primary control and auxiliary precautions: a comparative study of democratic institutions in six nations', in D. Beetham (ed.), Defining and Measuring Democracy, SAGE, 1994

Bibliography

REGARDING STATS, FUNCTIONS AND PROBLEMS OF PURE PROPORTIONAL
VOTING

Arend Lijphart, *Electoral Systems and Party Systems: A Study of Twenty-Seven Democracies, 1945–1990*, Oxford University Press, 1994

REGARDING RECENT ELECTIONS

I tabulated recent election stats for all systems myself following each election. Some of the material that contributed to that (in the order used in the text):
'Election results 2010', *BBC News*, news.bbc.co.uk/2/shared/election2010/results/
'Electoral results by party', Parliament of Canada, www.parl.gc.ca/parlinfo/compilations/electionsandridings/ResultsParty.aspx
'2000 presidential electoral and popular vote', Federal Election Commission (December 2001), www.fec.gov/pubrec/fe2000/elecpop.htm
'Wahlnachtsreport der Nachwahl im Wahlkreis 160 – Dresden I' (2 October 2005), www.wahlrecht.de/news/2005/nachwahl-2005.htm
'March 18 2007, general election results – Finland totals' (Elections to the Finnish Eduskunta (Parliament)), www.electionresources.org/fi/eduskunta.php?election=2007
'Polls close in Finnish election: live results', *Uutiset*, 19 April 2015, yle.fi/uutiset/polls_close_in_finnish_election_live_results/7938227
'Chamber: list results' (Federal Public Services, Belgium), polling2014.belgium.be/en/cha/results/results_graph_CKR00000.html
Luis Ramiro, 'The 2004 Spanish general elections' (RIIA/EPERN Election Briefing no. 04/01, July 2004, Royal Institute of International Affairs), www.sussex.ac.uk/webteam/gateway/file.php?name=epern-election-briefing-no-14.pdf&site=266
William Chislett, 'Elections in Spain: a political change in the framework of a major international crisis', www.iemed.org/observatori-en/arees-danalisi/arxius-adjunts/anuari/med.2012/chislett_en.pdf

REGARDING THE COSTS OF THE WARS IN AFGHANISTAN AND IRAQ

The wars in Afghanistan and Iraq are estimated to have cost Americans alone $4–6 trillion and to account for 20 per cent of US debt incurred between

2001 and 2012 (Ernesto Londono, 'Study: Iraq, Afghan war costs to top
$4 trillion', *Washington Post*, 28 March 2013, www.washingtonpost.com/
world/national-security/study-iraq-afghan-war-costs-to-top-4-trillion/
2013/03/28/b82a5dce-97ed-11e2-814b-063623d80a60_story.html). The
war in Iraq had already caused over 400,000 deaths by late 2013, most
of them as a direct result of violence ('Iraq study estimates war-related
deaths at 461,000', *BBC News*, 16 October 2013, www.bbc.com/news/
world-middle-east-24547256)

Chapter 3 – Buying and selling elections

REGARDING THE COST OF, AND CONTRIBUTORS TO, ELECTIONS

Ian Hughes, Paula Clancy, Clodagh Harris and David Beetham, *Power to
the People? Assessing Democracy in Ireland*, New Island Press, 2007
Jason Fekete, 'Orgy of spending', *National Post*, 10 November 2014,
news.nationalpost.com/news/canada/canadian-politics/
orgy-of-spending-expected-in-lead-up-to-federal-election-as-political-
parties-stockpile-tens-of-millions
Martin Linton, *Money and Votes*, Institute for Public Policy Research,
1994
Michael Marsh, 'Candidate centered but party wrapped: campaigning
in Ireland under STV', in S. Bowler and B. Grofman (eds), *Elections
in Australia, Ireland and Malta under the Single Transferable Vote*,
University of Michigan Press, 2000
'Almost €10 million spent by general election 2011 candidates', *The
Journal*, 18 October 2011, www.thejournal.ie/almost-e10-million-
spent-by-general-election-2011-candidates-256872-Oct2011/
'Election campaign spending by political parties', UK Political Info,
www.ukpolitical.info/Expenditure.htm
'General election 2015 explained: who finances the parties, who gets the
most and how much does the campaign cost', *Independent*, 17 April
2015
'PAC activity increase at 18 month point in 2004', Federal
Election Commission, 1 September 2004, www.fec.gov/press/
press2004/20040830pacstat/20040831pacstat.html
'PAC financial activity increases', Federal Election Commission,
30 August 2006, www.fec.gov/press/press2006/20060828pac/
20060830pac.html.

'PAC Table 4c, top 50 PACs by contribution to candidates and other committees, January 1, 2013 to December 31, 2014', Federal Election Commission, 4 March 2015, www.fec.gov/press/summaries/2014/tables/pac/PAC5c_2014_24m.pdf

'Registered party financial transactions reform', Elections Canada, www.elections.ca/WPAPPS/WPF/EN/PP/

'2012 US presidential campaign cost $7 billion – Election Commission', *RT*, 2 February 2013, rt.com/usa/seven-billion-us-elex-285 ($2 of this was spent by non-candidates)

REGARDING THE LINK BETWEEN DONATIONS, SUCCESS AND LEGISLATIVE ACTIVITY

Kenneth Benoit and Michael Marsh, 'For a few euros more: campaign spending effects in the Irish local elections of 1999' (2003), *Party Politics*, 9, 561

Lawrence Broz and Michael Hawes, 'US domestic politics and International Monetary Fund policy', in D. Hawkins, D. Lake, D. Nielson and M. Tierney (eds), *Delegation and Agency in International Organizations*, Cambridge University Press, 2006

Richard L. Hall and Frank W. Wayman, 'Buying time: moneyed interests and the mobilization of bias in Congressional Committees' (1990), *American Political Science Review*, 797

Skelly Wright, 'Money and the pollution of politics' (1982), *Columbia Law Review*, 82, 609

Thomas Stratmann, 'Can special interests buy Congressional votes? Evidence from financial services legislation' (2002), *Journal of Law and Economics*, 345

Financing and success of 2012 congressional candidates tabulated by myself from:

Peter Bell, 'New faces of the 113th Congress', *National Journal*, 5 November 2012, www.nationaljournal.com/congress/the-new-faces-of-the-113th-congress-20121105, and '2014 House and Senate campaign finance', Federal Election Commission, www.fec.gov/disclosurehs/

REGARDING THE EFFECT OF FINANCE ON REFERENDA

Amy Standen, 'California rejects labeling of genetically modified food –

supporters vow to fight on', *NPR*, 7 November 2012

Andreas Fagetti, 'Eine Watsche fuer di da oben', *Wochenzeiting*, 31 January 2013, www.woz.ch/1305/abzockerinitiative/eine-watsche-fuer-die-da-oben

Björn Hengst and Samiha Shafy, 'Swiss populist leader Blocher: we are a sovereign country', *Der Spiegel*, 17 February 2014 (trans. Daryl Lindsey)

Gerard O'Dwyer, 'Sweden caught in Swiss referendum controversy', *Defense News*, 23 February 2014, www.defensenews.com/article/20140223/DEFREG01/302230017/Sweden-Caught-Swiss-Referendum-Controversy

John Letzing and Robert Wall, 'Swiss voters oppose government's plan to buy Gripen fighter jets', *Wall Street Journal*, 18 May 2014, online. wsj.com/news/articles/SB10001424052702304422704579569912208819056?mg=reno64-wsj&url=http%3A%2F%2Fonline.wsj.com%2Farticle%2FSB10001424052702304422704579569912208819056.html

Julia Werdigier, 'Critics of executive pay put pressure on Novartis', *New York Times*, 18 February 2013, B3

Mark Bittman 'Buying the vote on G.M.O.'s', *New York Times*, 23 October 2013, opinionator.blogs.nytimes.com/2012/10/23/buying-the-vote-on-g-m-o-s/

Michael Marsh, 'Referendum campaigns: changing what people think or changing what they think about?', in C. de Vreese (ed.), *The Dynamics of Referendum Campaigns: An International Perspective*, 63

Niklas Magnussen, Catherine Bosley and Niclas Rolander, 'Saab declines after Swiss reject $3.5 billion jet order', *Bloomsberg News*, 19 May 2014, www.bloomberg.com/news/2014-05-18/saab-loses-3-5-billion-jet-order-as-swiss-reject-gripen.html

Paul Towers, '"Big 6" pesticide corporations top the list of food labelling opponents', Pesticide Action Network, 11 October 2012

Peter Stamm, 'Why the Swiss scorn the superrich', *New York Times*, 22 November 2013, A23

'Lisbon Treaty referendum 2008 analysis', Workers' Party of Ireland, June 2008, www.workerspartyireland.net/sitebuildercontent/sitebuilderfiles/lisbon_analysis.doc

'Yes and no groups spend at least 3.5 million euro on treaty campaigns', *Irish Times*, www.irishtimes.com/news/yes-and-no-groups-spent-at-least-3-5-million-on-treaty-campaigns-1.751483

REGARDING CAMPAIGN FINANCE REGULATION

Adam Liptak, 'The polarized court', *New York Times*, 10 May 2014, www.nytimes.com/2014/05/11/upshot/the-polarized-court.html?_r=0&abt=0002&abg=1

Canadian Press, 'Per-vote subsidy: ending funding for parties will change how politics is conducted experts say', *Huffington Post*, 10 April 2011, www.huffingtonpost.ca/2011/10/04/ending-per-vote-party-subsidy-canada_n_995143.html

Daniel Boffey, 'Tories accused of "trying to buy election" with 23% hike to campaign spending', *Guardian*, 13 December 2014, www.theguardian.com/politics/2014/dec/13/tories-david-cameron-buy-election-campaign-spending

Neal Devens and Lawrence Baum, 'Split definitive: how party polarization turned the Supreme Court into a partisan court', William & Mary Law School Research Paper no. 09-276, papers.ssrn.com/sol3/papers.cfm?abstract_id=2432111

William E. Nelson, Harvey Rishikof, I. Scott Messinger and Michael Jo (2009), 'The liberal tradition of the Supreme Court clerkship: its rise, fall and reincarnation?', *Vanderbilt Law Review*, 62, 1749

'The best lawyers money can buy', *New York Times*, 25 December 2014, www.nytimes.com/2014/12/26/opinion/the-best-lawyers-money-can-buy.html?_r=0

REGARDING CAMPAIGN BIAS

Martin Linton, *Money and Votes*, Institute for Public Policy Research, 1994

Chapter 4 – Participation

REGARDING PARTICIPATION IN MODERN DEMOCRACIES

Aaron Smith, 'Civil engagement in the digital age', Pew Research Center, www.pewinternet.org/2013/04/25/civic-engagement-in-the-digital-age/

Geraint Parry and George Moyser, 'More participation, more democracy?', in D. Beetham (ed.), *Defining and Measuring Democracy*, SAGE, 1994

Gwyn Topham, 'Budget 2013: fuel duty frozen again', *Guardian*, 20 March 2013, www.guardian.co.uk/uk/2013/mar/20/budget-

2013-fuel-duty-frozen

Henry E. Brady, Kay Lehman Schlozman and Sidney Verba, *Voice and Equality: Civic Voluntarism in American Politics*, Harvard University Press, 1995

Ian Hughes, Paula Clancy, Clodagh Harris and David Beetham, *Power to the People? Assessing Democracy in Ireland*, New Island Press, 2007

Lewis Anthony Dexter (1956), 'What do Congressmen hear: the mail', *Public Opinion Quarterly*, 16

British Social Attitudes Survey (Lucy Lee/Penny Young), bsa-30.natcen. ac.uk/read-the-report/politics/is-there-less-interest-in-british-politics. aspx

The website of the UK's Backbench Business Committee at www. parliament.uk/bbcom, in particular 'Transcript of the House of Commons Representations taken before the Backbench Business Committee, Backbench Debates', 11 October 2011, www.publications. parliament.uk/pa/cm201012/cmselect/ cmbackben/ucbbc1110/ucbbc1110.htm

The website of FairFuelUK: fairfueluk.com, particularly the entries on 'Quentin's Blog': 'The SUN questions Parliament "Why ignore 100,000 ePetition for FairFuelUK debate?"', 29 October 2011, fairfueluk.com/quentins_blog.php?entry_id=1319880748&title=the-sun-questions-parliament-why-ignore-100000-epetition-for-fairfueluk-debate and '10,000 frustrated FairFuelUK supporters eMail Parliament over the weekend', 30 October 2011, fairfueluk. com/quentins_blog.php?entry_id=1319993044&title=10000-frustrated-fairfueluk-supporters-email-parliament-over-the-weekend

The PR campaign that accompanied FairFuelUK was run by Peter Carroll Associates, www.petercarroll.co.uk/campaigns.html

REGARDING PARTICIPATION IN ANCIENT ATHENS

Martin Ostwald, *From Popular Sovereignty to the Sovereignty of Law: Law, Society and Politics in Fifth-Century Athens*, University of California Press, 1986

Mogens Herman Hansen (1981), 'Initiative and decision: the separation of powers in fourth-century Athens', *GRBS*, 22, 345.

Thucydides, *The Peloponnesian War* (trans. Rex Warner), Cassell, 1962

The following articles from Josiah Ober and Charles Hedrick (eds), *Demokratia: A Conversation on Democracies, Ancient and Modern*, Princeton

University Press, 1996:
- Kurt Raaflaub, 'Equalities and inequalities in Athenian democracy'
- Paul Cartledge, 'Comparatively equal'
- Philip Manville, 'Ancient Greek democracy and the modern knowledge-based organization: reflections on the ideology of two revolutions'
- Robert W. Wallace, 'Law, freedom and the concept of citizens' rights in democratic Athens'

The following contributions to the *Cambridge Ancient History*:
- E. M. Walker, 'The Periclean democracy', 5th edn, vol. V
- Marcus Tod, 'The economic background of the fifth century', vol. V, 1
- P. J. Rhodes, 'The polis and the alternatives', 2nd edn, vol. VI

The following articles from P. J. Rhodes (ed.), *Athenian Democracy*, Edinburgh University Press, 2004:
- Claude Mosse, 'How a political myth takes shape: Solon, "Founding Father" of the Athenian democracy'
- M. M. Markle, 'Jury pay and Assembly pay at Athens'
- P. J. Rhodes, 'Political activity in classical Athens'

Chapter 5 – Modern democracy and the international system

REGARDING THE UNITED NATIONS

Alberto Alesina and David Dollar (2000), 'Who gives foreign aid', *Journal of Economic Growth*, 5, 33

A. W. Brian Simpson, *Human Rights and the End of Empire: Britain and the Genesis of the European Convention*, Oxford University Press, 2004, Axel Dreher, Jan Egbert-Sturm and James Raymond Vreeland, 'Does membership on the Security Council influence IMF decisions: evidence from panel data', KOF Working Paper 151, ETH Zurich, 2006

Axel Dreher, Peter Nunnenkamp and Rainer Thiele, 'Does US aid buy UN General Assembly votes? A disaggregated analysis', Kiel Working Paper, Kiel Institute for the World Economy, April 2006

David Malone (2000), 'Eyes on the prize: the quest for non-permanent seats on the UN Security Council' *Global Governance*, 6, 3

Ilyana Kuziemko and Eric Werker (2006), 'How much is a seat on the Security Council worth? Foreign aid and bribery at the United Nations', *Journal of Political Economy*, 115(5)

Ofer Eldar (2008), 'Vote-trading in international institutions', *EJIL*, 19, 3

Sahar Okhovat, 'The United Nations Security Council: its veto power and its reform', CPACS Working Paper no. 15/1, December 2011

Strom Thacker (1999), 'The high politics of IMF lending', *World Politics*, 52(1), 38

A copy of Eisenhower's speech in which he refers to the military-industrial complex is available from the University of Virginia's Miller Center, Presidential Speech Archive, 'Dwight Eisenhower, Farewell Address (Jan.17, 1961)', www.millercenter.org/president/eisenhower/speeches/speech-3361

The obligation to control arms is laid out in Art. 26 of the UN Charter. The extent of this obligation is disputed among legal scholars, but it is generally agreed that some form of arms control is necessary, and that arms reduction should be pursued, so long as it is compatible with keeping the peace.

The Doomsday Clock reached its maximum of seventeen minutes from midnight at the end of the Cold War. However, since it started off at seven minutes to midnight and is now at three minutes to midnight, we have in sum total moved closer to total human obliteration under the Security Council's watch.

REGARDING THE CONTROVERSIAL RES. 678 ON IRAQ

Geoff Simons, *UN Malaise: Power, Problems and Realpolitik*, Macmillan Press, 1995, at 63 et seq.

Ofer Eldar (2008), 'Vote-trading in international institutions', *EJIL*, 19, 3

Phyllis Bennis, 'United Nations vs. United States', *Foreign Policy in Focus*, 1 December 2006, www.fpif.org/articles/united_nations_v_united_states

For confirmation that the Baltic states did not attend the Paris Summit, see ILM, 30, 190 (1991)

Regarding Kuwait's loans to the USSR, see 'Moscow and the Iraqi invasion of Kuwait', by Robert O. Freedman, in Robert O. Freedman (ed.), *The Middle East after Iraq's Invasion of Kuwait*, University Press of Florida, 1993, 74 at 94 et seq.

Regarding Saudi Arabia's loans to the USSR, see *Middle East Economic Survey*, archives.mees.com/issues/1053/articles/38318, XXXIV(9) (3 December 1990), for the extension of a $4 billion loan, and *Middle*

East Economic Survey, www.mees.com/issues/1091/articles/39365, XXXIV(47) for a $1.5 billion loan on 26 August 1991 to be used for balance of payments and project finance

Regarding the loan to China: In January 1990, White House, Treasury and State Department officials told the *Los Angeles Times* that the USA would oppose resuming a $700 million loan to China which had been frozen after Tiananmen Square (Jim Mann/Art Pine, *Los Angeles Times*, 10 January 1990). On 5 December 1990, the World Bank approved a $114.3 million loan to China. The USA did not object. The decision about the loan came within days of China abstaining on Res. 678 (Stephen Labaton, *New York Times*, 5 December 1990)

Regarding the expulsion of Yemenis from Saudi Arabia, see Gwenn Okruhlik and Patrick Conge (1997), 'National autonomy, labour migration and political crisis: Yemen and Saudi Arabia', *Middle East Journal*, 51(4), 554.

REGARDING THE IMF AND THE WORLD BANK

Axel Dreher in L. Yueh (ed.), *The Law and Economics of Globalization: New Challenges for a World in Flux*, Cheltenham Press, 2009, 161

Charles Lipson (1981), 'The international organization of Third World debt', *International Organization*, 35(4), 603

Erica Gould (2003), 'Money talks: supplementary finances and International Monetary fund conditionality', *International Organization*, 57, 55

Fatoumata Jawara and Aileen Kwa, *Behind the Scenes at the WTO: The Real World of International Trade Negotiations*, Zed Books, 2003

I. de Vegh (1943), 'The International Clearing Union', *American Economic Review*, 33, 534

Ibrahim Shihata, *The World Bank and the IMF Relationship – Quo Vadis?: Essays in International Financial and Economic Law*, London Institute of International Banking, 2002

James Vreeland, *The International Monetary Fund: Politics of Conditional Lending*, Routledge, 2007

John Benjamin Goodman, 'Monetary sovereignty: the politics of central banking in western Europe', Cornell University, 1992

Joseph Stiglitz, *Globalization and Its Discontents*, Penguin Books, 2002

Lawrence Broz and Michael Hawes, 'US domestic politics and International Monetary Fund policy', in D. Hawkins, D. Lake, D. Nielson and M. Tierney (eds), *Delegation and Agency in International Organizations*, Cambridge University Press, 2006

Leonce Ndikumane and James K. Boyce (1998), 'Congo's odious debt: external borrowing and capital flight in Zaire', *Development and Change*, 29

Michael Breen (2012), 'The international politics of Ireland's EU/IMF bailout', *Irish Studies in International Affairs*, 75

Robert Putnam (1988), 'Diplomacy and domestic politics: the logic of two-level games', *International Organization*, 42, 427

Stephen Schnably, 'Constitutionalism and democratic government in the inter-American system', in G. Fox and B. Roth (eds), *Democratic Governance and International Law*, Cambridge University Press, 2000

Udaibir S. Das, Michael G. Papioannou and Christoph Trebesch, 'Sovereign debt restructurings 1950–2010: literature survey, data and stylized facts', IMF Working Paper WP/12/203, 2012

The following articles from Ariel Buira (ed.), *The IMF and World Bank at Sixty*, Anthem Press, 2005:
- Davesh Kapur, 'Conditionality and its alternatives'
- Tim Kessler, 'Assessing the risks in the private provision of public services'

'Congo, Democratic Republic of: transactions with the Fund from May 01, 1984 to April 30, 2014', International Monetary Fund, www.imf.org/external/np/fin/tad/extrans1. aspx?memberKey1=197&endDate=2014-05-31&finposition_flag=YES

'Democratic Republic of Congo to get billions of dollars in debt relief', CNN, 2 July 2010, edition.cnn.com/2010/WORLD/africa/07/02/congo.debt.relief/

Shares at the IMF and the World Bank are subject to variations as they are recalculated before a vote. These variations are, however, very slight. Figures regarding country shares were taken from:

'IMF members' quotas and voting power and IMF Board of Governors', International Monetary Fund, 6 July 2014, www.imf.org/external/np/sec/memdir/members.aspx

'International Bank for Reconstruction and Development: voting power of Executive Directors', Corporate Secretariat, 28 May 2014, siteresources.worldbank.org/BODINT/Resources/278027-1215524804501/IBRDEDsVotingTable.pdf

Data on current country group configurations taken from:
International Bank for Reconstruction and Development:
  Voting Power of Executive Directors, Corporate Secretariat,
  10 April 2015, siteresources.worldbank.org/BODINT/
  Resources/278027-1215524804501/IBRDEDsVotingTable.pdf

IMF resources as a percentage of world trade for the years up to 2005
taken from:
Ariel Buira, 'The IMF and the World Bank at sixty: an unfulfilled
  potential?', in A. Buira (ed.), *The IMF and World Bank at Sixty*,
  Anthem Press, 2005, 5
I. de Vegh (1943), 'The International Clearing Union', *American
  Economic Review*, 33, 534
Sarah Babb and Ariel Buira, 'Mission creep, mission push and
  discretion: the case of IMF conditionality', in A. Buira (ed.), *The IMF
  and the World Bank at Sixty*, 59

After 2005, calculations were derived from the following figures:
The value of goods traded in 2012 was US$18.3 trillion, while the value of
services was $4.3 trillion (so $22.6 trillion in total) (WTO press release, 10
April 2013, Press/688, 'Trade to remain subdued in 2013 after sluggish
growth in 2012 as European economies continue to struggle', www.wto.
org/english/news_e/pres13_e/pr688_e.htm). Total IMF resources for 2012
were 518.5 billion SDRs (IMF's Financial Resources and Liquidity Position,
2012–March 2014, www.imf.org/external/np/tre/liquid/2014/0314.htm).
In March 2012, the exchange rate was US$0.645 to the SDR ('SDRs per
Currency Unit for March 2012, www.imf.org/external/np/fin/data/rms_
mth.aspx?SelectDate=2012-03-31&reportType=SDRCV). That means the
IMF's total resources were US$334,432,500,000 or 1.48 per cent of total
world trade. If one counts trade only in goods, the percentage would be
1.83 per cent.

Chapter 6 – Non-governmental organizations and the civil society chimera

REGARDING THE NATURE OF MODERN NGOS

Anara Musabaeva, 'Responsibility, transparency and legitimacy of
  socially-oriented NGOs in Krygyzstan', International NGO Training
  and Research Centre, January 2013

Ian Hughes, Paula Clancy, Clodagh Harris and David Beetham, *Power to the People? Assessing Democracy in Ireland*, New Island Press, 2007

Jan Aart Scholte, Robert O'Brien and Marc Williams (1999), 'The WTO and civil society', *Journal of World Trade*, 33, 107

Orysia Lutsevych, 'Briefing Paper, How to finish a revolution: civil society and democracy in Georgia, Moldova and Ukraine', Chatham House, January 2013

ECOSOC Resolution 1996/31, 'Consultative Relationship between the United Nations and Non-Governmental Organizations', 25 July 1996

CARE Annual Report, 2012 Donors, www.care.org/newsroom/ publications/annualreports/care-usa-annual-report-2012/images/ CARE_Annual_Report_2012_Donors.pdf

'Corporate Engagement' (Oxfam), www.oxfam.org.uk/get-involved/ how-your-company-can-partner-with-us/corporate-engagement

'Donors and Grantmakers' (Institute of Economic Affairs), www. ieakenya.or.ke/about/donors-and-grant-makers

'Funding' (EDCMP), bit.ly/12Da9lk

'Our Funding' (World Leadership Alliance, Club de Madrid), www. clubmadrid.org/en/our_funding

Figures regarding corporate and trade NGO participation at the WTO were compiled from 'Non-Governmental Organizations accredited to attend the Eighth WTO Ministerial Conference Geneva, 15–17 December 2011', WTO Doc. WT/MIN(11)/INF/6, 30 November 2011

REGARDING NGO LOBBYING ACTIVITY

Patrick Bond, *Against Global Apartheid: South Africa Meets the World Bank, IMF and International Finance*, 2nd edn, Zed Books, 2003

Susan Sell and Aseem Prakash (2004), 'Using ideas strategically: the contest between business and NGO networks in intellectual property rights', *International Studies Quarterly*, 48(1), 143

ERT Highlights (ERT), ertdrupal.lin3.nucleus.be/system/files/ uploads/2010%20October%20-%20ERT%20Highlights.pdf

The Gorlin paper that was used as the basis of corporate lobbying on the issue of intellectual property (Big Pharma and the Access Campaign) was originally commissioned by IBM's CEO John Opel. IBM was also a member of the ACTN's Task Force. The paper was later endorsed by the other members as well as by the Intellectual Property Committee.

Some of the cases brought by the United States for alleged infringement of the TRIPS agreement are:
- Pakistan – Patent Protection for Pharmaceutical and Agricultural Chemical Products, DS36
- Portugal – Patent Protection under the Industrial Property Act, DS37
- India – Patent Protection for Pharmaceutical and Agricultural Chemical Products, DS50
- Brazil – Measures Affecting Patent Protection, DS199

The case against Brazil appears to have related directly to HIV/AIDS drugs (see Remarks of Ambassador Zoellick in 'Brazil – Measures Affecting Patent Protection, Notification of a Mutually Agreed Solution', WT/DS199/4 G/L/454 IP/D/23/Add.1, at 2)

Some of the agreements reached prior to dropping these cases are available here:
- 'Brazil – Measures Affecting Patent Protection, Notification of a Mutually Agreed Solution', WT/DS199/4 G/L/454 IP/D/23/Add.1, 19 July 2001
- 'Pakistan – Patent Protection for Pharmaceutical and Agricultural Chemical Products, Notification of a Mutually Agreed Solution', WT/DS36/4 IP/D/2/Add.1, 7 March 1997
- 'Portugal – Patent Protection under the Industrial Property Act, Notification of a Mutually Agreed Solution', WT/DS37/2 IP/D/3 Add.1, 8 October 1996

Chapter 7 – How did things get to be this way?
Regarding the Roman Republican system

Alfred Heuss (1956), 'Der Untergang der roemischen Republik und das Problem der Revolution', *Historische Zeitschrift*, 1

Andrew Borkowski and Paul du Plessis, *Textbook on Roman Law*, 3rd edn, Oxford University Press, 2005

A. W. Lintott, 'Provocatio: From the struggle of the Orders to the Principate', in H. Temporini (ed.), *Aufstieg und Niedergang der Roemischen Welt*, 226.

E. S. Staveley, *Greek and Roman Voting and Elections*, Thames and Hudson, 1972

C. Nicolet, *The World of the Citizen in Republican Rome*, Batsford Academic and Educational, 1980

Corey Brennan, *The Praetorship in the Roman Republic*, vol. 1, Oxford University Press, 2000

David Stockton, *The Gracchi*, Clarendon Press, 1979

H. F. Jolowicz and Barry Nicholas, *Historical Introduction to the Study of Roman Law*, 3rd edn, Cambridge University Press, 1972

H. H. Scullard, *From the Gracchi to Nero*, 4th edn, Methuen and Co. Ltd, 1976

J. M. Kelly, *Roman Litigation*, Oxford University Press, 1966

M. Cary and H. H. Scullard, *A History of Rome down to the Reign of Constantine*, 3rd edn, Macmillan Press, 1975

Michael Crawford, *The Roman Republic*, 2nd edn, Harvard University Press, 1992

Plutarch, 'Tiberius Gracchus', in *Lives*, penelope.uchicago.edu/Thayer/E/Roman/Texts/Plutarch/Lives/home.html

Plutarch, 'Ciaus Gracchus', in *Lives*, classics.mit.edu/Plutarch/gracchus.html

W. Kunkel, 'Magistratische Gewalt und Staatsherrschaft', in H. Temporini (eds.), *Aufstieg und Niedergang der Roemischen Welt: Geschichte und Kultur Roms im Spiegel der neueren Forschung*, vol. 2, Walter de Gruyter, 1972

The keen observer will note that the centuries described in the main text add up to only 189 rather than 193. This is because in addition to the property classes, there were four centuries for artisans and musicians. Historians are not exactly sure when the artisan centuries voted, but it was probably with the second or fourth classes.

Much of our vocabulary regarding elections is rooted in Republican Roman times. For example, the toga was the folded garment that was the Roman equivalent of a business suit. While all togas were basically white, the toga worn during election campaigning was made even whiter by bleaching it in the sun and rubbing ground chalk into it. This was known as the *toga candida*, the root of the English word 'candidate'. The word 'competitor' also has its roots in Roman elections.

The extrapolation of average Roman wages and the fortunes of the Roman wealthy into current American dollars is based on an average wage of $34,500 as equivalent to an average Roman wage of 380 sesterces.

Bibliography

REGARDING THE FEDERALIST AND ANTI-FEDERALIST MOVEMENTS IN THE
EARLY UNITED STATES

Alexander Hamilton, Federalist Papers no. 71, in *The Federalist Papers*
Alexander Hamilton, Speech on 21 June 1788 Urging
    Ratification of the Constitution in New York, from *The
    Works of Alexander Hamilton*, vol. II, available at Online
    Library of Liberty (Liberty Fund), oll.libertyfund.org/titles/
    Hamilton-the-works-of-alexander-hamilton-federal-edition-vol-2
David J. Siemers, *Ratifying the Republic: Antifederalists and Federalists in
    Constitutional Time*, Stanford University Press, 2002
George Mason, quoted in James Fishkin, *Democracy and Deliberation:
    New Directions for Democratic Reform*, Yale University Press, 1991
Herbert J. Storing, *The Complete Anti-Federalist*, University of Chicago
    Press, 2008
James Madison, Federalist Paper no. 10, in *The Federalist Papers*
James Madison, Federalist Paper no. 63, in *The Federalist Papers*
Jennifer Nedelsky, *Private Property and the Limits of American
    Constitutionalism: The Madisonian Framework and Its Legacy*,
    University of Chicago Press, 1990
Sheldon Wolin, 'Fugitive democracy', in S. Benhabib (ed.), *Democracy
    and Difference: Contesting the Boundaries of the Political*, Princeton
    University Press, 1996
Sheldon Wolin, 'Transgression, equality and voice', in Josiah Ober and
    Charles Hedrick (eds), *Demokratia: A Conversation on Democracies,
    Ancient and Modern*, Princeton University Press, 1996

OTHER

Branko Milanovic, *The Haves and the Have-Nots: A Brief and Idiosyncratic
    History of Global Inequality*, Basic Books, New York, 2011
M. I. Finley, *The Ancient Economy*, Chatto and Windus, 1973

Chapter 8 – The way forward

REGARDING COSMOPOLITAN DEMOCRACY

David Held, 'Cosmopolitan democracy and the global order: a new
    agenda', in J. Bohman and M. Lutz-Bachmann (eds), *Perpetual Peace:
    Essays on Kant's Cosmopolitan Ideal*, MIT Press, 1997, 235
Ian Traynor, Bartłomiej Kuraś, Philippe Ricard, Ignacio Fariza

Somolinos, Javier Cáceres and Marco Zetterin, '30,000 lobbyists and counting: is Brussels under corporate sway?', *Guardian*, 8 May 2014, www.theguardian.com/world/2014/may/08/ lobbyists-european-parliament-brussels-corporate
Juergen Habermas, 'Kant's idea of perpetual peace with the benefit of two hundred years' hindsight', in J. Bohman and M. Lutz-Bachmann (eds), *Perpetual Peace: Essays on Kant's Cosmopolitan Ideal*, MIT Press, 1997, 113

REGARDING E-VOTING

Alexander Trechsel, 'E-voting and electoral participation', in C. H. de Vreese (ed.), *The Dynamics of Referendum Campaigns: An International Perspective*, Palgrave Macmillan, 2007, 159
'E-Voting' Republique et Canton de Génève, www.geneve.ch/evoting/ english/presentation_projet.asp
Vabarigii Valimiskomisjon, 'Statistics about internet voting in Estonia', www.vvk.ee/voting-methods-in-estonia/engindex/statistics
'E-voting pioneer Estonia plans mobile phone ballots', AFP, 11 December 2008, www.google.com/hostednews/afp/article/ AleqM5gTGWVyQTdroF3kfmgzTO8-Y_6F_g
Vabariigi Valimiskomisjon, 'Internet voting in Estonia', www.vvk.ee/ voting-methods-in-estonia/engindex/ #I-voting_by_means_of_ID_card
Estonian National Election Committee 'E-Voting System: General Overview', Tallinn, 2005–10, www.vvk.ee/public/dok/General_ Description_E-Voting_2010.pdf

REGARDING PARTICIPATORY BUDGETING

Richelle Harrison Plesse, 'Parisians have their say on city's first €20m "participatory budget"', *Guardian*, 8 October 2014, www.theguardian.com/cities/2014/oct/08/ parisians-have-say-city-first-20m-participatory-budget?CMP=twt_gu
'Funded Projects', Participatory Budgeting in New York City, pbnyc.org/ projects
'2014 Results – District 5', Participatory Budgeting in New York City, 28 April 2014, pbnyc.org/content/ 2014-vote-results-district-5
'2014 Results – District 44', Participatory Budgeting in New York City, 16 April 2013, pbnyc.org/content/vote-results-district-44

Bibliography

REGARDING CITIZENS' ASSEMBLIES

Iseult Honohan, 'What can the UK learn from the Irish Constitutional Convention?', *OpenDemocracy*, 8 October 2014, www.opendemocracy.net/ourkingdom/iseult-honohan/what-can-uk-learn-from-irish-constitutional-convention

Michael Pal (2012), 'The promise and limits of citizens' assemblies: deliberation, institutions and the laws of democracy', *Queen's Law Journal*, 38, at 259 et seq., queensu.ca/lawjournal/issues/pastissues/Volume38a/7-Pal.pdf

R. S. Ratner, 'British Columbia's citizens' assembly: the learning phase', *Canadian Parliamentary Review*, Summer 2004, www.revparl.ca/27/2/27n2_04e_ratner.pdf

Thorhildur Thorleifsdottir, 'From the people to the people, a new constitution', *OpenDemocracy*, 13 November 2012

Thorvaldur Gylfason, 'Iceland: direct democracy in action', *OpenDemocracy*, 12 November 2012

REGARDING DIGITAL DEMOCRACY TOOLS

'DEMOS: Democracy OS in the Buenos Aires city legislature', Democracy OS, blog.democracyos.org/

'Wellington City Council uses Loomio!', Loomio, 1 November 2013, blog.loomio.org/2013/11/01/wellington-city-council-uses-loomio/

Chapter 9 Disinformed is disenfranchised

REGARDING THE MERITS OF DELIBERATION

Amy Gutman and Dennis Thompson, *Why Deliberative Democracy?*, Princeton University Press, 2004

Guy Standing, 'The Precariat: why it needs deliberative democracy', *OpenDemocracy*, 27 January 2012, www.opendemocracy.net/guy-standing/precariat-why-it-needs-deliberative-democracy

Hélène Landemore, 'Democratic reason: the mechanisms of collective intelligence in politics', in *Collective Wisdom: Principle and Mechanisms*, Cambridge University Press, 2012

James S. Fishkin, *Democracy and Deliberation: New Directions for Democratic Reform*, Yale University Press, 1991

Beasts and Gods

John Dryzek, *Foundations and Frontiers of Deliberative Governance*, Oxford University Press, 2010
Joshua Cohen, 'Deliberation and democratic legitimacy', in James Bohman and William Rehg (eds), *Deliberative Democracy: Essays on Reason and Politics*, MIT Press, 1997

The following articles from S. Benhabib (ed.), *Democracy and Difference: Contesting the Bounds of the Political*, Princeton University Press, 1996:
- Iris Young, 'Communication and the other: beyond deliberative democracy'
- Seyla Benhabib, 'Toward a deliberative model of democratic legitimacy'

REGARDING THE MYTILENEAN DEBATES

Thucydides, *The Peloponnesian War* (trans. Rex Warner) Cassell, 1962, at 180–91

REGARDING THE EFFECTS OF MODERN MEDIA/GROUP PRESSURE ON PERCEPTION

Edward Bernays, *Propaganda*, Kennikat Press, New York, 1928
Edward S. Herman and Noam Chomsky, *Manufacturing Consent: The Political Economy of the Mass Media*, 2nd edn, Pantheon Books, 2002
Elizabeth Loftus (1979), 'The malleability of human memory', *American Scientist*, 67(3), 12
Shanto Iyengar and Donald R. Kinder, *News that Matters: Television and American Opinion*, University of Chicago Press, 1987
Solomon E. Asch (1955), 'Opinions and social pressure', *Scientific American*, 193(5), 31

REGARDING MEDIA OWNERSHIP

Ashley Lutz, 'These 6 corporations control 90% of the media in America', *Business Insider*, 14 June 2012
Ian Hughes, Paula Clancy, Clodagh Harris and David Beetham, *Power to the People? Assessing Democracy in Ireland*, New Island Press, 2007
Richard Allen Greene, 'Murdoch denies political influence, Cameron disagrees', *CNN*, 25 April 2012, edition.cnn.com/2012/04/25/world/europe/uk-phone-hacking/
Robert Weir, Press Reference, United States, www.pressreference.com/Sw-Ur/United-States-html

394

Norman Fowler, 'In the post-Murdoch era, we must reform media ownership', *Guardian*, 11 May 2012

Torin Douglas, 'Analysis: Murdoch and media ownership in UK', *BBC*, 22 December 2010, www.bbc.com/news/uk-12062176

William Irvine, 'Additional member electoral systems', in Arend Lijphart and Bernard Grofman (eds), *Choosing an Electoral System: Issues and Alternatives*, Praeger Publishers, 1984

Statistics from The Ownership of the News, Select Committee on Communications, House of Lords (UK), 1st Report of Session 2007–08, 27 June 2008, HL Paper 122-I

The top five owners of American media are: General Electric, NewsCorp, Viacom, Time Warner and CBS.

In Ireland, RTE accounts for 42 per cent of television viewership, while TV3 has 13.4 per cent. In Denmark, two government channels, TV2 and DR, account for 72 per cent of viewership. In Portugal, private channels SIC and TV1 have 28.3 and 29.5 per cent of market share respectively, while public channel RTP1 has 23.2 per cent. Ireland has fifty-four licensed radio stations, with ownership concentrated among Thomas Crosbie Holdings, UTV, Communicorp Ltd and Emap Plc. Independent News and Media Plc accounts for 43 per cent of papers sold in Ireland.

REGARDING TACTICS FOR MEDIA MANIPULATION

Dan Morain, 'Voucher concept has come a long way', *LA Times*, 10 October 1993, articles.latimes.com/1993-10-10/news/ mn-44434_1_school-voucher-concept

Isabel Hardman, 'The Tory "rally" that wasn't: these photos reveal how modern campaigning works', *Spectator*, 7 April 2015, blogs.spectator. co.uk/coffeehouse/2015/04/how-election-campaigning-works/

Jane Mayer, 'Covert operations', *New Yorker*, 30 August 2010, www.newyorker.com/ reporting/2010/08/30/100830fa_fact_mayer?currentPage=all

Lori Robertson, 'In control', *American Journalism Review*, February/ March 2005, ajrarchive.org/article.asp?id=3812

Nick Davies, *Flat Earth News*, Vintage Books, 2008

Sean Quinn, 'Who sits where?', 9 March 2009, fivethirtyeight.com/ features/who-sits-where/

'The Cato Institute's impact', Cato Institute, www.cato.org/support/ impact

'An open letter to Canadian journalists', Canadian Association of Journalists (June 2010), signed by: Hélène Buzzetti, President, Canadian Parliamentary Press Gallery; Mary Agnes Welch, President, Canadian Association of Journalists; Brian Myles, President, Fédération professionnelle des journalistes du Québec; Kim Trynacity, President, Alberta Legislature Press Gallery; Christine Morris, President, New Brunswick Press Gallery; David Cochrane, President, Newfoundland Press Gallery; Réal Séguin, President, Quebec Press Gallery; Wayne Thibodeau, President, Press Gallery of the Prince Edward Island Legislative Assembly; Karen Briere, President, Saskatchewan Legislature Press Gallery Association, www.caj.ca/an-open-letter-to-canadian-journalists/
'Trauermarsch in Paris: Fotos von Spitzenpolitikern in abgesperrter Strasse aufgenommen', Spiegel-Online, www.spiegel.de/politik/ausland/charlie-hebdo-marsch-durch-paris-mit-staatschefs-auf-einsamer-strasse-a-1012649.html
The Institute for Justice is a real organization funded partially by the Koch Brothers that focuses on bringing court cases against legislation that the organization does not agree with.

REGARDING ONLINE COMMUNICATION

Andy Williamson, 'The internet and the British election: politicians get their clicks', The World Today, February 2010, 14
Col. Alastair Aitken, 'Mastering a new kind of warfare', The British Army 2014, British Ministry of Defence, army.newsdeskmedia.com/Images/Upload/files/TheBritishArmy2014.pdf
Ewen MacAskill, 'British Army creates team of Facebook warriors', Guardian, 31 January 2015, www.theguardian.com/uk-news/2015/jan/31/british-army-facebook-warriors-77th-brigade
George Monbiot, 'Reclaim the cyber commons', Guardian, 14 December 2010
George Monbiot, 'Robot wars', Guardian, 23 February 2011
George Monbiot, 'These Astroturf libertarians are the real threat to internet democracy', Guardian, 13 December 2010, www.theguardian.com/commentisfree/libertycentral/2010/dec/13/astroturf-libertarians-internet-democracy
Kim Sengupta, 'New British Army unit "Brigade 77" to use Facebook and Twitter in psychological warfare', Independent, 31 January 2015, www.independent.co.uk/news/uk/home-news/return-of-the-chindits-mod-reveals-cunning-defence-plan-10014608.html

Bibliography

Peter Levine, 'The internet in public life', in Verna V. Gehring (ed.), *The Internet and Civil Society*, Rowman and Littlefield, 2004

P. J. Bednarski, '$1 billion in online political spending in 2016, Borrell study says', *MediaPost News*, 30 June 2014, www.mediapost.com/publications/article/229055/1-billlion-in-online-political-spending-in-2016.html

Michael Bristow, 'China's internet "spin doctors"', *BBC News*, 16 December 2008

Scott K. Parks, 'American Majority holds Dallas workshop', *Dallas Morning News*, 5 October 2009, www.dallasnews.com/sharedcontent/dws/news/localnews/stories/DN-americanmajority_05met.ARTo.State.Edition2.4ba21b6.html

Tom Porter, 'British Army's new 77th Brigade will wage online PSYOP war with terrorists', *International Business Times*, 31 January 2015, www.ibtimes.co.uk/british-armys-new-77th-brigade-will-wage-online-psyop-war-terrorists-1486044

'Today's top headlines: 8.9 million Australians go online for their daily news', Nielsen, 2 February 2014, www.nielsen.com/au/en/insights/news/2014/todays-top-headlines-8-9million-australians-go-online-for-their-daily-news.html

The Ownership of the News, Select Committee on Communications, House of Lords (UK), 1st Report of Session 2007–08, 27 June 2008, HL Paper 122-I

The Australian online news sites references are: News.com.au (owned by NewsCorp); Smh.com.au (owned by Fairfax); Nine msn news websites; Yahoo!7 news websites (a conglomerate of pre-existing news outlets); ABC news websites; Herald Sun (owned by NewsCorp); The Age (owned by Fairfax); Mail Online; Couriermail.com.au (owned by NewsCorp); and BBC

ON PAY FOR PARTICIPATION

Alison Crawford, 'Revenue Canada rejected secret tax haven files', *CBC News*, 10 June 2013, www.cbc.ca/news/canada/revenue-canada-rejected-secret-tax-haven-files-1.1308967

Bastian Brinkmann, '13 Milliarden am deutschen Fiskus vorbeigeschleust', *Süddeutsche Zeitung*, 10 March 2014, www.sueddeutsche.de/wirtschaft/schaetzung-zur-steuerhinterziehung-im-jahr-milliarden-am-deutschen-fiskus-vorbeigeschleust-1.1908150

Rajeev Syal, 'UK's tax gap rises by £1 billion to £35 billion', *Guardian*, 11 October 2013, www.theguardian.com/politics/2013/oct/11/uk-tax-gap-rises-hmrc-avoidance-nonpayment

Military Expenditures Database, Stockholm International Peace Research Institute, www.sipri.org/research/armaments/milex/milex_database

'Revenue Canada offers rewards for tips against offshore tax cheats', *CBS News*, 15 January 2014, www.cbc.ca/news/politics/revenue-canada-offers-rewards-for-tips-against-offshore-tax-cheats-1.2497955

Chapter 10 – Democracy and dissent

REGARDING INDIVIDUAL RIGHTS IN ATHENS

Alan Sommerstein, *Aristophanes: Lysistrata and Other Plays*, 2nd edn, Penguin Books, 2002

Andrew Wolpert, *Remembering Defeat: Civil War and Civic Memory in Ancient Athens*, Johns Hopkins University Press, 2002

Aristotle, *Politics*, 3rd edn, Clarendon Press, 1968

A. R. W. Harrison, *The Law of Athens*, vol. II, 2nd edn, Bristol Classical Press, 1998

Peter Krentz, *The Thirty at Athens*, Cornell University Press, 1982

Plato, *The Republic and Other Works* (trans. B. Jowett) Anchor Books, 1973

Pseudo-Xenophon, *Constitution of the Athenians*, 2nd edn, London Association of Classical Teachers, 2004

Robin Waterfield, *Why Socrates Died: Dispelling the Myths*, W. W. Norton, 2009

The following articles from Josiah Ober and Charles Hedrick (eds), *Demokratia: A Conversation on Democracies, Ancient and Modern*, Princeton University Press, 1996:
- Mogens Herman Hansen, 'The ancient Athenian and the modern liberal view of liberty as a democratic ideal'
- Robert W. Wallace, 'Law, freedom and the concept of citizens' rights in democratic Athens'

The following articles from P. J. Rhodes (ed.), *Athenian Democracy*, Edinburgh University Press, 2004:

Bibliography

- Claude Mosse, 'How a political myth takes shape: Solon, "Founding Father" of the Athenian democracy'
- Mogens Hansen, 'How did the Athenian Ecclesia vote?'

The following contributions to the *Cambridge Ancient History*:
- J. B. Bury, 'The age of illumination', vol. V
- Marcus Tod, 'The economic background of the fifth century', vol. V

Socrates' thoughts were, of course, not recorded by himself but rather by his student Plato.

The counter-attack on the Thirty Tyrants was not just carried out by Athenian citizens. The movement consisted in large part of metics (foreign residents of Athens) and slaves. Fears that the Thirty might rise again from Eleusis were entirely justified. They did eventually attempt another attack from Eleusis, but were defeated by the Athenian army.

REGARDING ECONOMIC BALANCE

Alexis de Tocqueville, *Democracy in America*, Harper and Row, 1966

Aristotle, *Politics*, 3rd edn, Clarendon Press, 1968

Branko Milanovic, *The Haves and the Have-Nots: A Brief and Idiosyncratic History of Global Inequality*, Basic Books, 2011

Charles de Secondat, Baron de Montesquieu, *The Spirit of Laws*, vol. 1, trans. T. Nugent, G. Bell and Sons, 1914

Darel Tai Engen (2005), '"Ancient Greenbacks": Athenian Owls, the Law of Nikophon and the Greek economy', *Zeitschrift fuer Alte Geschichte*, 359

E. Cohen, *Athenian Economy and Society, a Banking Perspective*, Princeton, 1992

James Tobin, 'A proposal for International Monetary Reform', in James Tobin (ed.), *Essays in Economics*, MIT Press, 1982, 494

Jean-Jacques Rousseau, *The Social Contract* (trans. Maurice Cranston) Penguin Books, 1968

Joseph Stiglitz, *The Price of Inequality*, W. W. Norton, 2013

Kirsty Shipton (1997), 'Private banks in fourth-century Athens: a reappraisal', in *CQ*, 47, 396

Marcus Tod, 'The economic background of the fifth century', *Cambridge Ancient History*, vol. V

Mogens Herman Hansen (1979), 'Did the Athenian Ecclesia legislate after 403/2 B.C.?', *GRBS*, 20, 27

Mohammed Nafissi (2004), 'Class, embeddedness and the modernity of
ancient Athens', *Comparative Studies in Society and History*, 378

M. Cary and H. H. Scullard, *A History of Rome down to the Reign of
Constantine*, 3rd edn, Macmillan Press, 1975

M. I. Finley, *The Ancient Economy*, Chatto and Windus, 1973

M. I. Finley, *The Ancient Economy*, 2nd edn, University of California
Press, 1999

M. M. Markle, 'Jury pay and Assembly pay at Athens', in P. J. Rhodes
(ed.), *Athenian Democracy*, Edinburgh University Press, 2004

P. J. Rhodes, 'Political activity in classical Athens', in P. J. Rhodes (ed.),
Athenian Democracy, Edinburgh University Press, 2004

Robin Waterfield, *Why Socrates Died: Dispelling the Myths*, W. W. Norton,
2009

Sheldon Wolin, 'Transgression, equality and voice', in Josiah Ober and
Charles Hedrick (eds), *Demokratia: A Conversation on Democracies,
Ancient and Modern*, Princeton University Press, 1996

Thomas Piketty, *Capital in the Twenty-First Century*, trans. Arthur
Goldhammer, Harvard University Press, 2014

David M. Ewalt, 'Thirty amazing facts about private jets', *Forbes*, 13
February 2013, www.forbes.com/sites/davidewalt/2013/02/13/
thirty-amazing-facts-about-private-jets/2/

Edward N. Wolff and Maury Gittleman, 'Inheritances and the
distribution of wealth or whatever happened to the great inheritance
boom?', Working Paper 445, US Bureau of Labor Statistics, January
2011, www.bls.gov/ore/pdf/ec110030.pdf

Kevin Maguire, 'Where do you rank in the official earnings list?
Figures reveal huge pay gap between rich and poor', *Daily
Mirror*, 9 January 2014, www.mirror.co.uk/news/uk-news/
uk-average-salary-26500-figures-3002995

Mandi Woodruff, 'Heirs and heiresses of the wealthiest people
in America', *Yahoo Finance*, 9 December 2013, finance.yahoo.
com/news/heirs-and-heiresses-of-the-wealthiest-people-in-
america-134134504.html

Patrick Collinson, 'UK incomes: how does your salary compare?',
Guardian, 25 March 2014, www.theguardian.com/money/2014/
mar/25/uk-incomes-how-salary-compare

Peter Stamm, 'Why the Swiss scorn the superrich', *New York Times*,
22 November 2013, A23.

Bibliography

Richard Dyson and Matthew Holehouse, 'House price boom ripples out of London, across Britain', *Telegraph*, 9 April 2014, www.telegraph. co.uk/finance/personalfinance/houseprices/10756343/House-price-boom-ripples-out-of-London-across-Britain.html

Tony Barber and George Parker, 'EU leaders urge IMF to consider Tobin Tax', *Financial Times*, 11 December 2009, www.ft.com/ cms/s/0/76e13a4e-9725-11de-83c5-00144feabdc0.html? nclick_check=1

'Ehemaliger Chefoekonom der UNO wirbt fuer 1:12 Initiative', *Aargauer Zeitung*, 31 October 2013, www. aargauerzeitung.ch/dossiers/abstimmung-1-12-initiative/ ehemaliger-chefoekonom-der-uno-wirbt-fuer-112-initiative-127333020

'Finanzprofessor sagt 1:20 waere wahrscheinlich angebrachter', *Aargauer Zeitung*, 20 October 2013, www.aargauerzeitung.ch/ dossiers/abstimmung-1-12-initiative/finanzprofessor-sagt-120-waere-wahrscheinlich-angebrachter-127293675

'Inheritance tax facts', Mercury Wealth Management, www.nigelbourke. co.uk/emagazine/ihtguide/14.html

Philosophers like Montesquieu and Aristotle did not necessarily endorse democracy as a system of government; however, they still had well-developed ideas about what would be necessary to make a state a democracy.

Comparing an ancient economy to a modern one can be difficult. Everything in the ancient world was made by hand and transported by nothing faster than a horse or oxen. Therefore, many things required an enormous amount of time and energy to make. The value of a piece of clothing in the ancient world would be comparable to a custom-made garment today, not a mass-produced one. For these, and other reasons, when translating ancient economic values into modern ones, only rough approximations are possible. However, for the purposes of this book, rough approximations are adequate, because we are primarily looking at the differentials within each society and not between them.

For the calculations here, I set the Athenian wage for unskilled labour of 250 drachmae a year as equivalent to the amount earned on a US minimum wage of $7.65 an hour that – erring on the side of optimism – would include paid vacation and sick leave. Assuming a forty-hour working week, this would deliver an annual income of approx. $15,300. All other calculations were based on the assumption of 250 drachmae as being equivalent to US$15,300.

Regarding the tax burden: in North America, even low earners pay nearly 30 per cent in income tax and social service charges, as well as sales tax of up to 13 per cent on everything they purchase, and other consumption taxes on property, fuel, cigarettes, etc. Upper-middle-class earners typically pay 45 per cent in income tax and social services, in addition to consumption taxes. In European countries, effective tax rates of 50 per cent for upper-middle-class earners, in addition to consumption taxes of over 20 per cent, are more typical. For the super-rich, however, the effective tax rate is often much lower: something like 10–15 per cent, as they derive much of their income from capital gains, which are usually subject to low tax rates and divert other sources of income into tax havens, where it is either untaxed or taxed at much lower rates. As billion-aire Warren Buffett has noted, he pays less tax than his secretary does (Chris Isidore, 'Buffett says he's still paying lower tax rate than his secre-tary', *CNN Money*, 4 March 2013, money.cnn.com/2013/03/04/news/economy/buffett-secretary-taxes/). If middle-class citizens can sustain an effective tax burden of 50 per cent (including income and sales tax and social services fees) for any reasonable time, there is no reason to believe that the super-rich cannot.

Index

selection system, 35-7, 40, 88, 137; office holding time limit, 39; oligarchic coup 404BC, 335; participatory equality weaknesses, 142; political participation level, 26; power dispersed, 149; prejudiced writers, 272 'people power, 15; *principles*, 16; private property respect, 344; progressive taxation, 349, 351; randomness democracy key, 39; relatively egalitarian wages, 352; right to free speech, 339; social mobility, 147; super-rich obligations, 350; wealth scale, 345

Athens, classical, Assembly, 25, 27, 139, 143, 366; assembly-Courts symbiosis, 34; collective decision-taking, 29; debates, 293; decision-making, 147; efficiency of, 26; 'foreign policy' decisions, 144; online mimicked, 288-9; pragmatism of, 28; randomness, 40

Attaway, Fritz, 227

Australia, 166; Senate, 73; UN SC seat lobbying, 165

Backbench Business Committee, House of Commons, 128, 131

'bad apples', discourse, 4

'bailouts', investor beneficiaries, 203-4

Balladur, Edouard, 223

Bank of International Settlements, 357

banking syndicates, IMF loans, 187

Belgium, votes-seats disparity, 81

Bernays, Edward, 290

Bhutan, modern, 14

Bildt, Carl, 216

Bivings PR group, 317

Blair Tony, 7, 214, 303-4; Global Legacy Award, 213

Blocher, Switzerland, 112

Boeing, election spending, 94; political donations, 93

Brazil, IMF shares, 179

Brigade 77, British Army propaganda unit, 316; online media 'shaping', 317

British Council, 215

British House of Lords Committee on Communication, 314

Brown, Gordon, 304

Bulletin of Atomic Scientists, 160

Bush clan, 287; G.W. Bush, 6, 62, 86

Business Alliance for a Yes Campaign, Ireland, 111

California Proposition 37, 109; defeat, 110

Cameron, David, 304, 311

Canada, 46, 56, 280; British Columbia voting system change, 69; Conservative Party, 61, 117; corporate financing, 91; donor regulation circumvented, 118; Federal elections 1896, 61; Federal election 1980, 53; Federal election 1988, 57, 86; Federal election 2008; International Development Agencies, 215; Liberal Party, 61NAFTA rules power, 58; online Assembly proposed, 323; parties' corporate backing, 9; Security Council lobbying expense campaign spending, 164-5; states elections, 54

candidate-donor relation, 108

Cardiff University, 306, 307

CARE International, donors to, 213

Cathgus, 243

Cato Institute, 308; op-eds frequency, 309

CDU, Germany, 77

censors, Roman corrupt, 255

Index

Index

Hoplites, 146
Hortensius, 256
Hubcap: income guaranteed, 201;
Pakistan, 200
Hurtado, Osvaldo, 192, 216

Iceland: Constitutional Council, 285;
Constitutional Council, over-ruled,
286; crowdsourcing constitutional
change, 17; medieval, 14
IFIs (international financial
institutions) privatization loans,
199
IMF (International Monetary
Fund, 98, 153, 182, 194; creation
of, 171; directors, 176-7; Ghana
stand-by 1983 arrangement, 204;
hijacked, 370; investor bailouts,
203; -Italy 1970s negotiations,
193; largest shareholders, 179;
'Letters of Intent, 191; limited
resources, 183; loan approval
vetos, 184; loan conditions
('Stand-by Arrangements'), 187-8;
'moral hazard', 205; neoliberal
contradicted, 189; NGOs image
use, 209; private bank shares, 183-
4; private finance dependent, 190;
reckless lending, 186 SDRs, 174;
UN vote leverage, 168; unequal
vote weighting, 178; USA power,
280
income inequality, severity of, 360
India, 46; nuclear weapons, 160
individuals, as citizens, 331; official
narrative of, 327
Indonesia, Enron forced payment, 198
inheritance(s), 354-6
Intellectual Property Committee, 227
intellectual property rights, global
regime, 228
intergenerational inequality, 354, 359

international banking-campaign
contributions, 98
International Chamber of Commerce,
UN accreditation, 212
International Clearing Union,
proposed, 172, 174
international decision-making, NGO
involvement, 233
international lending, irresponsible
lending, 185
Iranian Supreme Council, 10
Iraq, 2003 invasion, 6, 86; British
government supported, 87; British
people opposed, 7;
Ireland, 73, 104; bailout, 204;
citizen-representative relation, 135;
Constitutional Convention 2013-
14, 285; EU referendum, 110; local
elections money impact, 105-6;
NGO government funding, 219;
Northern Republicans, 64; 1997
election cost, 90; privatizations,
193; STV votong system, 69
Irish Business and Employers'
Confederation, 111
'isegoria', 27-8, 137, 293, 317, 330
ISIS, 317
Isocrates, 139
Israel, nuclear weapons, 160
issues, not-packaged, 365

Japan: foreign aid leverage, 169; IMF
shares, 176; wage differentials, 359;
World Bank power, 177
Job Training Partnership, USA 1982,
98
journalism, JCB technique, 307
judges, Athens randomly selected, 31
Julius Caesar, assassination of, 267
juries, 41; classical Athens, 30-2,
339; duty compensated, 140-1, 321;
Roman bribed, 256

Index